For Geoff Lamb

# From Versailles to Pearl Harbor

Related titles from Palgrave:

| | |
|---|---|
| Chamberlain and Appeasement | *R.A.C. Parker* |
| Eastern Europe and the Origins of the Second World War | *Anita J. Prazmowska* |
| The Second World War | *A.W. Purdue* |
| The Soviet Union and the Origins of the Second World War | *Geoffrey C. Roberts* |
| France and the Origins of the Second World War | *Robert J. Young* |

# From Versailles to Pearl Harbor

The Origins of the Second World War in Europe and Asia

Margaret Lamb and Nicholas Tarling

palgrave

First published 2001 by
PALGRAVE
Houndmills, Basingstoke, Hampshire RG21 6XS and
175 Fifth Avenue, New York, N.Y. 10010
Companies and representatives throughout the world

PALGRAVE is the new global academic imprint of
St. Martin's Press LLC Scholarly and Reference Division and
Palgrave Publishers Ltd (formerly Macmillan Press Ltd).

ISBN 0–333–73839–x hardback
ISBN 0–333–73840–3 paperback

This book is printed on paper suitable for recycling and made from fully managed and sustained forest sources.

A catalogue record for this book is available from the British Library.

Library of Congress Cataloging-in-Publication Data

Lamb, Margaret.
    From Versailles to Pearl Harbor: the origins of the Second World War in Europe and Asia / Margaret Lamb and Nicholas Tarling.
        p. cm.
    Includes bibliographical references and index.
    ISBN 0–333–73839–X—ISBN 0–333–73840–3 (pbk.)
        1. World War, 1939–1945—Causes. I. Title: Origins of World War 2 in Europe and Asia. II. Title: Origins of World War Two in Europe and Asia. III. Tarling, Nicholas. IV. Title.

D741 .L32 2001
940.53′11—dc21

00–048341

10  9  8  7  6  5  4  3  2  1
10 09 08 07 06 05 04 03 02 01

Printed and bound in Great Britain by Creative Print and Design Wales

# Contents

List of Maps                                                              viii

Preface                                                                     ix

Introduction                                                                 x

Maps                                                                       xii

Chapter 1:   The First World War                                            1

Chapter 2:   The Peace Settlements                                         21

Chapter 3:   The Implementation of the Peace Settlements                   45

Chapter 4:   The Depression                                                71

Chapter 5:   The End of Collective Security                                92

Chapter 6:   Appeasement                                                  112

Chapter 7:   The War of 1939                                              138

Chapter 8:   The War of 1941                                              160

Chapter 9:   Conclusions                                                  182

Epilogue                                                                  194

Notes                                                                     201

Suggestions for Further Reading                                          221

Index                                                                     232

# List of Maps

1  Europe, 1921–35                          xii

2  Europe, 1935–9                           xiii

3  Japan and Manchuria                      xiv

4  South-east Asia                          xv

# Preface

There are many books on the origins of the Second World War. Our reasons for adding to the number are twofold.

We believe that the Asian factor is significant in the making of the war in Europe. Even a book that focused on the origins of the war of 1939 could not omit it or play it down. In particular, the threat that Japan presented to the status quo in East Asia made it more difficult for the British to face Hitler's Germany and Mussolini's Italy, and contributed to the policy of appeasement. A war with Germany could have been an invitation to further Japanese aggression. The alienation of Italy threatened the Mediterranean route to the East and faced the British with the nightmare prospect of a war against three powers.

East Asia is clearly significant in the transformation of the European war into a world war. It was there that the USA was most conspicuously concerned, and that had helped to constrain Britain's handling of the East Asia crisis in the 1930s. When the European war began, however, and particularly when France surrendered, it became clear that the real focus of American interests was in Europe. In an attempt to ensure its security, the USA both built a two-ocean navy and sought to encourage Britain to continue its resistance to Germany. While that might lead to open participation, it might also avoid it. In the event it led to the former, but by an unexpected route. The steps the USA took in 1940–1 led the Japanese to attack both the USA and the UK as part of an attempt to seize the resources of South-east Asia.

The book owes much to the research of others. It also owes a great deal to our students at the University of Auckland, who continually prompted us to clarify our thinking and our presentation. If we have to any extent succeeded, that would provide a third reason for writing the book.

The maps were drawn by Jan Kelly of the University Geography Department, to whom we offer our thanks.

M.L.
N.T.

# Introduction

At the conclusion of the Second World War, the world was dominated by two superpowers, the USA and the Soviet Union. World politics was set in a pattern that lasted nearly fifty years, only recently replaced by one in which a single power, the USA, enjoys 'primacy' as more or less the undisputed leader. The end of the war had itself marked the end of a long period of change in world politics that had begun well before the opening of the First World War.

The nineteenth-century pattern of world politics was one in which Europe was dominant, and in which one European power, Britain, the first industrial society, was ahead of the others and enjoyed 'primacy'. But towards the end of the century that pattern was being challenged both within Europe and beyond it, above all because industrialisation spread to other countries. The most epoch-making change was the emergence of an industrialised USA, which contemporaries came to believe would, along with the vast Russian empire, dominate the world politics of the future. Germany's industrialisation was also very rapid. Its leaders concluded that, even as Europe's position in the world was changing, it, not Britain, must be the leading power in Europe and, as such, share 'world power'.

In some sense both wars were fought to decide how power should be redistributed among these contenders. The wars, it has been suggested, were wars of British 'succession', deciding what power or powers should replace Britain's nineteenth-century primacy. What was at the time seen as 'the Great War' became the 'First World War' because, despite its unprecedented scale and vast sacrifice of life, it failed to decide that question. A second world war, even more destructive and causing far greater loss of life, was to follow before the United States and the Soviet Union emerged indisputably as the successors, creating a bipolar world.

Though in some ways similar, the two wars were also distinctive. In the second, but not in the first, Japan was a major contender. The Great War was indeed a world war in the sense that, in addition to the USA, it drew in non-European states and peoples. That was inevitable, given the extent to which the European states had worldwide interests and investments, and

Britain and France had worldwide empires. Participation encouraged nationalist feelings in many of the European colonies and dependencies. It also offered special opportunities to Japan, as the one Asian state that, maintaining independence of European rule, had begun to modernise itself and to industrialise.

In what came to be called the 'inter-war' period, particularly in the 1930s, both the rise of nationalism and still more the expansionism of the Japanese threatened the British. At the same time they faced the re-emergence of a German challenge, and their relations with Italy deterio-rated. Japan was not a world power, but it now affected world politics. The British did not 'appease' Japan, but the threat it offered promoted their attempts to appease Italy and Germany. That policy was abandoned in 1939, and war followed in Europe. Japanese action and reaction ensured that it became a second world war in 1941. This book accepts that, in Akira Iriye's words, 'Asian affairs were distinct from . . . developments elsewhere', but it emphasises, perhaps more than most, how 'intertwined' they were.[1]

The two world wars were distinctive in another way. Attempts to analyse the causes of the war solely in the context of changing conditions and circumstances are vain: human factors are also involved. And they, of course, varied. Major changes were under way in the distribution of power in the world, and in turn they made it more difficult to handle other changes – such as nationalist struggles or civil wars – that contributed to instability. But both sets of changes are best seen as, in F. H. Hinsley's terms, challenges to statesmanship.[2] The Second World War, like the first, was not simply the result of circumstances nor of human decisions. This history aims to take account of circumstances and decisions and of their inter-relationship.

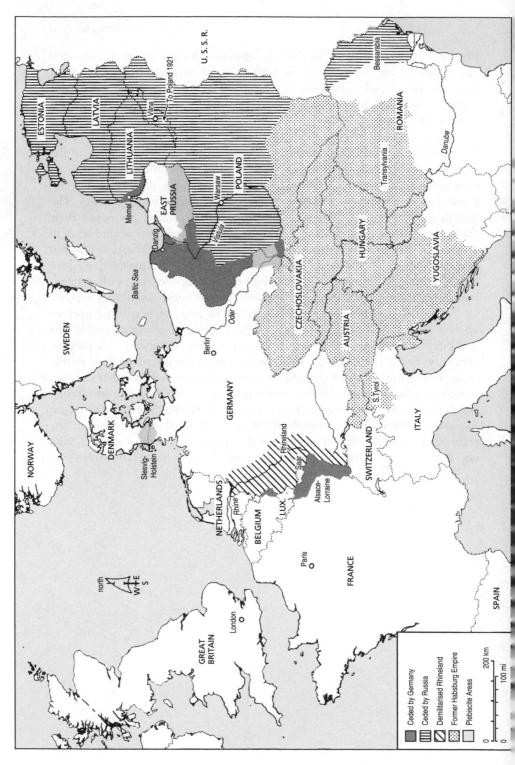

north
N
W+E
S

NORWAY

SWEDEN

DENMARK
Slesvig-
Holstein

GREAT
BRITAIN
London ○

NETHERLANDS

BELGIUM
LUX.

Rhine

Rhineland

Saar

Alsace-
Lorraine

Paris ○

FRANCE

SWITZERLAND

SPAIN

ITALY

S.Tyrol

AUSTRIA

GERMANY

Berlin ○

Oder

Baltic Sea

Memel

EAST
PRUSSIA

Danzig

Vistula

Warsaw ○

POLAND

To Poland 1921

Vilna ○

ESTONIA

LATVIA

LITHUANIA

U. S. S. R.

Bessarabia

ROMANIA

Transylvania

Danube

HUNGARY

CZECHOSLOVAKIA

YUGOSLAVIA

Ceded by Germany
Ceded by Russia
Demilitarised Rhineland
Former Habsburg Empire
Plebiscite Areas

0        100 mi
0    200 km

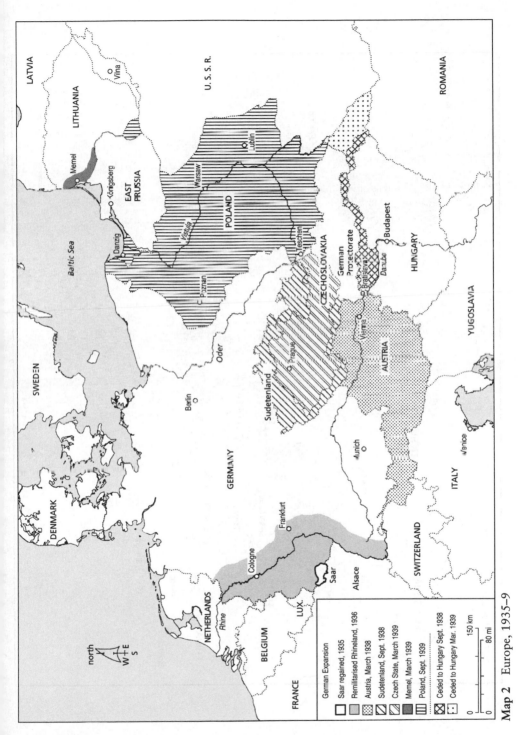

Map 2  Europe, 1935–9

xiii

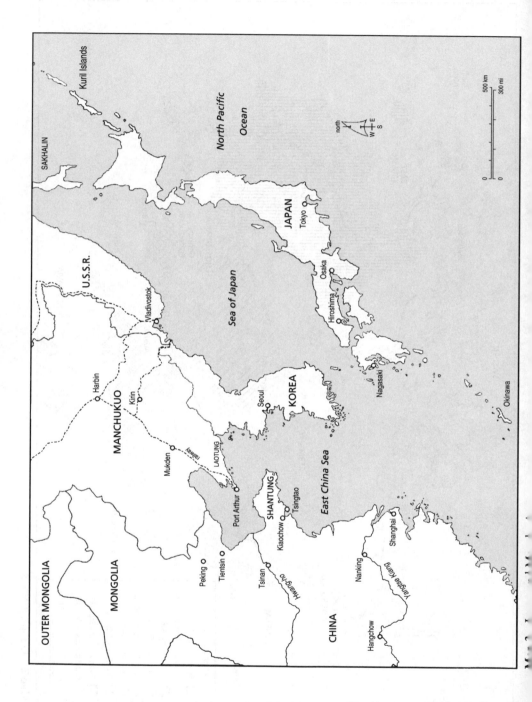

OUTER MONGOLIA

MONGOLIA

U.S.S.R.

MANCHUKUO

Harbin

Kirin

Mukden

railway

LAOTUNG

Vladivostok

SAKHALIN

Kuril Islands

North Pacific

Ocean

north

N

W E

S

500 km

300 mi

0

0

Sea of Japan

JAPAN

Tokyo

Osaka

Hiroshima

Nagasaki

Okinawa

KOREA

Seoul

Port Arthur

Peking

Tientsin

Tsinan

Hwang-ho

SHANTUNG

Kiaochow

Tsingtao

East China Sea

CHINA

Nanking

Yangtse Kiang

Shanghai

Hangchow

xiv

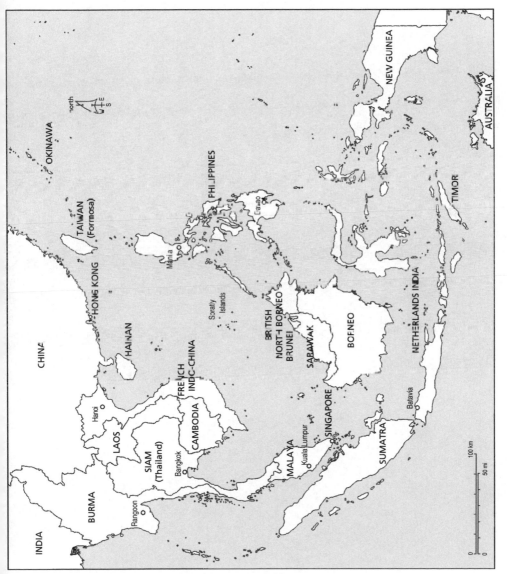

**Map 4** South-east Asia

*Chapter 1*

# The First World War

## The major powers before the First World War

Britain was the most successful of the nineteenth-century European powers in expanding its territory overseas, but that very success brought an increasing nervousness and sense of vulnerability as well as prestige and status as a world power. As early as the 1830s, the possession of India had led to growing fears about the threat of Russian expansion in Central Asia. The development of intense imperial rivalry with France in Africa and Asia, disagreements with the United States over the Canadian–American boundary and over Central America, pressures from Germany to make colonial concessions, and the perception that the Russian threat had extended to Manchuria and China as well as the Middle East caused the British to reconsider their whole diplomatic position. They decided that they were no longer able to stand aloof from the alliances of the other European powers and alone defend their interests against a number of potential enemies. When the attempt to conclude an agreement with Germany failed, they made an alliance with Japan in 1902 to help protect their interests in the Far East and settled their differences with the United States in 1902 and 1903, with France in 1904 and with Russia in 1907. Although the memories of years of rivalry and friction could not be expunged, Britain's relations with France and the USA steadily improved. And with France the resulting diplomatic and military co-operation increasingly bound the two states together prior to 1914. With Russia, however, Britain's relations continued to be determined largely by fear. Britain remained nervous about Russia's growing influence in Persia and its desire to control the Straits of the Bosphorus and Dardanelles, but was constrained in its expression of opposition by a fear of provoking a Russo-German rapprochement and by the recognition of its own weakness in Central Asia. Whatever the difficulties, the foreign secretary, Sir Edward Grey, believed that the agreement with

Russia had to be maintained because 'if it was to go everything would be worse'.[1] Continuing anxieties about its position in the Middle East and Asia as well as apprehension about Germany in Europe led Britain to support France and Russia in the decade prior to 1914.

The economic balance amongst the major powers was also changing. Britain might be the major imperial power but the economic predominance it had enjoyed in the earlier part of the nineteenth century was being successfully challenged by the United States and, to a lesser extent, by Germany. A few economic prophets looking at the indicators of territorial size, population and potential resources predicted that it would be Russia rather than Germany that would join the United States as the major powers of the twentieth century. In terms of their future performance upon the world scene, however, there was some uncertainty about both of those powers. The economic growth of the United States was indeed phenomenal; so much so that one economist has calculated that, even without the adverse effects of the 1914–18 war upon the European powers, its economic output would have equalled that of the whole of Europe by 1925.[2] Although Britain remained the financial centre of the world until the outbreak of the war, it was clear that the United States was going to have a growing impact upon the economic life and the financial stability of other powers. How would the United States use that power?

Diplomatically and militarily the United States had chosen to exercise its influence mainly over matters relating to its own immediate region but it had shown increasing interest in the Pacific with its annexation of Hawaii and the Philippines in the 1890s, its attempt to maintain the 'open door' for trade with China in 1902, and its mediation at the end of the Russo-Japanese war in 1905. There were no such indications of a desire to become involved in European affairs. Americans seemed content to follow the advice of George Washington to eschew involvement in the rivalries and quarrels of the European powers. Protected from Europe by a vast expanse of ocean and by a sizeable navy, it was content to have an army establishment that was about half that of the least of the European major powers, Italy. An indication of its military potential, however, was the speed with which its navy, described as little better than a collection of washtubs in the 1880s, had been transformed into a modern navy surpassed only in size by those of Britain and Germany in 1914. While American intervention in the European scene appeared unlikely, the foundations of its power to exercise a decisive military influence in the future if it chose to do so were already laid.

The position of Russia was also problematical but in a different way . Diplomatically and militarily Russia was clearly a major player on the European and indeed the world scene. A successful imperial drive to the east from the mid nineteenth century had expanded its territory across central Asia to the coasts of the sea of Japan, and a successful war against the Ottoman empire in 1877, ostensibly on behalf of the Balkan Christians, had allowed Russia to extend its influence in that area. Tied into the alliance system of the European powers by agreements first with Germany and then from the early 1890s with France, the Russians were involved in all the major diplomatic crises of the late nineteenth and early twentieth centuries. Considerable resources had been poured into making it a major military power. Its army was by far the largest in Europe, its navy was being modernised, its industry was being developed with a particular eye to armaments production, and railways were being extended to facilitate the transport of troops. The question mark about Russia was whether its fundamental economic and financial situation, its political and social stability, and even its military planning and leadership were equal to the demands which would be placed upon them if Russia became involved in a major war.

Russia had already suffered the humiliation of having been defeated by the Japanese in 1905 and this had been followed by revolutionary outbreaks of such magnitude at home that the Tsar had agreed to the summoning of a consultative assembly, known as the Duma. The steady development of a constitutional type of monarchy, however, did not take place. The Tsar reverted to autocratic methods and to such extreme repression to deal with the growing political and industrial discontent that one leading industrialist exclaimed in May 1914, 'One can only hope that our great country will outlive its petty government.'[3]

In the years immediately prior to 1914 it was the growth of German power which appeared to be the most obvious danger to the stability of Europe. Its economic development since unification in 1871 had been impressive. Its population growth was outstripping that of Britain and particularly that of France. By the eve of the war, its coal production nearly equalled that of Britain and its output of steel exceeded the combined totals of Britain, France and Russia. In the newer electrical and chemical industries, Germany was even more dominant. Such economic development enabled Germany to expand its armed forces with comparatively little strain when it chose to do so. Its warship tonnage rose from 285,000 in 1900 to 1,305,000 in 1914 and its total military and naval personnel from 694,000 men in 1910 to 891,000 men in 1914. Such clear signs of power in themselves created nervousness amongst the other states but what made the situation appear threatening was the way in which the German government conducted its external relations. The attempts to intimidate France over Morocco in 1905 and 1911, the more successful bullying of Russia during the Bosnian crisis of 1908–9, the pushing of German interests in the Turkish empire and the failure to reach an agreement with Britain over naval rivalry in 1912 fed the perception that Germany was an aggressive, dangerous and untrustworthy power. According to the admittedly anti-German British Foreign Office official, Eyre Crowe, the dominating influence at the second Hague Peace Conference in 1907 had been 'fear of Germany' as that country had 'followed the traditional course, cajoling and bullying in turn, always actively intriguing'.[4] The German perception, of course, was different. They believed that their industrial and commercial growth necessitated political and military expansion and resented British opposition to it.

Germany's use of its potential power was not the only threat to the stability of Europe in the early twentieth century. The rise of a nationalist ideology which defined the nation in ethnic and cultural terms and asserted that the boundaries of state and nation should coincide challenged the existence of the multinational Ottoman, Russian and Austro-Hungarian empires. During the nineteenth century, the Ottomans had gradually been forced to retreat from their European lands by the creation of the independent states of Greece, Serbia, Romania and Bulgaria – developments which had been brought about by the nationalist aspirations of these peoples and the intervention of the major powers. The settlements still left many nationalist aspirations unfulfilled. Czechs, Slovaks, Romanians, Serbs and other South Slavs still lived under Hapsburg rule. Poles were ruled not only by the Austrians but also by the Germans and the Russians. The threat to the empires aside, nationalist aspirations contained other seeds of conflict. In an area where peoples had intermingled for centuries there were no clearly defined national boundaries, which led to bitter rivalries between the newly created nation states and differences amongst the still subject peoples about the best solution for their problems. Some wished to join an existing nation state; others wanted to form a new state: and many were still looking for concessions within the Austro-Hungarian empire rather than for a separate existence outside it prior to 1914. The tensions and conflicts between the nationalist groups had more far-reaching implications when major powers believed that their interests would be affected by the outcome. Prior to 1914, these powers were Austria-Hungary and Russia. For Austria-Hungary it was a question of its very existence, but Russia also believed that it had vital and abiding interests in the Balkan region. It was not only an affinity with fellow Slavs which was a powerful influence in some quarters but there was also a belief that Russia's gaining control of the Balkans and the Straits was essential for the state's economic and strategic well-being.

The assassination of the Archduke Franz Ferdinand, the heir to the Austro-Hungarian throne, led to an international crisis and the outbreak of war in 1914 because the pre-existing tensions and alliances affected the way in which the powers reacted to the situation. Austria-Hungary attempted to use the occasion to humble and control Serbia whose nationalist ambitions were seen as a threat to the empire. Russia's whole prestige as a great power demanded that it support its fellow Slavs and thwart further Austrian expansion in the Balkans. Most importantly, Germany decided to support its ally Austria-Hungary and run the risk of precipitating a major war. The French promised support to their ally Russia which began to mobilise. At that point, German military planning determined the rapid outbreak of the war. France, it had been agreed, had to be defeated first before the Russians completed what was expected to be their slow mobilisation. The Germans declared war on Russia and on France and immediately put into operation their planned attack on France by invading neutral Belgium. The British decision to support France and Russia was ostensibly in support of Belgium whose neutrality Britain had guaranteed in 1839. The real reason may well have been a fear of the consequences of standing aside. The triumph of either side could pose a threat to Britain. If Germany and Austria won, the danger would come from a dominant Germany but if France and Russia won, there was a danger that they would revert to their previous anti-British attitudes. In the latter case, 'What about India and the Mediterranean?', asked Eyre Crowe. The foreign secretary summed up the situation: 'If we did not stand by France and stand up for Belgium against this aggression, we should be isolated, discredited and hated; and there would be nothing before us [...] nothing but a miserable and ignoble future'.[5]

## The war of 1914–18

When war began in August 1914, few anticipated that it would last for four years, that the nature of the fighting would result in millions of casualties or that the number of combatant states would continue to grow. The most important additions were the Ottoman empire and Bulgaria which joined Germany and Austria-Hungary, and Romania, Italy, Japan and the United States which joined Russia, France and Britain. The former group were commonly referred to as the Central Powers and the latter as the Entente Powers. On both sides, there had been an expectation of victory after a short, decisive war. When that did not occur both sides endeavoured to obtain the greatest possible amount of manpower, military, technological and financial resources.

The prolongation of the war had far-reaching effects. The pre-war state system was destroyed and the prestige of the major European powers throughout the world was undermined. Repeatedly defeated by Germany in the field, the Tsarist regime was unable to survive the demands and pressures of the long war. Its more liberal successor had little time to consolidate its position before it was overthrown by the Bolshevik seizure of power in October 1917. At the end of the war, the Bolsheviks' hold upon power was still precarious. They had chosen to make peace with Germany at the Treaty of Brest-Litovsk in March 1918, surrendering a large part of the former empire in the Baltic and eastern Europe. Their internal enemies, the supporters of the two previous regimes and some of the subject nationalities who were fighting for independence, were being aided by Russia's former allies who had hoped to obtain a government which would take Russia back into the war. The Austro-Hungarian empire had also collapsed. Its subject nationalities, encouraged as the war progressed by the propaganda and promises of support from the empire's opponents, had gradually withdrawn their support, defected from its armies and proclaimed their independence. The German empire too had ceased to exist. With the collapse of their allies in the east, Austria-Hungary, Bulgaria and the Ottoman empire, and with the promise of increasing American reinforcements to their opponents in the west, the German high command recognised that it could not win the war and prevailed upon the German government to seek an armistice in October 1918. In the ensuing month while the armistice negotiations continued, the popular discontent with the effects of the war and the desire to present a more democratic regime to the Americans led to pressure upon the German emperor to abdicate and to the establishment of the German republic.

The two major European powers who had emerged on the winning side, Britain and France, had not emerged unscathed. The French had come near to defeat and had been shaken by mutinies in the French army and by some crumbling of morale and determination on the home front in 1917. Britain's financial and economic position, weakening before the war, was now thoroughly undermined. In this war, it had not been sufficient for it to fulfil its traditional role of relying on the navy and financing allies on the continent; it had also been called upon to make large contributions to the land armies. Britain's financial reserves could not cope with such demands. Nor could its population resources. Like its allies, it had to seek financial assistance from the United States and had been glad to receive reinforcements of manpower from the empire and particularly the dominions. For their final victory, Britain and France had relied upon the economic and financial assistance of the United States and on the promise of increasing military reinforcements. It brought fears that 'the Americans...would be the real victors' and that 'economically all European peoples are being ruined to the benefit of Japan, North America and new peoples'.[6]

The collapse of the three empires in Europe and the defeat of the Ottoman armies in the Middle East meant that the scale of the peace settlement had to be immense. The kind of peace treaties which had followed Bismarck's wars in the 1860s – the exchange of small pieces of territory and the imposition of war indemnities – provided totally inadequate models. As far as redrawing the map of Europe alone was concerned, the nearest equivalent was the settlement in 1815 following the more than twenty years of the French revolutionary and Napoleonic wars. On that occasion Lord Castlereagh, the then British foreign secretary, had openly stated that the settlement would be dominated by the major victorious powers owing to their 'natural weight'. In 1918, the powers in that position were Britain, France and especially, by virtue of its financial and economic strength, the United States.

## War aims

The war aims of Britain and France had grown with the years and had been a matter of continuing debate, much of it away from public scrutiny. The French had initially thought in terms of the return of Alsace-Lorraine, which, after their defeat in the Franco-Prussian war in 1871, they had had to cede to the newly united Germany. The progress of the 1914–18 war and particularly the defeat of their ally, Russia, had led the French to ponder whether the return of that territory alone would provide them with sufficient security against Germany in the future. Some thought in terms of trying to redress further the economic imbalance between France and Germany by the creation of an Entente economic bloc which would protect French industry and discriminate against Germany, and by the continuation in peacetime of the inter-allied pooling of shipping and raw materials which had finally been achieved at the beginning of 1918. Others were more ambitious. They sought to acquire the Rhineland and the coal-producing region of the Saar. Much depended on France's allies. At the beginning of the war, they had all agreed not to make a separate peace or to publicise peace terms without prior agreement. The Russians, who had chosen to make a separate peace, could be ignored. In some ways that saved embarrassment as the Russians had developed large appetites and demanded not only promises of support for their future control of Constantinople and the Straits of the Bosphorus and the Dardenelles but also a free hand in shaping their western boundary. Other allies had still to be considered. At the beginning of the peace negotiations, Clemenceau, the French premier, warned his colleagues that 'France will have to make sacrifices not to Germany, but to her allies.'[7]

For the British, drawing up a wish list for the end of the war had proved particularly difficult. In public, the British government said little that was specific until Lloyd George's speech to the Trades Union Congress in January 1918. Much of what he said was echoed three days later in President Wilson's more famous Fourteen Points. Lloyd George, in an effort to assure domestic opinion that the country was not being called upon to suffer continuing sacrifices in a war for conquest and gain, spelled out the terms for what he saw as a moderate and just peace. There was no question of trying to destroy Austria-Hungary or Germany, but they would have to withdraw from all the countries which they had occupied and the 'great wrong' done to France over Alsace-Lorraine would have to be reconsidered. Poland should become independent, the national minorities of Austria-Hungary should have self-government, the German colonies should be allowed self-determination and the whole basis of the future Europe should be that government was with the consent of the governed. Germany and her allies would have to pay some penalty in that Belgium should be indemnified for her invasion and others should receive reparation for 'injuries done in violation of international law'.[8] In more confidential discussions, opinions varied about the possible extent of that reparation. Some thought of compensation for Belgium alone, others of payment for all of the physical damage which Germany had inflicted during the fighting and a few mentioned the whole cost of the war. The problem was to decide which policy would most favour British interests and particularly the restoration of its trade in the future. Security was as important as trade and for that the British looked to the destruction of the German fleet and for the restoration of a balance of power in Europe. What that should mean in practice provoked considerable discussion. Should Germany keep its 1914 frontiers and its colonies or should it lose the latter and also have its territories in Europe severely curtailed? There was no firmly agreed policy when the war came to an end.

Some states who had joined the Entente side had specific objectives from the beginning. Romania and Italy both had aspirations at the expense of the Austro-Hungarian empire. Romania wanted Transylvania with its considerable Romanian population. Italy, which had abandoned its pre-war allies Germany and Austria-Hungary, asked a high price for its adherence to the Entente side. It wanted not only Trieste and the Trentino, to which it had some nationalist claims, but also the South Tyrol and large parts of the Dalmatian coast, its claim to which had to rest mainly on security and strategic considerations. Influenced by the need to obtain further support at a crucial stage of the fighting in 1915, and not unwilling to establish the Italians as a counterpoise to a possible Russian domination of the Balkans, Britain and France had agreed to support these claims at a future peace settlement. By 1918, however, any immediate Russian threat had evaporated and the Austro-Hungarian state had collapsed. The Italian claims were largely at the expense of the newly constituted union of the South Slavs, a group to whom the Allies had been giving considerable encouragement in the latter stages of the war. These were not the only commitments which the exigencies of war had extracted from the Entente powers. The Italians had also been promised a share of the Ottoman empire should it disintegrate. In varying degrees of formality, the Poles and the Czechs and the Slovaks had had promises of independent statehood. Britain, in particular, had been prolific with promises. Japan had been offered support for her claim to the former German concessions in China. The French, the Arabs and the Jews had all been promised support for their particular claims to the Ottoman lands in the Middle East. In that area, Britain's commitments conflicted with each other in spirit if not in letter.

The United States, which had not been a party to the wartime bargaining, introduced a new set of war aims. Its participation in the fighting on the Entente side had been somewhat reluctant. President Wilson had hoped to preserve American neutrality and to mediate a compromise peace that would lead to a just and permanent settlement. He had little understanding of Clemenceau's view that ideas on what constituted justice were variable and depended on one's perspective. Wilson believed that his view of what was just was right. When the Germans declared unrestricted submarine warfare and attempted to involve Mexico in any war between themselves and the United States, Wilson led his country into the war on the British and French side, but as an 'associated power' not as a full ally. The publication by the Bolsheviks at the end of 1917 of the secret agreements and territorial bargains of the Entente powers increased Wilson's desire to distance himself from the former acts of his associates. In the Fourteen Points and in a series of major speeches throughout 1918, he took a highly moral and idealistic tone. Apart from specific provisions like those for the evacuation and restoration of Belgium, the return of Alsace-Lorraine to France and independence for Poland, he called for a different kind of peace settlement from those in the past. There should be 'open covenants of peace openly arrived at' and 'peoples and provinces' should not be 'bartered about...as if they were mere chattels' and, above all, 'impartial justice' should be meted out with 'no discrimination between those to whom we wish to be just and those to whom we do not wish to be just'.[9]

Such sentiments were music to the ear of the German government when they reached the point of wishing to bring the war to an end, although they themselves had followed no such precepts when they concluded their own peace treaty with the Bolsheviks in March 1918. It is significant that the German approach for an armistice was to the Americans alone. They asked for peace negotiations to be on the basis of the Fourteen Points. Britain and France had some reservations about the Fourteen Points and the nature of the German approach, but they knew that they could not continue to fight without American support. They concentrated, therefore, on obtaining the best possible military terms for the armistice and some modifications of the Fourteen Points which they believed would better protect their vital interests. On the military side they were very successful; the terms were so crippling that any German attempt to renew the war would have been impossible however unpalatable the final peace terms might be. The modifications to the Fourteen Points were few but crucial. It was made clear that the 'restoration' of evacuated territories which was referred to in the Fourteen Points meant that Germany was liable to pay 'compensation...for all the damage done to the civilian population of the Allies and their property by the aggression of Germany by land, by sea and by the air'.[10] The Germans, however, had the satisfaction of surrendering not unconditionally but with the expectation that the peace terms, based on the Fourteen Points and Wilson's subsequent addresses, would be openly negotiated and would not be draconian.

The end of a war which had cost so much in human lives and economic resources evoked mixed reactions. In Britain and France many looked for compensation for the great sacrifices that the war had demanded, which was reflected in the simple slogan 'Germany will pay'. In Germany itself, on the other hand, after so much effort and sacrifice, many had difficulty in believing that the country had been defeated while others quickly set to work to try to counter any claim that Germany had been responsible for the conflict.[11] President Wilson and his supporters believed that they should learn lessons from the recent past and remove what they perceived to have been the causes of the war – the build-up of armaments, the existence of alliances, the grievances of subject nationalities and the lack of a formal mechanism for the settlement of international disputes. His solution was to be the establishment of a League of Nations through which disputes could be debated, mediated and resolved. The first task, however, was to draw up a peace settlement which would have to provide the basis for any new international system and reflect the changes which the war had brought to Europe and to the other parts of the world.

### Asia before the war

Unprecedented in scale and duration, the war came to involve not only the USA but also the colonial territories of the Europeans from which they drew wealth and manpower. It also came to involve states that were becoming independent, like the Dominions, and states that were still independent, like China and Japan. In the Second World War China and Japan were to be major combatants. But even in the First World War their actions were not simply reactions to the actions of the Europeans. Japan in particular had become a player on the international scene, though the Europeans had a poor understanding of it.

Before the war Asian countries had been undergoing a transformation that in some respects resembled what the West had undergone or was undergoing. Indeed its concepts came from the West: that of the nation-state; and that of the industrial system. To the challenges those concepts presented Asian countries responded in different ways, as indeed did European.

At the time of the First World War most of the Indian subcontinent was under the control of the British, exerted either directly or through native princes. The capacity of the Indians to respond to the new concepts was thus limited. But, though they were not in control of their own government, the alien government, sometimes in spite of itself, sometimes more willingly, offered opportunities they could turn to account. The idea of nationhood, which Sir John Seeley believed must sound the death-knell of British control, was nevertheless introduced, part and parcel of the albeit limited spread of education and the founding of the Congress in the 1880s.

10

The Indian economy was shaped by the needs of the British, but the railways they built – initially with a strategic purpose – had a revolutionary effect. For the British India was a source of strength, but it was also a source of weakness. It provided manpower, but the mutiny of 1857 stressed that it was not entirely reliable. Nor was its external security easy to guarantee. Its needs rather differed from Britain's own: they were those of a continental state, not bounded only by sea, nor defensible only by sea. Britain, essentially a sea-power, was always apprehensive lest failure on or beyond the frontiers of India should coincide with or even precipitate a challenge within the frontiers. That added to the concern about Russia, a potential threat in the north-west.

The position of China was quite different, though that was partly a result of British policy. India was seen as an exception; China must not become another India. Britain's policy in the nineteenth century was thus to uphold its independence under the Manchu dynasty and provide for commercial opportunity. China was not formally subordinated to Europeans, but it made 'unequal treaties', under which it was admitted into the European world of nations on a less than fully equal basis. The Manchu dynasty was able to turn the resources of European diplomacy to some account, fitting it into an older policy of using barbarians to control barbarians. It was much less able to take up the challenge of modernisation that Europe also presented. Defeat at the hands of the Japanese in 1894–5 demonstrated the inadequacy of its policy of 'self-strengthening'. The dynasty then attempted reform, only to precipitate its overthrow by Chinese revolutionaries in 1911.

The Japanese response to the nineteenth-century challenge differed again. Following a visit from four USA warships under Commodore Matthew Perry in 1853, the ruling Tokugawa clan abandoned its tradition of seclusion and accepted unequal treaties without the bouts of violence to which the Europeans had submitted the Manchus. Revolution had, however, followed within Japan, and the Tokugawa had been overthrown in 1868. Ruling in the name of the Meiji emperor, the new government was an oligarchy drawn from rival clans. For the time being it maintained the treaties, while seeking to strengthen Japan to ensure its survival in a changing world. It overthrew the old feudal structures and created a Western-style army and navy, with a direct line to the emperor, described in terms of 'right of supreme command'. It led the way in industrialising Japan, often by highly interventionist means. It suppressed revolt and only reluctantly introduced an electoral system. Even liberals supported a more democratic approach only because they thought wider participation would strengthen the state.

The Japanese differed about foreign policy. It was not the basic aim that was at issue: the preservation of Japan's independence, strength and prosperity, equality with other nations. The question was the strategy.

Seclusion had been abandoned. What foreign policy was to replace it and when? The industrialisation which the oligarchy introduced into Japan required a commercial relationship with other parts of the world, particularly, but not solely, within the East Asian region. Japan lacked resources of its own, and industrialisation made it dependent on a high level of foreign trade. But how could that be ensured? and even if it could be, was it enough?

The failure of China's self-strengthening, moreover, presented risks for Japan. France had taken over northern Vietnam in the 1880s, and the advance of Russia's power to the Far East, demonstrated by the commencement of the Trans-Siberian railway in 1891, might, it was feared, bring neighbouring Korea and Manchuria within its grasp. Could China preserve Taiwan from the Western powers? Even in order to provide for its own security, Japan would surely have to become more active. Such activity could take two forms: working with China against the West in a 'pan-Asian' style; or pre-emptive moves at China's expense. The idealistic former notion never prevailed, though it was never quite forgotten, but Japan's policy tended to follow the second more realistic line. Western concepts enforced this conclusion. Japan's long-suppressed tradition of economic expansion was modernised by the adoption of Malthusian doctrines on population: Japan was perceived as a country with too many people and too little food.[12] Merely economic expansion, too, had not sufficed for the Western nations with which Japan was seeking to make itself equal. Should not Japan, too, become an imperial power? Ambitious aims conceived in the frustration of the late Tokugawa years were given a new imperialistic slant. The attitude of the Western powers with interests in Asia had, however, also to be considered, and the oligarchy generally took a cautious approach. On the other hand Japan became part of their calculations, too. None would have welcomed the pan-Asian policy: even the British, concerned to maintain the integrity of China, did not want to see it revolutionised, and thus, they expected, made more anti-Western. To the more realistic policy upon which the Japanese in the event resolved they were likely to respond in an expedient fashion, sometimes welcoming, sometimes opposing, sometimes constraining.

The war with China of 1894–5 was a triumph for Japan. It demonstrated the weakness of China, the need for reform, even for revolution. But it also demonstrated the weakness of Japan. For it became apparent that, whatever the aims it conceived for the East Asian region, they could not be realised if other powers opposed them, and that, even if China could be defeated, its compliance with Japan's demands might be undermined by other powers. In the treaty of Shimonoseki (1895), China recognised the independence of Korea, and ceded to Japan Taiwan, the Pescadores, and the Liaotung peninsula in southern Manchuria. But the Triple Intervention followed: France, Germany and Russia pressed the Japanese government to return south Manchuria to China, and it assented to what nationalists were bound to see as a mutilation of Japan's victory.

This episode was striking: it not only inaugurated a forceful Japanese policy on the mainland; it linked the politics of Europe and Asia in an unprecedented but precedent-setting way. Germany had joined France, Russia's new ally, in supporting it in the Far East, and Japan bowed to this unusual and indeed temporary combination. The episode not only rankled at the time; its memory influenced Japan in the future. Japanese governments recognised more fully than ever that the realisation of their ambitions depended on the relationships with and among the Western powers. That expediency was to influence their policy for another forty-five years. Indeed it was so strong a feature of their foreign policy that it may have misled other powers into discounting the frustration that the intervention had also prompted and the risk that it would overcome the caution inherited from the early Meiji period. Japan was an actor on the world scene, but it seemed to be playing only a small and deferential part.

The initial response of the Japanese government was to make an alliance with a European power, Britain. Following the Boxer uprising of 1900, several powers intervened in China, most worryingly Russia, which failed to withdraw its troops from Manchuria afterwards. To counter the threat, Britain was ready to make an alliance with the Japanese, even though their attitude to the integrity of China was ambiguous. Some of the Japanese preferred to negotiate with Russia, but the Katsura government concluded the alliance of 1902. It did not deter Russia. Instead it made it possible for Japan to fight a war with Russia alone without the renewed risk of the intervention of other European powers. At great cost in lives and treasure, it won: 'Jap the giant-killer', *Punch* exclaimed. Within Japan the government was criticised for gaining too little, and nationalists saw the treaty of Portsmouth that concluded the war as a humiliation. But the Chinese empire lost southern Manchuria, including Port Arthur; the Russian empire was shaken by the 1905 revolution; and the European empires were jolted when their subjects realised that an Asian power could defeat a European power.

The Western powers should indeed have taken even more account of this war: it implied that short wars and rapid victories had become unlikely, as the Polish banker and author Ivan Bloch had pointed out, a lesson neglected in 1914. They also took too little account of its impact on Japan. The extent of the conflict indeed made the Japanese cautious about further conflict with the Russians. They had, however, been victorious, even if disappointed. This was the war that the Japanese remembered, not the First World War, which saw little conflict in Asia; and unlike that war, it did not suggest the need to end wars.[13] In the First World War, indeed, they were able to revert to an older policy, of benefiting from the weakness of others without themselves engaging in major conflict. China's government was overthrown; Europe was absorbed in a succession of crises.

The Chinese revolution of 1911 was, of course, designed to strengthen China, the weakness of which had been demonstrated so vividly by recent events; but overthrowing the Manchus was insufficient. The new republic relapsed into instability, civil war and warlordism. Should Japan take up the pan-Asian cause or continue to take advantage of China's weakness? The latter course remained the more tempting. Nor were the European powers well placed to restrain Japan, whatever policy it adopted. Britain was its ally. The terms of the alliance had been modified in 1905, partly perhaps in the hope of exercising some kind of restraining influence on the Japanese. But its focus on Europe, and in particular the reduction of its naval forces to meet the threat of the German navy in European waters, reduced Britain's capacity to sustain its policy in respect of China. Japan had come to terms, too, with France and Russia, Britain's Entente partners from 1907. The mediation that led to the treaty of Portsmouth had demonstrated USA interest. In 1900 it had endorsed, in the Hay notes, what in origin were British principles, the integrity of China and the Open Door, equal commercial opportunity in China. But like the European powers the USA, too, had accepted the outcome of the Russo-Japanese war: Japanese dominance in Korea and south Manchuria. There was no evidence that the USA would interpose its growing power in order to uphold the principles Hay had enunciated.

In South-east Asia the USA had interposed. Three years after the Japanese acquisition of Taiwan to the north, it had acquired the Philippines in 1898. Acquiring the Philippines, however, made it a colonial power. Though the imperialism of the USA was more liberal than that of its neighbours, its presence in effect protected them from any direct challenge by the Japanese. The challenges the colonial powers faced from within were limited, though the Chinese revolution and the Japanese victories had some effect.

Most of South-east Asia was indeed under the control of Western powers by the end of the nineteenth century. Though Britain was the most powerful of them, it had not monopolised the region. It had found it convenient that the Dutch, a minor power, should control the islands of Indonesia, Netherlands India. It had also accepted the long-established Spanish control of the Philippines, preferring, if it had to be terminated, that it should be replaced by USA rule rather than by German rule or the rule of an independent Latin-American style republic. Even the ambitions of Britain's longstanding rival, France, had not been opposed in Vietnam and Cambodia, and it was only when the French threatened the independence of Siam (Thailand) that the British sought to constrain them. The independence of Thailand had become a cardinal point in Britain's policy. That was because the Thais, responding positively to Britain's approaches, had made commercial treaties in 1826 and 1855. Britain's policy in Burma was indeed less liberal: it was an Indian policy, seeking security for the continental empire through a substantial measure of submission. When that was not forthcoming, the British felt they had to teach the Burmans a lesson, and bit by bit they annexed the kingdom. That, however, boosted Thailand's prospects, for it became a buffer state between the British and French empires.

The other focus of British activities, more characteristically commercial in orientation, was the island of Singapore, acquired in 1819. But, partly in order to keep major powers away from the important routes through the Straits of Melaka and the South China Sea, the British intervened on the Malay peninsula and also, yet more reluctantly, in north-western Borneo. In 1888 they established protectorates over the three Borneo states, the raj of Sarawak, the sultanate of Brunei and the state of North Borneo, and in 1895–6 they set up the Federated Malay States, with a capital at Kuala Lumpur.

Their own caution, coupled with the American acquisition of the Philippines, limited any threat the Japanese might present to colonial South-east Asia at this time. But the colonial systems, in part unintentionally, themselves brought about changes. Whatever their political complexion or their economic purpose, they were bound to start a process of modernisation, which it would be difficult to curb and control.

### Asia and the war

While it lost what empire it had at the outset of the war, Germany sought to subvert the empire of others. Before the war, the German emperor had endeavoured to present himself as the friend of Islam, and the Turkish leaders joined in the war against the Entente in October 1914. That marked the culmination of the long deterioration in the relations of Britain with Turkey which had once been the pillar of British policy in the Middle East and the bulwark of its empire in India. But the risk was larger still. The king-emperor had more Muslim subjects than any other ruler, and the British had always been anxious to avoid provoking, and to avoid others provoking, an anti-European Islamic reaction which would fall largely upon them. Their nervousness in India was increased by Sikh extremism. This, too, the Germans sought to encourage. There was, of course, no chance that it would undermine the raj, but it would help to divert Britain's attention, and perhaps some of its military strength, from the European front. Increasingly, indeed, Britain needed to use Indian forces outside India, in other non-European territories and in Europe itself. They felt it necessary to make a political gesture that would reward and strengthen India's loyalty. That, in fact, speeded up the re-shaping of the empire.

15

The empire that the British had built up in the nineteenth century was a heterogeneous collection of settler colonies, imperial possessions and protectorates. To it, perhaps, no general rule could apply, though decentralisation was a common feature. In the case of the settler colonies, that was combined with the concept of self-government, and by the early twentieth century 'Dominion status' conferred a substantial degree of independence on Australia, New Zealand, Canada and, the latest recruit, South Africa – so much so, indeed, that the empire, so far as these territories were concerned, was a kind of unwritten alliance. What would happen to the other territories? The British had already convinced themselves that they could safely share some power with their Indian subjects. The war speeded up the process and committed them, in Montagu's declaration of 1917, to the granting of self-government within the empire in the future. That was a major step in the evolution of what the South African leader, Jan Smuts, called the British Commonwealth of Nations.

If Britain's antagonist prompted change in Asia, so did its ally. Japan's role reflected the ambiguity in the Anglo-Japanese alliance. Originally designed to limit the Russians, its purpose had shifted, and increasingly the British saw it as a means of influencing Japan, so that its policy should continue along the existing lines, avoiding pan-Asianism, pursuing an expedient diplomacy. On the outbreak of the war it was difficult to turn aside Japan's rather too enthusiastic proffer of help, and it absorbed the German concession in Shantung. The following year the government – led by the one-time popular-rights politician Okuma Shigenobu – took advantage of the continued chaos in China and the continued absorption of the European powers in the war by presenting China with the Twenty-One Demands. Japan had avoided pan-Asianism, but stepped up its realist policy at the expense of China, and incidentally of other powers. The demands required China's assent to any subsequent arrangement over the German concession in Shantung, the aim being to avoid anything like the Triple Intervention; sought a strengthening of Japan's position in Manchuria; and insisted on a Chinese pledge not to cede any port or island to a foreign power. In the words of Chiang Kai-shek, the nationalist leader, the Twenty-One Demands were 'the grand culmination of all the unequal treaties',[14] but the government of Yuan Shih-kai accepted most of them. These were days of national humiliation, and boycotts of Japanese trade followed in Shanghai and on the Yangtse. Britain, upholder of the integrity of China and the Open Door, was in no position to oppose its ally, and in a sense the demands marked Japan's continued moderation, for it could have gone further. But its actions weakened the Chinese government, and also radicalised Chinese nationalism.

The war intensified that radicalism in another way. For the Bolsheviks who had seized power in Russia, revolution there was but the prelude to world revolution. 'And if our Soviet republic perishes', Alexandra Kollontay told the seventh party congress, 'another will raise our banner... Long live the revolutionary war!'[15] The humiliating peace with the Germans that led the Allies to intervene also prompted a 72,000 strong Japanese expedition to Siberia, despite opposition from Yamagata, the last of the military wing of the Meiji oligarchs. But if the Russian revolution was initially an opportunity for the Japanese, in the longer term it was a challenge. For it gave Chinese nationalism a communist backing.

The entry of the USA into the war made it ever more clearly a worldwide conflict, but also enhanced its ideological character. So far the USA had been no more willing to restrain Japan than before the war, and at the time of the Twenty One Demands it simply declared that it would not recognise any agreement reached between China and Japan that impaired American rights, China's integrity or the Open Door. USA entry into the war made Japan more apprehensive. Now it would need USA assent for retaining the Shantung concession at the conclusion of the war. In the event, the Lansing–Ishii agreement of 1917 reaffirmed the Open Door, but recognised that geographical propinquity gave Japan 'special interests'. It still seemed unlikely that America's commitment to self-determination and nationality, and to the idealism of the Fourteen Points, would lead it to take up China's cause. China's own declaration of war was designed, however, to enhance its status in the peace negotiations. Wilsonian policy, too, had to counter the appeal of the Russian revolutionaries. If the President's Fourteen Points were an answer to 'the voice of the Russian people',[16] they seemed to have meaning for the Chinese, too, even though so far the USA had done little save repeat its verbal endorsement of the integrity of China and the Open Door.

Though no territorial change took place, South east Asia was not unaffected by the war. Indeed its experience reflected or replicated that of other parts of Asia. The most dramatic event was the mutiny in Singapore in 1915, though its importance was more symbolic than real. A mutiny in an Indian regiment was disconcerting, even if it could be blamed on subversive Sikhs or Germans, or on disputes among the British officers, rather than on nationalist feeling. It was readily suppressed, but it demonstrated Britain's weakness in the area during the war. The help of allies, particularly Japan, was only half welcome. Pan-Asians among the Japanese made more of the help they gave than the British liked. 'What is the significance to be attached to the fact that the flag of the Rising Sun was set up in the centre of Singapore?', a Japanese journalist asked his readers.[17]

The ambivalence in the Anglo-Japanese relationship was clear in respect of Netherlands India, too. The Germans did not breach the neutrality of the Dutch as they did that of the Belgians, and the Netherlands did not take part in the First World War. The British Consul-General in Batavia indeed believed the Dutch were too tolerant of subversive German activity in the Indies. Was there not a case, he suggested, for a partition of Netherlands

India? The Dutch could retain Java, but the future of Sumatra, Borneo and Sulawesi could be determined by Britain and Japan. The concept was rejected in London. The aim of the Anglo-Japanese alliance was to preserve as much of the status quo as possible, not to dislodge it: 'If the Netherlands Indies are not too friendly, they are harmless. It would be quite another matter if the islands were in the hands of the Japanese.'[18] The British had long preferred the Dutch to a major power. Breaking with that policy was rejected, even though the Dutch were on the unfriendly side of neutral, and the Japanese were Britain's allies. It was not in this way that the Japanese could realise their shadowy ambitions in South-east Asia, firmer though they became with the development in Sumatra and Borneo of the oil resources that they themselves so notably lacked.

The war drew in other peoples as time passed. Siam joined in the war, like China, when the USA did: it was important for the Thais to secure a place at the peace conference. Short of manpower, the French had recruited some 545,000 colonial troops by armistice day, and seventeen Indo-Chinese battalions were fighting in the Balkans and on the Western front.[19] The most rigid of the colonial powers, the French, characteristically made no political concessions in return. Even the Dutch introduced a People's Council in 1916, though giving it limited powers.

## Britain and the powers at the end of the war

Outside Europe Britain, the leading nineteenth-century power, seemed stronger than ever at the end of the war. The Turkish empire had disintegrated and the German empire had been destroyed – and the strength of the British empire had always derived in part from the lack of effective opponents. Yet, perhaps all the more for the weakness of its political and constitutional links, it had also depended on Britain's naval power, and on its financial and economic linkages. The latter had been weakened by the war effort, while the former, also affected by the strain on Britain's economy, now faced new rivalries. In the nineteenth century the rival navies were all European, and Britain's own security, and that of its empire, could be defended at the same time. Now the expansion of the Japanese navy, and still more that of the USA navy, had diffused the focus of naval power across the world. Worldwide commitments could not be sustained simply by having the greatest navy in Europe. How was Britain to meet them?

Before the war one response had been apparent: Britain would select priorities. The first of these was, of course, the defence of Britain itself, and the second was the defence of its possessions. Compromise must be accepted. In effect Britain had accepted USA dominance in the Caribbean and Japanese dominance in East Asian waters. Post-war the pattern must even more be one of prioritisation and compromise. Britain had never expected its nineteenth-century primacy to endure for ever. Adjustment had long been part of its diplomacy. That, of course, implied that other powers should follow a similar kind of approach, accept change over time, pursue a prudential diplomacy. Would the Japanese be content to build on the gains they had made before and during the war? Would they put their emphasis more on economic success than on political adventure? Certainly the war had brought them economic as well as political advantages, and they had now for the first time become a creditor nation.

In their dependent territories the British continued to believe that they could handle the domestic situation. They had promised constitutional advance in India, but believed that they could determine its phasing, and a similar view applied perhaps even more strongly in South-east Asia. In the Middle East the same was true, both in respect of Egypt and of the remnants of the Turkish empire over which they had acquired control. Their position in Asia, they continued to believe, was more likely to be threatened from outside the frontiers than from inside. If there was no direct threat from the Japanese, the main threats would be American example and communist propaganda. The latter the British took most seriously. Otherwise, the war had not, it seemed, undermined the empire, nor the confidence that, guided by the British, it would slowly evolve more or less along the lines set by Britain's relationships with the settler dominions.

Certainly there was no alteration of the basic model, to which indeed the war gave a new impetus, the British Commonwealth of Nations – the 'British entente', as Alfred Zimmern was to call it. But if, on the one hand, there was now even less chance than before the war that the model could be changed and a more formal and coherent structure set up, the British did not, on the other hand, take the step of speeding up its application to parts of the empire other than the settler dominions, Montagu's declaration on India being the exception to prove the rule. The problems such a step would involve offered many grounds for caution, but if imperial policy was to remain one of progressive evolution towards self-government, it might have strengthened rather than weakened the British if they had undertaken and implemented it more positively. The impression was given that Britain would yield only if pressed, and that it was increasingly apprehensive over the risk of dislodging what remained of the status quo. The war left a legacy of caution as well as of change.

### Diplomacy and war

The war began in Europe. It might be seen not as a continuation of European diplomacy, but a result of its failure. Over time the relative power of states alters – for example as a result of national unification or industrialisation – and their relations with each other have to alter accordingly. To regulate them is the task of diplomats. How far can their interests be reconciled by adjustment or by negotiation? Are differences so great that independence or security are put at risk? Can states sacrifice even those interests for the sake of peace? For if changes cannot be accepted in the course of peaceful diplomacy, the use of force is a likely outcome.

There had been great changes in the pre-war world, and the diplomacy of the day had failed to preserve peace. A short war had seemed a possible answer, but it proved to be more extensive than expected. Not only the statesmen but the system itself seemed to be at fault. Moreover an overall 'settlement' seemed to be necessary. A great deal was indeed expected of it.

In Asia conflict had been on a smaller scale. Yet some Asians had witnessed the fighting among Europeans, and even taken part in it, and their hold was weakened in that and other ways. Japan, in which the building of the nation state and industrialisation were furthest advanced, had been able to make considerable gains. But it was not alone in its high expectations of the 'settlement'.

# Chapter 2

# The Peace Settlements

The statesmen who met in Paris in 1919 to draw up a peace settlement faced a daunting task. Lloyd George, the leader of the British delegation, claimed that 'it is not one continent that is engaged – every continent is affected'.[1] The collapse of the four empires of Germany, Austria-Hungary, Russia and Turkey and the demands of previously subject national groups necessitated a major redrawing of the map in Europe and the Middle East. In Africa, China and the Pacific, the future of Germany's former possessions had to be considered. Many diverse and often conflicting hopes and aspirations depended on the outcome of the negotiations. Some were inevitably disappointed and those disappointments fuelled the criticism of contemporaries and have influenced the judgement of historians. The fact that the settlement was followed twenty years later by another major war has led to the assumption that it must have been fatally flawed. There has been less agreement on the nature of the flaws. Its treatment of Germany has been criticised both as too harsh and as not severe enough. The peacemakers have been accused of failing to appreciate the full strength of nationalist aspirations but they have also been blamed for too easily acquiescing in the break-up of the multinational Austro-Hungarian empire. Most frequently the settlement has been criticised for failing to fulfil expectations that it would be the first major act of the new open diplomacy of which Wilson had been the advocate.

The settlement was embodied in a series of treaties made with the main enemy states: the treaty of Versailles (28 June 1919) with Germany, the treaty of St Germain (10 September 1919) with Austria, the treaty of Trianon (4 June 1920) with Hungary, the treaty of Neuilly (27 November 1919) with Bulgaria and the treaty of Sèvres (10 August 1920) with Turkey, revised in the treaty of Lausanne (24 July 1923). The terms of the treaty with Germany were largely determined by the heads of the main delegations, Woodrow Wilson of the United States, Clemenceau of France, Lloyd George of Great Britain and to a lesser extent Orlando of Italy and the representatives of Japan. The other treaties were mainly left to their sub-ordinates as Wilson and Lloyd George were limited in the time that they could spend away from their own countries. The order in which the treaties were negotiated was a reflection of the perceived priorities and of the complexities of the issues. All the powers accepted that the settlement with Germany had to be made first but there could be no absolute isolation of issues. A state's policy in one area was influenced by its interests and relationships in another. For the British, the non-European settlement was almost as important as the European one: while the future security of Britain itself was most likely to be affected by developments in Europe, Britain's status as a great power was believed to be dependent upon its imperial possessions and the safety of its access to them.

### The League of Nations

The covenant or constitution of the League of Nations was, at Wilson's insistence, an integral part of each treaty. It was to be the basis for the new international order, replacing the system of secret diplomacy and alliances and the untrammelled exercise of national sovereignty which it was believed had contributed to the coming of war. The concept which emerged was essentially an Anglo-American one which stressed the deliberative, consulta-tive functions of the new body rather than providing it with coercive powers. Members agreed to respect each other's independence and integrity. Matters of mutual interest and potential conflict could be discussed in the Assembly, and where compromise solutions could not be reached, the League Council was to provide the option of arbitration. If that were not successful and a state resorted to war, then it was envisaged that trade and financial sanctions would be applied, but military sanctions required the unanimous support of the whole Council which could only recommend to member governments what forces they might individually contribute.

The French had had a very different scheme in mind. They had envisaged a strong executive and a League army with its own independent general staff which could enforce League decisions and protect members against aggressive powers. Wilson had been well aware that any proposal which would impinge upon national sovereignty was unlikely to win approval in the United States. Lloyd George was nervous about additional commitments on Britain's overstretched resources. Both were suspicious that the French wished to use the League mainly as a means of enforcing a settlement on Germany. Against the combined opposition of the United States and Britain, Clemenceau was forced to give way. As a result, the French leadership had little faith in the League. Marshal Foch expressed the opinion that 'it was a queer Anglo-Saxon fancy not likely to be of the slightest importance in practice', and Lloyd George believed that Clemenceau had no faith or hope in it.[2] The French would therefore look for other means to safeguard their future security.

In public, British politicians, aware of the considerable public support for the League, expressed confidence in it but in private members of the government were more reserved. Leo Amery referred to it as 'moonshine' and Lord Milner as 'flapdoodle', and Arthur Balfour considered that 'You cannot and no rational man would suggest that the League of Nations is constituted to deal with a world in chaos or with any part of a world which is in pure chaos'.[3] The British would continue to try to ensure their security by the more traditional methods of protecting Britain's naval position and favouring the maintenance of a balance of power.

Constituted as it was, the success of the League in maintaining future peace was going to be very dependent upon states submitting to its authority and its decisions. It would need the preservation of an overwhelming desire for peace and a belief that the benefits of that peace far outweighed the promotion of any national interests that might be achieved by the use of force. In 1919, there was some optimism that the growth of democracy would help to promote that state of affairs and that the public opinion of the civilised world would be innately pacifist and the best protection against future aggression. Some saw the continuing support of the USA for the League as crucial. Sir Maurice Hankey, the British cabinet secretary, who refused the offer to be the first Secretary-General of the League, expressed the fear that if Wilson failed 'to carry his policy in America . . . the League will probably fail also'.[4]

### The Treaty of Versailles

Of the 440 clauses of the Treaty of Versailles, the most important determined Germany's future boundaries with France and Poland, its relationship with Austria, the fate of its armed services and the extent of the reparations which it would have to pay to its former enemies. In the West, the main territorial changes were not unexpected. Alsace-Lorraine was returned to France and a few border districts were given to Belgium. The Saar valley was put under the special administration of the League for a period of fifteen years, after which it would be returned to Germany or remain with France depending on the results of a plebiscite. The ownership of the mines of the area was given to France which was to receive compensation for them should the plebiscite favour a return to Germany. The west bank of the Rhine and a 50-km belt on the east bank were to be demilitarised. The west bank with bridgeheads at Cologne, Coblenz and Mainz was to be divided into three zones and occupied by Allied and American troops, who would evacuate a zone every five years if Germany fulfilled its other obligations under the treaty. In the east, Germany ceded Posen and part of West Prussia to Poland, and Memel to Lithuania, while the port of Danzig was made a free city under the control of the League of Nations. Plebiscites were to be held in Upper Silesia, Allenstein and Marienwerder to determine the fate of those territories. Germany's union with Austria was forbidden: its colonies were confiscated and were to be ruled as mandate territories under the League of Nations. Severe restrictions were placed on Germany's future military strength – its army was to be reduced to 100,000 men and its navy to 15,000. The kind of ships and weapons it could manufacture or possess were limited and were to be subject to allied control and inspection. Economically, too, Germany was restricted. It had to sacrifice a proportion of its merchant and fishing fleets. Any German investment or property in the countries controlled by ex-enemies was liable to appropriation. The obligation to pay reparations was set out in what became known by the unfortunately emotive term 'the War Guilt clause': 'The Allied and Associated Governments affirm and Germany accepts the responsibility of Germany and her Allies for causing all the loss and damage to which the Allied and Associated Governments and their nationals have been subjected as a consequence of the war imposed upon them by the aggression of Germany and her allies.'[5] It had been designed not so much to apportion blame for the outbreak of war as to establish the principle of Germany's responsibility to pay compensation. No specific sum was named. The final amount and the method and time of payments were to be decided by a Reparations Commission, which was to make its report in or before May 1921.

The treaty, as the French diplomat Jules Cambon, had foreseen, was *'une improvisation'*. In the end it had been put together in some haste, a combination of the decisions on separate issues rather than the result of mature consideration of the treaty as a whole. It reflected the differing views of the 'Big Three' (as Wilson, Clemenceau and Lloyd George came to be called) and the fact that each one had compromised over some issue for the sake of preserving allied unity and of achieving a settlement in a reasonable space of time. That had been thought necessary because of the unstable internal political situation within Germany and the threat of the spread of Bolshevism, which was equated with the breakdown of the whole political and social order. As democratic leaders, the 'Big Three' were subject to the pressures of their own domestic politics and of public opinion, which had had hopes and expectations aroused by wartime propaganda and the promises of a new post-war world. Clemenceau relinquished the French claim to the whole of the Rhineland and the Saar in the face of determined Anglo-American opposition, although it brought him bitter recriminations within France from those who believed that he had sacrificed future French security. 'When confronted with the Rhineland question Mr Wilson shook his head in an uncompromising fashion, and Mr Lloyd George assumed a

24

determined air of antagonism', Clemenceau explained.[6] In accordance with the new emphasis on national self-determination, the British and Americans argued that there was no ethnic justification for such a claim and that it would arouse similar bitterness amongst the Germans as the annexation of Alsace-Lorraine by Germany had aroused amongst the French. For the French the compromise solution of the demilitarisation of the Rhineland was designed to go some way to giving France security, and the free access to Saar coal was compensation for the mines which had been destroyed by the retreating German army in northern France in 1918. In addition, an Anglo-American guarantee of aid was given to France in the event of its being subject to unprovoked aggression. Although the Germans objected to this part of the settlement and were particularly concerned at their loss of control over the iron industry of Lorraine there was not the same intensity of opposition as to some other parts of the treaty. The Fourteen Points had prepared them for the loss of Alsace-Lorraine; the economically important Rhineland remained a German possession; and the loss of the Saar was expected to be temporary. The power which later saw itself as the main loser was France. When the American Senate refused to ratify the whole treaty which President Wilson had negotiated, the Anglo-American guarantee became invalid. The sacrifice of claims to the whole Rhineland and the Saar seemed to have been in vain and it led to a redoubling of French efforts to obtain security by other means.

The German–Polish frontier was the subject of considerable debate and acrimony between the three delegations and even within the British delegation itself. In the Fourteen Points, Poland had been promised an independent state with territories that were inhabited by 'indisputably Polish populations' and 'free and secure access to the sea' and a guarantee of economic independence. The problem was that the territories which would provide the new state with access to the sea and a major port were not 'indisputably Polish'. Posen had a mixed German–Polish population and Danzig was almost totally German. The mineral-rich and important economic area of Upper Silesia was also inextricably mixed in population. If the Poles were treated generously, then it was recognised that a large German minority would be left within the new Polish state and that East Prussia, regarded by many Germans as the cradle of their state, would be left in isolation. If the territory were left with Germany, then there would be a Polish minority and a considerable question as to whether Poland's secure access to the sea would be safeguarded in the future. France was unequivocally in favour of generous treatment of the Poles. With the collapse of its former ally, the Russian empire, France saw a strong Poland as a necessary constraint on Germany in the east and as part of a bulwark against the possible spread of Bolshevism from Soviet Russia. On this issue, Wilson largely supported the French in wanting a strong substantial Polish state. Whether his views were coloured by a moral zeal to redress the wrong of the eighteenth-century partition of Poland, by some inaccuracies in his geographical knowledge or by the size of the Polish vote in the USA is open to question. The British, and particularly Lloyd George, were less sympathetic to the Polish claims. Irritated by what they saw as Polish greed and unconvinced of the Poles' ability to govern themselves, they believed that the least possible number of Germans should be left within the new Polish state. Lloyd George argued passionately that the alternative would risk Germany's very acceptance of the treaty, and would lead to the growth of a strong German desire for revenge that would threaten the future stability of the whole region. In that event, he tellingly asked, 'Would we make war for Danzig?'[7] As a result of his efforts and in response to the German representations, Wilson modified his views to allow the compromise of League authority over Danzig and the holding of plebiscites in disputed areas. Ultimately Allenstein and Marienwerder chose to remain in Germany and Upper Silesia was divided between Poland and Germany after prolonged Anglo-French friction over the holding of the plebiscite.

The concessions did little to reduce German resentment about this aspect of the treaty. Admittedly, there was a considerable number of Germans left within the new Polish state, and the loss of part of its second most important industrial area, Silesia, adversely affected Germany's ability to cope with the economic demands of the treaty and its own recovery. Much of the settlement, however, could have been anticipated from the Fourteen Points. There was no easy solution to the complicated problems of drawing a boundary along lines of nationality in areas of mixed population, while giving some consideration to the economic and strategic requirements of both states. The extent of the German resentment can perhaps only be explained fully by the widespread German 'hatred and contempt for the Poles'.[8]

The reparations agreement arose out of the need for another compromise between the main delegations. The French, faced by budget deficits, the need to rebuild the war-devastated areas of northern France and huge debts to Britain and to the USA, had appealed to those powers for assistance. The former was faced with economic problems of its own, and the latter, influenced by what the British chancellor of the exchequer referred to as a 'lot of Wall Street toughs', refused any continuation of the wartime economic co-operation or to link reparations with the repayment of war debts.[9] The French therefore increased their demand for reparations. Politically there was little option. For France to be restored someone had to pay, and the French public expected that burden to fall on Germany, both the aggressor and the loser in the war, rather than on themselves. There was undoubtedly an attraction too in imposing a heavy bill on Germany that would take years to pay, and which would hinder its economic recovery and therefore reinforce French security. Given that situation, the French were naturally reluctant to acquiesce in the American suggestion that reparations should be set at a modest figure based on Germany's immediate capacity to pay.

French intransigence was long thought to have been mainly responsible for the failure to agree on a specified sum in 1919. France, however, was not totally intransigent. Clemenceau wavered in his reparations policy. He saw the possibility that Germany's failure to meet substantial reparations demands could be a means of prolonging the occupation of the Rhineland, but his economic advisers saw some advantage in a more moderate and immediate settlement and even had tentative direct negotiations with the Germans.[10] Britain, in 1919, was the more unwilling to settle for a modest sum. Lloyd George, whose own views may well not have been as moderate as he later claimed, was also imprisoned by British opinion and his own previous policy. During the election campaign which he had fought at the end of the war, he and his supporters had promised that 'Germany should pay' and, if he had any inclination to forget, he was reminded by a telegram from 233 MPs in April 1919. There were two related problems. How much should Germany pay? How much could Germany pay? The attitude of the British did not make for moderation on either count. In an attempt to increase their share of reparations – Britain had suffered little civilian damage – they demanded that war pensions should be included in the categories for compensation. Britain as much as France was unwilling to contemplate basing any assessment of Germany's capability to pay on its immediate post-war situation. For Lloyd George the answer was to make no immediate decision. He admitted that 'any figure that would not frighten them [the Germans] would be below the figure with which he and M Clemenceau could face their peoples in the present state of public opinion. If figures were given now they would frighten rather than reassure the Germans.'[11]

Their solution was to leave the financial decisions to the reparations Commission but to establish the principle of Germany's responsibility to pay by including the so-called War Guilt clause. It was probably one of the most unfortunate decisions of the whole settlement. Germany could rightfully claim that the uncertainty would have a most damaging effect upon its economic planning, particularly because of the fear that any recovery could be made the basis for a higher claim. The idea of signing a 'blank cheque' and of accepting German responsibility for the war made reparations doubly unacceptable. At the same time, it was a dangerous assumption that it would be easier to reach an agreement on a final figure in the future.

The other main aspects of the treaty reflected the particular desires of Britain and France. Britain was determined that the German navy should cease to be a threat to its own naval position. The British Dominions, which had been loyal allies in the war, had their eyes upon Germany's former colonies and it was only in deference to Wilson's views that they obtained them as mandate territories under the League of Nations rather than as outright acquisitions. For France any idea of allocating the Austrian and the Bohemian lands to Germany, whatever the claims of national self-determination, was anathema. What was the point of winning the war and trying to constrain Germany in some ways if it were allowed extra territories elsewhere? The British and the Americans acquiesced with comparatively little discussion. Colonel House, who was deputising for Wilson at the time of the decision over Bohemia, was said to be more concerned 'to bring about peace quickly than ... to haggle over details', and Lloyd George seemed 'to know but little about it'.[12] Underlying the whole approach of the victorious powers to the settlement was the view that Germany should not make gains at the end of a war which it had provoked. Wilson's view of justice required some punishment for past misdeeds, and the fact that the United States had felt compelled to enter the war against Germany was evidence of some German culpability. Germany's total territorial losses under the treaty deprived the country of some 14.5 per cent of its previous arable land, 74.5 per cent of its iron ore, 68 per cent of its zinc ore, and 26 per cent of its coal production.[13] For the Germans, the extent of these territorial and economic losses, their unilateral disarmament, the lack of any 'free and open discussion of colonial claims', and the failure to allow freedom of choice to the Germans of Austria and Bohemia were unjust impositions and a hypocritical abandonment of the promises and principles of the Fourteen Points.[14]

Castigating the treaty as 'injustice without example', the Germans accepted the peace treaty with the greatest reluctance. No government had been willing to accept the responsibility of appending its signature but, faced with military advice that any thought of armed resistance was totally futile, the coalition of moderate left-wing parties of the new Weimar Republic capitulated. The Germans could rightfully claim that it was a *diktat*, that there was little of the 'open covenants of peace openly arrived at' that they had been promised in the Fourteen Points. The constraints on the time of the Allied leaders and their belief that a quick settlement was necessary meant that the Germans had been given a mere two weeks to make comments on a draft treaty, and then little modification had resulted from their remarks. In that respect there seemed little difference from the way in which defeated powers had been treated in the past. The fact that the old imperial Germany had been replaced by the new democratic Germany also appeared to have had little effect. It was still assumed that it should have no continuing association with its former colonies and it was denied membership of the League of Nations. For a German public which had difficulty in realising that militarily it had been defeated when no foreign armies had appeared on German soil, any treaty which implied defeat would have been hard to accept. Versailles, with its overall demands and especially its demands relating to Poland and reparations, was totally unacceptable.

One of the serious consequences of the settlement on internal German developments was that the signing of the peace treaty was a political albatross around the neck of the moderate left-wing parties in the new republic. In their determination to continue the fight to obtain modifications of the treaty, successive governments emphasised its harsh aspects without a corresponding emphasis on the extent of Germany's military impotence at the time of its signature. In so doing they played into the hands of those opponents of the Weimar regime who claimed that the politicians who had signed the armistice and the treaty had betrayed Germany. Germany's losses under the treaty were undoubtedly considerable in territory, manpower and economic potential. Compared, however, with the terms of the treaty of Brest-Litovsk and the terms which it is now known Germany was proposing to impose on the rest of Europe had it emerged victorious from the war, Versailles was not draconian. Germany remained far superior to France in the size of its population and, while it retained the Rhineland and part of Silesia, it possessed far greater economic resources. Germany was left with the potential to emerge as a first class power again. Indeed, for some that has been the main criticism of the treaty. As one contemporary Frenchman remarked, 'it was too lenient for its severity'.[15] Bitter and resentful, Germany was not so weakened that it had to accept its fate. What was more, it was no longer bordered by powerful states in the east but by the new, often weak and unstable successors to the old empires.

### The settlement in eastern Europe

In eastern Europe, the treaties of St Germain and Trianon confirmed the break-up of the Austro-Hungarian empire and allocated its former lands between the new states. Czechoslovakia, made up of the former Austrian provinces of Bohemia and Moravia and of the Hungarian ones of Slovakia and Ruthenia, was a miniature version of the old empire with its three million Germans, some half a million Hungarians, Ruthenians and other small minority groups, as well as the majority Czechs and Slovaks. Romania was greatly enlarged at the expense of its neighbours, securing Transylvania from Hungary, Bessarabia from Russia and South Dobruja from Bulgaria. All three acquisitions were areas of mixed populations and in the Dobruja the Romanians themselves were very much in the minority. Yugoslavia was created as a result of the wartime decision of the main south Slav groups – the Serbs, Croats and Slovenes – to form a united state. It was made up of the former states of Serbia and Montenegro, the Austrian provinces of Slovenia, Bosnia and Dalmatia and the Hungarian provinces of Croatia and the Voivodina. The Istrian peninsula which the Yugoslavs had also claimed was granted to Italy and the port of Fiume, the subject of immense acrimony, was left for a future settlement between them. Austria, which also lost the South Tyrol to Italy and Galicia to Poland, was left as a small insignificant state, scarcely viable as an economic unit. Hungary lost about two-thirds of its pre-war territories and something approaching three million Hungarians were to live outside its borders. Bulgaria lost territory to Yugoslavia and to Greece, which deprived it of access to the Aegean. All three defeated powers, like Germany, had to accept responsibility for the payment of reparations.

The conclusion of a settlement for eastern Europe had been much more complicated and difficult than the leading peacemakers had anticipated. As Wilson later admitted: 'When I gave utterance to those words (that all nations had a right to self-determination) I said them without the knowledge that nationalities existed which are coming to us day after day'.[16] Throughout the former empires peoples had become intermingled and there was no easy drawing of borders along 'lines of nationality'. Problems similar to the one over the German–Polish border occurred many times over. The existence of minorities in some states was going to be inevitable unless the wholesale movement of peoples were contemplated. The complaint of the defeated powers, and with much justification, was that decisions over disputed areas had always been in favour of the newly created states. The reasons for that were manifold. There were the wartime commitments which Britain and France had made to Romania and Italy which they believed they had to honour. There was a particular lack of sympathy for Hungary which had had a communist government from March to August 1919 and was therefore thought likely to import the virus of Bolshevism into central Europe. In some instances possession proved to be nine points of the law. All the claimants, especially the Romanians, had some kind of forces in the field, while Austria and Hungary were in no position to resist, and the major powers possessed comparatively few troops on the ground with which they could have enforced any unpalatable decisions. As time passed, the American and British leadership, the former preoccupied with the domestic fight over the treaty and the latter preoccupied with difficulties elsewhere, took less interest in this part of the settlement and the French were firm supporters of the new states.

The major dispute amongst the victorious powers had been about the Italian claims. The Italians wanted Fiume in addition to the territories which had been promised to them during the war. Wilson had been outraged at the flagrant breach of the nationality principle with respect to the South Tyrol, which was largely German in population and had agreed to its cession to Italy only after dramatic scenes at the conference table which had left the Italian delegate, Orlando, in tears. It was the first time that he had heard of any statesman trying 'to sob his way to empire', commented Balfour, the British foreign secretary.[17] To some extent it succeeded. In the face of Italian intransigence Wilson gave way over the Tyrol in the futile hope that that would lead to Italy's moderating its claims to Dalmatia and Fiume where there were large Slav populations.

Prior to 1914, eastern Europe and the Balkans had been regarded as a potential danger to the peace of Europe because of the frustrated ambitions of the subject nationalities. The creation of nation states had not removed but merely altered the nature of the problems. Many of the minorities were more conscious of their minority status now that they were subjects of a nation state rather than subjects of a multinational empire. It was not only those who had been dominant groups in the past, such as the Hungarians and Germans, who felt discriminated against, but also supposed beneficiaries of the new system such as the Slovaks in Czechoslovakia and the Croats and Slovenes in Yugoslavia. The Slovaks soon complained of Czech and the Croats and Slovenes of Serb domination. In addition, there was increased international rivalry in the area. It was caused not only by Hungary and Bulgaria who were looking for an opportunity for revenge and to regain the territory which they believed was rightfully theirs, but also by antagonism between the new states themselves. Czechoslovakia and Poland, Yugoslavia and Romania, Yugoslavia and Italy all had border disputes. The nationalist rivalries militated against the economic development of the region. The former trading patterns and transport systems of the empire had been dislocated and the existing ill-will led to the failure of attempts to replace them by a suggested Danubian economic federation. While the eastern European states remained economically weak, internally divided and at odds with each other, there was always the future danger that they would be susceptible to the intervention and domination of larger powers.

### The settlement in the Middle East

The defeat of the Ottoman empire in the war ushered in far-reaching changes in the Middle East. By the treaty of Sèvres, the Ottomans accepted humiliating terms. An international commission was to control the zone of the Straits, another financial commission was to control Turkish finances and strict limitations were placed on their armed services. They had to give up all their Arabian lands and cede Thrace and the control of Izmir to the Greeks. The Anatolian heartland itself, while remaining under Turkish suzerainty, was to be divided into French and Italian spheres of influence. The severity of this proposed settlement prompted Churchill to say that 'the whole attitude of the Peace Conference to Turkey was so harsh that Right had now changed sides'.[18] After a successful Turkish nationalist uprising under Kemal Pasha, that treaty was repudiated and, by the treaty of Lausanne, a new basis for a settlement in the Near East was negotiated. Eastern Thrace and Izmir were returned to the new Turkish Republic. All financial restrictions were removed and the only military restriction was to be a demilitarised zone around the Straits. In the Arabian lands, however, Turkish control was not restored, but nor were the Arabs given independence. Instead, the area was divided into mandate territories under the League with Syria and Lebanon being allocated to France and Palestine and Iraq to Britain.

The negotiation of the treaty of Lausanne, which proved to be the basis of a very stable settlement, was a remarkable achievement given the disastrous policy which the Allied leadership had followed in that region at the end of the war. Lloyd George had encouraged the Greeks to land troops at Izmir and attempt to gain a base on the mainland. Izmir admittedly had a large Greek population but the surrounding countryside was solidly Turkish. His encouragement of the Greeks, which has not been easy to explain, seems to have arisen from a mixture of traditional beliefs that Britain needed a potential ally to protect its naval and imperial interests in the Mediterranean and from an emotional attachment to his Greek counterpart Venizelos. The support of Wilson and Clemenceau for the policy appears to have been for no better reason than their determination to frustrate what were seen as the exceedingly voracious Italian ambitions in that area. When the Greek adventure miscarried, the frustrated Italians and the French, who were at odds with the British elsewhere, were happy to reach an accommodation with the new Turkish regime. Britain, where support for the Greeks had always been mixed with apprehension about the repercussions of an anti-Turkish policy upon the Muslims of India, was forced to follow suit. Isolated in Europe, with the promise of assistance from New Zealand alone of the dominions and with rumblings of discontent at home at the prospect of further overseas adventures, the British government received a timely reminder of the limitations of its power. The new settlement was surprisingly satisfactory to the British. Their main naval interests were protected by the agreement about the Straits. Turkey severed what had appeared to be a dangerous reliance upon the Soviet Union (or Union of Soviet Socialist Republics – USSR – as Russia had become in December 1922) by joining the League. The immediate potential cause of ongoing Greco-Turkish tension, the question of minorities, was solved by the somewhat drastic policy of a forcible exchange of populations. In many ways the Allies had endeavoured to treat Turkey in much the same way as it had been treated throughout the nineteenth century. Unlike Austria and Hungary , which could only complain that they were not considered as new nation states but as the rump of the old empire, Turkey had forced the Entente powers to recognise that it was a new independent nationalist state with which a new settlement had to be negotiated.

In the Middle East, the outline of the settlement was influenced by the presence of the British army in that theatre of the war. The problems arose from the conflicting expectations which had been aroused by the British wartime promises to the Arabs, the French and the Jews. In the conflict between the Arab hopes of British support for their independence and French demands that Britain honour its commitment to support French control of Syria, the British had to make a choice. Unpalatable as it might be to the residual anti-French sentiments of many of the British leaders, the reality of the situation was that in global terms, Britain needed the support and co-operation of the 'bullying, lying, cajoling' French more than it needed that of the Arabs.[19] No independent Arab states were created and France obtained the mandates it wanted. The Americans refused any mandates and so the British accepted the mandate over Palestine in addition to the one in the potentially oil-rich area of Iraq. In 1917 Britain had promised to support the establishment of a national home for the Jewish people in Palestine but the existing Arab population was bitterly opposed to the idea. With the Jewish Zionist organisation, which had been the driving force behind the national home project, pushing for more Jewish immigration, the scene was set for increasing Arab–Jewish tension. One member of the British cabinet, Robert Cecil, correctly foresaw that 'Whoever goes there will have a poor time'.[20]

The settlement of the former Ottoman lands was little influenced by the ideas of the new diplomacy. The major concession in that direction was the creation of the mandates rather than more direct means of control. Britain's policy was influenced by its nineteenth-century views that its strategic and commercial interests, and particularly its possession of India, required the protection of Suez and the Persian Gulf from any potentially hostile power. The Ottoman empire's decision to join Germany in the war had finally brought to an end the increasingly difficult policy of supporting Turkey as a barrier to the infiltration of other powers in that area. French claims, based on historical contacts and growing financial interests, had to be taken into account. The result was something very akin to an old-fashioned imperial division of territory – but it had not been achieved without extreme acrimony and residual bitterness. The Arab sense of betrayal was the foundation for the ongoing suspicion and hostility of the Arab world towards the Western powers. The Italians felt cheated of the share of the Ottoman empire which they thought they had been promised. It was the part of the settlement which fuelled their discontent with what they came to describe as their 'mutilated victory'. Despite the final settlement which gave France most of what it required, Anglo-French relations had been soured. Successful British pressure to reduce French claims under their wartime agreements had not been followed by the expected *quid pro quo* of British support over the Rhineland. The separate French agreement with Kemalist Turkey had been seen by the British as little short of treachery. Anglo-French rivalry in the Middle East took its toll on their relationship in Europe. The British frequently reminded the French that what happened in the Middle East was as important to them as what happened in Europe, and one French diplomat went so far as to say that 'if we had not deserted England in the Middle East, she would not have abandoned us in Europe'.[21] For both powers their additional responsibilities in the Middle East were a questionable advantage at a time when they were aware of the limits of their resources.

### The settlement overall

The disappointment of so many hopes has led to considerable vilification of the peace settlement and the statesmen who made it. In some ways, however, it was a remarkable achievement. Many complex issues were dealt with and an agreement reached in a relatively short space of time. To reach agreements, compromise was necessary and the whole settlement was a compromise between the old secret diplomacy which had been practised by the European powers and the new, more open, diplomacy which was advocated by President Wilson. Concessions to the new way of ordering relationships between states and deciding the fate of peoples were seen in the setting up of the League, the consideration given to questions of national self-determination, the holding of plebiscites and the institution of mandates. It was some acknowledgement that the drawing of boundaries and the transfer of peoples from one jurisdiction to another simply by the will of the great powers and the fortunes of war was no longer as acceptable as it had been in the past. Old habits and ways of thinking about how to manage relationships, however, had not disappeared. A British diplomatic historian goes so far as to say that the 'dream of a "new diplomacy" remained ... no more than a dream' and Isaiah Bowman, an American adviser at the conference, admitted that the introduction of the so-called new diplomacy meant that 'the great stakes of diplomacy remain the same. We simply discuss them in different terms'.[22] The British continued to think in terms of establishing a balance of power and the French looked for specific security provisions in the form of reparations, the establishment of potential allies in eastern Europe and an Anglo-American guarantee, while the Americans were swayed by considerations of their own economic advantage.

One of the inherent problems in the settlement was that, being a compromise, no one of the major signatories had any fierce loyalty to it. The defeated powers were naturally hostile, and particularly so because of the expectations which had been aroused for a different kind of peace treaty. As one German delegate admitted, 'we can never sign this peace in earnest'.[23] By the time all the treaties had been signed, the victorious powers also had doubts. In America the Senate refused to ratify the Versailles treaty. There was some criticism of the concessions which Wilson had made to his European associates but the main attack was directed at the Covenant of the

League of Nations. Some saw it as perpetuating great power domination but others were appalled that the vote of 'a nigger' from Liberia, Honduras or India would equal that of the 'great United States'.[24] Wilson himself did nothing to moderate opposition by his uncompromising and self-righteous defence of the treaty. The major issue, however, was the preservation of American sovereignty. One of the most implacable opponents of the treaty, senator William Borah, said: 'I may be willing to help my neighbour... but I do not want him placed in a position where he may decide for me when and how I shall act or to what extent I shall make a sacrifice'.[25] In particular there was a fear that they would lose control of immigration into the United States. The League, it was said, would result in 'efficient and economical Japanese operating our street railways... Chinese craftsmen... laying bricks in the construction of our buildings'.[26]

In 1921, the United States made a separate treaty with Germany which excluded the League articles. The United States had signalled that it was not prepared to abandon its independent pursuit of its own interests and security in favour of more co-operative and collective action. The British, deprived of the anticipated continuation of Anglo-American co-operation, began to question whether it was practically possible, morally right or in their best interests to enforce the settlement. The French, having now lost the Anglo-American guarantee, were afraid that they had not made enough provisions for their security. The Italians, despite their considerable gains, were aggrieved that all their demands had not been met and were openly revisionist. The Soviet Union, whose Bolshevik government had not been invited to the peace conferences, was hostile to the League, to the settlement and to the powers who had made it. The crucial question therefore was how the settlement was to be implemented and enforced.

The important role of the United States, and the more limited participation of the Japanese, in drawing up a peace settlement which largely affected Europe was a significant indication of the changing position of the European powers in the world. When it came to the making of a settlement in the Far East, the major negotiating roles which were played by Japan and the United States, despite the interests of France, Britain and the Soviet Union in the area, provided an even clearer indication of the end of European predominance.

### The Washington Conference

Germany believed that the Versailles treaties denied it the peace promised by Wilson's Fourteen Points. His idealistic sentiments had stirred hopes in Asia that were also disappointed. Japan itself urged that 'racial equality' should be included in the Covenant of the League of Nations, less as a protest at the anti-immigration laws in Australia and the USA than as a means of pursuing the post-Meiji search for equality with other nations. Australia opposed it, however, as a threat to the 'White Australia' policy, and was backed by Britain, on the not entirely straightforward ground that it would imply the League's interference in the domestic affairs of its members. Wilson thought Billy Hughes, the Australian prime minister, a 'pestiferous varmint', but gave in. Japan confessed its 'poignant regret',[27] and concentrated on the Shantung issue. There, of course, it was acting in the old 'imperialist' style that Wilsonian idealism rejected.

Again, one reason for participation in the war on the part of China, and of Siam, too, was the hope that in the peace negotiations Wilsonian idealism would work against the old diplomacy and move towards the undoing of the unequal treaties: if Asian states took part in the war, they should surely be put on the basis of equality, particularly in a world avowedly based on the principles of self-determination and nationality. That did not occur. Over Shantung the treaty provided for a compromise that did not satisfy the Chinese: it recognised China's sovereignty and Japan's privileges. Wilson had concluded that he must yield to Japan, lest it failed to accept the League and settlement as a whole: 'If Japan went home, there was the danger of a Japan–Russia–Germany alliance, and a return to the old "balance of power" system in the world'.[28] The Japanese government had indeed put forward the claim to 'racial equality' partly to make the idea of joining the League more acceptable to those Japanese who saw it consolidating Anglo-American dominance.[29]

'Today it is a worldwide trend to honor pacifism and reject oppression. Everywhere in the world the so-called Americanism is advanced', Makino Shinken declared, 'and conditions have definitely altered since the days of the old diplomacy.'[30] The Japanese accepted that, and they also accepted the Washington agreements of 1921–2. In some ways they were a counterpart of the Versailles settlement in Europe, and an extension of the new diplomacy into the Far East. Versailles had dealt with issues that arose in considering a peace settlement. The new agreements sought to deal with the implications for East Asia of other developments that the war had prompted. The terms of the agreements marked major changes in the approach of the British, less in that of the USA, but more in that of the Japanese. Like Versailles, Washington was a matter of compromise: would it endure? Again the agreements disappointed the Chinese and left the Russians out of account. Indeed the Bolshevik government convened a kind of rival Congress of the Toilers of the Far East. Did that omission invalidate the Washington system?

Three main agreements were made at Washington. In a four-power treaty, the USA, Britain, France and Japan agreed to respect each other's rights in the Pacific in respect of insular possessions and dominions; to confer on any dispute; and to communicate in the case of threats from other powers. A five-power treaty related to naval power and included Italy as well. It prescribed a ratio for the battleships, battle cruisers and aircraft carriers that each power might possess: 10 USA; 10 UK; 6 Japan; 3.5 France; 3.5 Italy. It also prescribed the status quo for naval fortifications in East Asia, including those at Hong Kong (UK) and in the Philippines and at Guam (USA). A nine-power treaty, involving also Belgium, the Netherlands, China and Portugal (the possessor of Macau) committed the parties to the integrity of China and the Open Door or equal commercial opportunity.

Like Versailles, the agreements were partly designed to accommodate the interests of the victorious powers, the relative position of which had changed in the course of the war. The major shift was, of course, the relative decline in the power of Britain and the activation of US potential marked, for example, by its naval building. Both powers faced strong pressures for a post-war curbing of expenditure and for disarmament. In addition Britain needed to avoid competing in naval building with the USA, an arms race which it could not win. A deal with the United States that curbed its naval building would have to include other concessions, too.

One of the sensitive issues was the Anglo-Japanese alliance. Originally helping Britain to focus on the growing threat in Europe, in that respect it was now no longer relevant. It could still have some value in containing Russia, now in the hands of a communist regime that might take up the old expansionist policies of the tsars in new ways. Even more clearly it could perform the function it had already come to perform, that of encouraging the Japanese to act with moderation and with consideration for an ally, the connection with which had been of such great value. Against that it was possible to argue, as, with some chronological inaccuracy, did Meighen, the Canadian prime minister, that the alliance had not really restrained Japan: 'there is Korea, there is Formosa, there is Manchuria, there is Shantung. There are the 21 Demands'.[31] But the main argument against its continuance was American opposition to it, and conflict with the USA could not be risked. 'Canada will be the Belgium', as Meighen improbably added.[32] The 1911 arbitration treaty between the USA and the UK had been designed to preclude a conflict: the alliance, renewed that year, had specified that neither signatory would fight a third power with which it had such a treaty. But, more seriously, the alliance seemed to the Americans not merely to impose an ineffective constraint on Japan, but also to epitomise the system of imperialist diplomacy the USA had set itself to displace. The four-power treaty thus replaced the alliance with a wider but looser commitment, while the five-power treaty fixed a ratio in the building of capital ships. On the substance of the nine-power treaty, the USA and the UK were, of course, agreed. The Hay notes of 1900, which had set out the basis of the US government's policy, and which it had continued verbally to endorse, had been an iteration of Britain's nineteenth-century policy towards China. In this respect the objectives of the old diplomacy and the new appeared to coincide.

If, however, the USA and the UK came to terms, were the terms also acceptable to Japan? In the post-war recession, there, too, reductions in naval expenditure made some sense, and there was concern over the expense of a forward policy. But before the negotiations began, the aged Okuma had questioned the intentions of the United States of America, and urged the government of the day to reject any impairment of Japan's legitimately acquired rights.[33] The four-power treaty, moreover, signalled the end of the alliance that had been a pillar of Japan's diplomacy for twenty years, demonstrating the 'equality' the Japanese had long sought: 'It pleases the Japanese to think that they are on the same footing as the Great Powers because they are the Ally of one of them', as Sir C. Eliot had patronisingly put it in 1920.[34] Whether or not it affected that view, the termination of the alliance – 'divorce...with no unfaithfulness to justify it' as F. S. L. Piggott put it[35] – implied a check to the imperialist policy on the mainland, both helping and constraining as it had been.

Why then did Japan accept the treaties? There were general and specific reasons. First, participation in the new diplomacy signified equality as did participation in the old: if the old alliance was dismantled, Japan was a Washington signatory along with the USA and the UK. Second, the naval deal was made advantageous. One factor the Japanese had to consider was the possible expansion of the US navy. If that continued, Japan would have to expand its own navy, and the British follow suit. Yet the UK did not see the USA as a serious threat, and an unrestrained race would precipitate an Anglo-American alliance that would shatter Japan's security. So ran the argument of Kato Tomosaburo, the naval minister.[36] It was better, he concluded, to accept an accommodation that limited the naval building of the USA and the UK as well as Japan. The ratios agreed, moreover, assured Japan's security: given the commitments of the UK and the USA in other parts of the world, Japan would retain the capacity to dominate the Western Pacific. The Japanese government accepted the proposal when it was accompanied by the offer to forego modernising fortifications in the insular possessions of the UK and the USA in East Asia, thus further guaranteeing Japan's security. This the USA agreed to on the understanding that Japan adopted the undertakings of the nine-power treaty.

In these ways the Japanese accepted the implications for East Asia of the shifts in political power and ideology that the war had precipitated. They had made great gains, economic and political, during and immediately after the war. Now, like the British, though in a different way, they had to accommodate to the growth of US power. In face of that, Japan did not attempt to maintain its old methods. Instead, it retained the relatively cautious and accommodating policy of collaborating with the Western powers that it had pursued at least since 1902. Now that they had changed their approach, Japan changed accordingly. It secured naval hegemony in the Western Pacific, but committed itself to a non-violent approach to the protection of its interests on the mainland.

The maintenance of the 'Washington system' indeed depended on the continuance of the 'Washington spirit'. If, for example, the Japanese should abandon the conciliatory approach they had adopted to their interests on the mainland, the new arrangements would indeed be found to impose fewer curbs on them than the old. The displacement of the Anglo-Japanese alliance removed the restraint as well as the encouragement implied by the connection with a traditional partner, and it was replaced by an undertaking shared by more powers but involving less commitment. The Washington treaties in fact marked a further stage in the withdrawal of the British from East Asia, already begun before the First World War. Now Britain's interests in Asia shifted: the focus was on the Middle East, the source of oil, India, and Malaya, the source of rubber. Though Hong Kong and the treaty concessions were retained, Singapore was now the most advanced base, and, under the five-power treaty, the nearest to East Asia that could be modernised. Singapore, indeed, had come to have a new importance, though that was a sign of Britain's relative weakness rather than its strength. Now that naval power was no longer contested merely among Europeans, it had become necessary to have a naval base outside Europe, and the search for that, already undertaken, had led to the choice of Singapore. It was, however, a base with a difference. Britain could place only limited forces there on a regular basis. The main objective was to provide a base to which Britain might move its main fleet from the Atlantic to the Pacific in case of crisis. The building of the Singapore base was rather perilously predicated on meeting two-ocean demands with a one-ocean fleet. Moreover, the British built the base only reluctantly and slowly. The dry dock was opened only in February 1938.

US power now counted more in East Asia than British, and any change in Japan's policy would have to take that into account. Would that power be effectively exerted in support of the 'Washington system' if the 'Washington spirit' evaporated? There was a question over US policy in Asia, as there was in Europe. The five-power treaty meant that the United States of America could in any case develop no modern base west of Pearl Harbor in Hawaii, and under the Jones Act of 1916, it was already committed to the independence of the Philippines, though as yet no definite date had been set. The nine-power treaty endorsed the integrity of China and the Open Door, seen at least since the Hay notes as the basis of US policy in the region. But though Wilsonian idealism and also missionary endeavour stressed an emotional commitment to China, US interests there were limited: even in the 1930s China represented but 4 per cent of US trade. Moreover, isolationism and economic self-sufficiency marked the policy of the USA after Wilson's defeat, and it was far from certain that it would intervene to restrain Japan

39

if it infringed the treaty. Indeed secretary of state Hughes told the US delegation to Washington that the USA 'would never go to war over any aggression on the part of Japan in China'.[37] The Washington treaties were thus scarcely more substantial than the Hay notes themselves or the protest against the Twenty-One Demands. They lacked effective sanction unless and until the USA was prepared to back them up. They were a kind of moral commitment, their effectiveness depending on continued endorsement by the treaty partners. The diplomacy of imperialism, Thorne declares, was to be succeeded by 'confusion'.[38]

The fact that, like the Versailles settlement, the Washington settlement did not involve all the powers in the region it purported to cover again weakened the chances that it would in substance endure. The major absentee was, of course, Russia, an active participant in the Far East since the late seventeenth century, and its absence was a drawback to the new system in East Asia as fundamental as its non-involvement in the new European system. In the wake of the treaties Japan indeed withdrew from Siberia. Yet the gesture was but one step towards coming to terms with the Soviet Union. Was it possible to supplement the Washington system by developing bilateral relations with the Russians, given their rivalry with Japan in the past, their new ideological stance, and their interest in the future of China?

Nor were the Chinese themselves satisfied with the Washington settlement, endorsing though it did the integrity of their country, and amplified though it was in 1922 by an agreement with Japan for the return of Shantung to China and the sale of the railway, though with a fifteen-year Japanese lien upon it. For Chinese nationalists Versailles was disappointing, and Washington inadequate. The Chinese resented the inferior status which, though they had declared war on the Germans, they still retained. The aim of the nationalists was a strong and prosperous China, undoing the unequal treaties for a start. The approach of the Washington signatories was far more gradualist than the nationalists were ready to accept, so far as the treaties, and the rights they involved, were concerned. The signatories stated that they wanted to provide every opportunity for China to develop 'an effective and stable government' – a phrasing which stopped well short of 'a strong and prosperous China' – and to assist in achieving such reforms as would warrant relinquishing extraterritorial rights. But the recovery of full rights had become a great rallying cry in China, and the Washington system was weakened by what nationalists saw as its failure to redeem their country. In turn its ability to satisfy the Japanese was weakened. In face of an aroused Chinese nationalism, they might feel unable to sustain a conciliatory approach.

Moreover the struggle of the Chinese nationalists was intensified by the Bolsheviks' adoption of Lenin's theses on the colonial and undeveloped countries. The failure of the revolution in Russia to set off revolution elsewhere in Europe turned their attention towards countries outside Europe:

they might hope to undermine the hold of capitalism in Europe, particularly that of the British, by undermining it in Asia, and seeking, in Lenin's words, 'temporary understandings, even alliances, with the bourgeois democracy of the colonies and backward countries'. In China the Comintern, the communist international organisation based in Moscow, found the ground prepared by the nationalist resentment of the Versailles treaty. The year 1915 had been marked by days of national humiliation; 4 May 1919, the date of the treaty that made over the German concessions to Japan, gave its name to a whole movement designed to redeem China by a re-examination of its cultural base, and stimulated student riots and anti-Japanese boycotts. The struggle against imperialism now seemed an endeavour that Russians and Chinese could pursue in common.

The viability of the Washington system thus depended in part on the domestic politics of China: it also depended on the domestic politics of Japan. Would the Japanese continue to endorse the pacific approach their government had adopted? At what point, if any, would they conclude that it was not serving Japan's interests? Over the making of Japan's policy, though not its basic aims, there had long been disputes: between advocates of pan-Asian idealism and *realpolitik*, of diplomacy and action. In the event elements of all the approaches had been combined, but the emphasis was on a cautious opportunism. That was inherited from the oligarchy that had come to rule Japan in the early Meiji years, while 'popular rights' advocates had tended to be associated with a more impatient and expansive kind of policy.

The Twenty-One Demands were indeed delivered by a government led by Okuma, and its foreign minister, Kato Komei, an advocate of party rule. The military oligarch, Yamagata Aritomo, had wanted a more moderate approach, emphasising the need to base the relationship with China on 'coexistence and co prosperity'.[39] Okuma rejected the intervention of the elder statesman: 'The genro [elder Statesmen] have no responsibility for national affairs. It is the cabinet ministers who are responsible for national affairs,' he declared.[40] The expedition to Siberia was decided upon in the face of initial opposition from Yamagata. The opportunities offered by the war brought out the expansive aspirations long associated with the popular rights movement. It connected wider political participation with the strengthening of Japan. Asserting the role of the parties and the responsibility of the cabinet over against the genro was now associated with a foreign policy that also rejected the genro's moderation.

Yet it was the party governments of the so-called Taisho democracy that accepted the Versailles settlement and the Washington treaties. At first sight there seems to be an inconsistency between their approach during the war and their approach after it, and if that were the case, the chances that Japan would continue to uphold the agreements might be diminished. The inconsistency is, however, less than it appears. The new approach seemed to be the best way to pursue Japan's interests. In 1913 Kato had admired the

41

British party system as a means of 'contributing to the state'.[41] Now the democratic powers, Britain, France and the USA, were victorious, and the empires had been overthrown, including the German empire upon whose constitutional example the oligarchs had drawn. The governments that had won were the governments that had popular support. Parliamentary government had proved itself, and Japan would gain by adopting the approach its exemplars followed.

There was, however, an implicit threat to the Washington system. '[P]arty leaders endorsed "international cooperation" in the 1920s because their supreme commitment was to the defence and enhancement of Japan's imperial interests.'[42] If party politics had been seen not as a good in itself, but as a means of strengthening the state, the same was true of the new Americanism in international affairs. It was an approach that had to be justified, not by its intrinsic morality, but by its ability to contribute to the strength and prosperity of Japan. If it did not, even party politicians might find it difficult to sustain, while others would withdraw any support they had offered for running the Japanese government by political parties, and yet others reinforce the opposition they had never abandoned.

### Netherlands India and the identic notes

The Washington system did not cover Netherlands India. There the Dutch had been apprehensive of Japan during the war, particularly in view of its alliance with Britain. At the end of the war they felt more confident: 'when they realised that they had got through the war with their neutrality inviolate and therefore that the Indies were safe once more, a strong reaction set in in favour of encouraging the inflow of Japanese capital', as Frank Ashton-Gwatkin of the British Foreign Office put it.[43] In this, perhaps, the Dutch were endeavouring to reduce their reliance on British and American capital; more clearly, they were renewing a long-standing policy, clear since the 1870s, which recognised that commercial opportunity in Netherlands India was the best guarantee against political challenge from other powers.

The Japanese, Ashton-Gwatkin thought, were interested in the oil of the Indies and its trade. They had 'no definite political ambitions in this region. But they are obsessed by the idea that their country is one day destined to be mistress of the Pacific and of its islands. They regard Holland as a very weak Power, and her colonial empire as doomed to disruption. Japan must have a say in the disposal of this rich empire. So she is steadily increasing her knowledge of the country, her vested interests therein, and the numbers of her merchants and colonists.' Japan was also keeping an eye on the Indonesian nationalist movement, the main concern of the

Dutch at this juncture.[44] A conciliatory approach applied here, as on the mainland.

The Dutch were, however, concerned that the Washington treaties did not cover the Indies. At first they suggested a wider treaty, but that the Americans ruled out. Extending the four-power treaty, moreover, seemed likely to reduce its value in the eyes of the Japanese as a substitute for their alliance with Britain. The powers adopted another Dutch suggestion, the presentation at The Hague by the four powers of identic notes, declaring their intention of respecting the island possessions of Holland in the region of the Pacific. Balfour in Washington thought that the public announcement that none of the signatories proposed to rob Holland was 'embarrassingly superfluous',[45] but the Dutch were satisfied. It might be no more than another piece of paper. That would again depend, like the treaties themselves, on the maintenance of the 'Washington spirit'. Could Japan realise its aims through the new diplomacy?

### The durability of settlements

The scale and duration of the First World War had called for a large scale and enduring settlement. In many respects Versailles and Washington fell short. Not all the powers were involved. It was not possible even to achieve the aims of all that were, since they were at odds or in conflict.

Settlements can never be expected to be complete in the sense that they need never be changed. The power and relative position of states are bound to change over the years. A settlement can be expected to endure if it allows for this. That suggests it has to be based on a consensus strong enough to permit adjustment, and to be followed by a pattern of diplomacy that effects it. The task of preserving it will be harder if there is no consensus to start with and the changes, sought perhaps partly as a result, are too great for diplomacy to resolve. It will be easier if it proves to be in the interests of powers to sustain it, demonstrating both a capacity to do so, and a flexibility of approach.

In the old diplomacy a treaty was 'binding', but in the sense that it remained in the interests of the parties to continue to adhere to it. It created an expectation as to how a state might act rather than an obligation to act. The new diplomacy sought to go beyond that. The League of Nations, even as set up, sought to regulate the behaviour of states by setting them in a quasi-legal framework.

That might indeed be a means, as Wilson had hoped, of seeking adjustments in the settlement. In some sense, however, it risked making them more difficult to secure, since they became a question of legality rather than expediency. It was unrealistic in another way. A system of law requires a means of enforcement rather than a code of behaviour, but a world of nation states does not readily provide that. Would 'public opinion' suffice, as many hoped? What if that opinion were persuaded that national interests were at stake? What if sanctions were infringed or ineffectual? It was a system that needed to involve all, and it did not. It was also a system that required its members to act in its spirit. However desirable, that was bound to be uncertain.

*Chapter 3*

# The Implementation of the Peace Settlements

In the decade between the signing of the major peace treaties and the onset of the Great Depression, the statesmen of Europe attempted to come to terms with the major changes which had occurred and to reconstruct the economic and political life of the continent on the basis of the new settlement. The outbreak of another major war only ten years later suggests that the statesmen of the 1920s were not successful in laying the basis for a stable lasting peace. Some historians argue that considerable progress had been made in solving disputes and easing tensions and that it was the Great Depression of the early 1930s which produced new economic and political causes of international instability. Others believe that the tensions and disputes of the Great War era were never resolved and that there was a mere 'illusion of peace'.[1] All agree, however, that the difficulties that the statesmen faced were immense. In the aftermath of the war all governments needed to restore national finances, stimulate economic growth and maintain domestic political and social stability. Foreign policy had to respond to and reflect these domestic needs and pressures.

The harshness of the treaty of Versailles and French attempts to force German compliance with its terms were long seen as the main reason for the failure to establish the basis in the 1920s for a longer lasting peace. A powerful support for this argument was provided by the publication in 1919 of *The Economic Consequences of the Peace* by the British economist John Maynard Keynes. In a colourful, vituperative and persuasive style, he denounced the peacemakers for creating a treaty that was so harsh on Germany that it would prevent the economic recovery of that country and with it the economic recovery of the whole of Europe. The Germans were not slow to make use of his material in their own skilful propaganda in the 1920s which depicted the French as vengeful and vindictive, driven by no other purpose than a desire to crush totally a beaten foe. The Germans won the race to publish selected official documents on the origins of the war and in so doing built up a case against German war guilt and strengthened the case for revision of the treaty.[2]

With the fuller opening of government and other archives in Britain, France and Germany in the last thirty years, historians have considerably expanded the nature of the discussion of international relations in the 1920s. In the process they have modified the view that French policy was 'the major barrier to the reestablishment of peaceful stability in Europe'.[3] The French were driven by fears about security, by financial and economic vulnerability, and were forced unwillingly into the desperate measure of the occupation of the Ruhr in 1923 by the intransigence of the Germans in failing to fulfil any of the treaty terms, and by the lack of understanding and support from Britain and the United States. More criticism has been directed at these latter powers. The United States, by not recognising any connection between war debts and reparations and by refusing to cancel or moderate the former, failed to provide the kind of imaginative financial leadership which could have transformed the whole history of reparations and the course of economic reconstruction. Britain admittedly was preoccupied by its own problems of economic decline and overstretched resources, but it did not liberate itself from old prejudices and fears and had insufficient knowledge and understanding of the new post-war European situation. Driven by the desire to achieve its own economic revival and to fight a rearguard action against the emergence of American financial ascendancy, it was prepared to allow German economic resurgence despite the possible military implications. At the same time it failed to respond to the French fears for their future security by refusing to replace the Anglo-American guarantee with a British one. Some historians take a more sympathetic view of Britain's position. Germany has ceased to be seen mainly as a victim. German governments used all the means which they had at their disposal to avoid compliance with the treaty terms. According to Carole Fink, a severe critic of Weimar Germany, it was not looking for stability on the basis of the treaty terms or some modifications of them, but rather 'The revisionist diplomacy of the Weimar Republic, from the signing of the Versailles Treaty to the advent of the Nazis, amounted to the prolongation of the Great War by other means.'[4]

There has also been greater emphasis on the fundamental nature of the conflict of national interests. What Germany believed was necessary for its national recovery and indeed security – the end of economic constraints, of military occupation and of unilateral disarmament – France and Poland perceived as a danger to their security. There is also the recognition that states subscribed to contradictory assumptions and pursued contradictory objectives. As far as the former Allied Powers were concerned, there was a desire to return to some kind of balance of power which implied restriction on Germany's full use of its economic and human resources but there was also a desire for a return to prosperity which necessitated a German economic recovery so that it could pay reparations and play its part in the stimulation of international trade. There was adherence to the principle of a new international order which was based on the collaboration of independent democratic nation states, but there was also a belief that European security was dependent on the continuation of some constraint on Germany's exercise of its full sovereignty.

### Britain, France and the peace treaty

The conditions under which international relations were conducted in post-war Europe were very different from those of pre-1914. Diplomacy was much less of a secret affair than it had been in the past. In the League of Nations, the new small states expected to have their voices heard. The negotiations at big international conferences where states were represented by their leading politicians were more open to public scrutiny, which increased the influence of domestic politics on decision making and perhaps limited the opportunities for compromise. The world of alliances between major states had disappeared. Germany's former ally Austria-Hungary had disintegrated. France's former ally was now ruled by a Bolshevik or communist regime which had alienated the French by withdrawing from the war and repudiating all the financial obligations of its predecessor. Relations with the new Russia, soon to be known as the Union of Soviet Socialist Republics (USSR), was difficult for all of the powers. Many members of the new Soviet government had previously proclaimed their intention of trying to foment revolution and the overthrow of capitalist governments throughout the world, yet that same government now sought to establish diplomatic and economic relations with the capitalist states. The element of uncertainty in dealing with the Soviet regime was a constant contributory factor to the instability of the period. The position of the United States was equally unsatisfactory. After the Senate had rejected the treaty of Versailles, the United States ceased to be intimately involved in European political decision making but its financial position could not be ignored. American businessmen, financiers and bankers maintained a steady participation in European economic affairs. Politics and economics were intimately connected and the views of what was potentially the greatest power in the world would always have to be considered.

The immediate problems of implementing the peace settlement, however, fell to Britain and France. Much would depend on their ability to co-operate and work together. That did not prove easy as their relationship was bedevilled by historical animosities, personal antagonisms and above all by

47

a different perception of what was required to preserve peace and stability in Europe. Residual suspicion of the French was strong in the British Foreign Office, which opposed the construction of a Channel tunnel on the grounds that Anglo-French relations 'never have been, are not and probably never will be sufficiently stable to justify the construction'. In the country as a whole, Lloyd George believed that there was 'widespread hostility' towards the French. Nervousness about French military ambitions resurfaced. According to Sir Maurice Hankey, France had become 'the impersonation of militarism and Prussianism'.[5] Lord Curzon, the foreign secretary, and successive prime ministers Andrew Bonar Law and Stanley Baldwin all found it difficult to establish any rapport with Poincaré, the French premier. The suspicion was not all on one side. The French equally believed that 'perfidious Albion' had not changed and that it wished to use the situation to establish itself as the arbiter of the continent. Paul Cambon, the veteran French diplomat and former ambassador to Britain, warned his fellow countrymen against constantly letting the British see how much they distrusted them.[6] The main problem in Anglo-French relations, however, was that while each state wished to preserve the peace and international stability, they pursued different strategies to achieve it.

In the case of France, the predominant factor was its insecurity. The country was in serious financial difficulties as a result of having financed the war largely by borrowing. The important industrial areas in the north needed rebuilding after the devastation caused by the fighting and the deliberate damage inflicted by the Germans during their withdrawal. No French government was prepared to take the political risk of suggesting that France, the victor in the war, should shoulder the responsibility for that reconstruction: if the United States and Britain refused to ease the burden of debt repayment, then Germany would have to pay more of the cost. In addition France was very conscious that it remained inferior in population and resources compared to Germany and that it had no firm guarantees of support from other powers, as the Anglo-American guarantee had been rendered invalid by the decision of the American Senate. For France peace and stability would depend on its building up protection against future German resurgence. It sought to do that in three main ways: by developing new alliances; by seeking to prevent an untrammelled German economic revival; and by attempting to strengthen the League of Nations. In all three measures, France received little support from Britain.

For British governments, the main consideration was the growing awareness of the potential conflict between the extent of the country's commitments and the now more limited extent of its resources. In the immediate post-war period, the demands of reconstruction in Britain and in Europe had to vie with the demands of a host of problems elsewhere. In Ireland there was civil war, in India serious disturbances and growing demands for independence, in Egypt insurrection, in the Near East a crisis over Turkey, and in the Far East the situation was bringing about a major reconsideration of Britain's policies and relationships. Bonar Law, the new Conservative leader, summed up the situation at the end of 1922, 'We cannot act alone as policeman of the world. The financial and social condition of this country makes that impossible'.[7] That economic and social condition weighed heavily on successive British governments. The challenges to its financial and economic situation which had existed before the war but which had been hidden by the extent of its overseas investments and income from shipping were now laid bare. Britain was a debtor as well as a creditor nation. Many of its markets and much of its carrying trade had been lost during the war and were hard to replace. The social benefits which had been expected from victory in the war, largely as a result of the politicians' own rhetoric, were not forthcoming. As a result there was growing industrial unrest and clear signs of opposition to Britain's continuing close involvement in European affairs.

In accordance with the prevalent economic thinking of the day, the British government decided that in those circumstances government spending would have to be cut and that one of the main areas which should be targeted was military expenditure. As early as 1919, the armed services were directed to draft their estimates on the assumption that the British empire would not be engaged in a major war for ten years and that no expeditionary force would be required on the continent. Cutting the military budget was acceptable to a wide spectrum of the population: to orthodox economists; to those who believed in disarmament and put their faith in the League; to those who believed that the priority in government spending should be on improving conditions at home; and to those who did not wish to face the possible alternative of an increase in taxation. In what was thought to be a winning election slogan in 1922, Bonar Law was urged to promise 'Honest Government, Drastic Economy, National Security and No Adventures abroad or at home'.[8] 'No Adventures' was important. Militarily, Britain was already in danger of being overstretched. In the graphic description of Michael Howard, the British empire had become 'a brontosaurus with huge vulnerable limbs which the central nervous system had little capacity to protect, direct or control'.[9] The British government wanted no more commitments, no extension of its obligations – and in the French proposals about alliances and the strengthening of the League, there was danger of both.

For economic recovery, retrenchment was not sufficient. Many accepted the Keynesian argument that British economic resurgence depended on a general European one in which Germany would have to play a vital part. High reparations would dislocate trade, would probably deprive Britain of markets, especially for coal, and would militate against a German and therefore a British recovery. Austen Chamberlain, the British chancellor of the exchequer, wrote to his sister, 'You must get Keynes' book...it is very indiscreet, but it is ably & indeed brilliantly written....There is only too much truth in Keynes' gloomy picture.'[10] French attempts to tie the German economy to the French one were equally unacceptable. Britain was also prey to a number of fears about the Soviet Union. Whatever the nature of the Russian regime Britain did not want to lose its share of the potential Russian market. Continuing Anglo-French pressure upon Germany they feared would lead the latter to grow closer to the Soviet Union and gain a privileged economic position in that country. The British also had fears that Germany itself would succumb to communism – fears which were played upon by the Germans as they sought to persuade British officials that mitigation of the treaty terms would reduce the chances of such a catastrophe.[11] Reconstruction and stability for Britain, therefore, meant accepting some modification of the treaty of Versailles and working towards the full reintegration of Germany into the European political and economic scene.

French efforts to achieve additional security through new alliances had only limited success. Although Britain refused to replace the Anglo-American guarantee with an Anglo-French treaty, France concluded a military agreement with Belgium in 1920, an alliance and a secret military convention with Poland in 1921 and an agreement with Czechoslovakia in 1924. The Polish agreement was the most significant and the one of which the British most disapproved. While Poland was bound to assist France in the event of German aggression, France was equally bound to assist Poland in similar circumstances and in addition to attempt to preserve German neutrality in the event of a Polish–Russian quarrel. The latter was not unlikely. In the Russo-Polish war which had erupted in 1920 over the unsettled Polish eastern boundary, the Poles had gained a very unexpected victory, the so-called miracle of the Vistula, and had seized the opportunity in the peace treaty to claim territory which was not largely Polish in population and which the Russians believed was more rightfully theirs. Poland, therefore, had placed itself in the unenviable situation of having potentially powerful enemies on both of its flanks. The British had had little sympathy with what they saw as Polish irresponsibility although the cabinet had recognised that, in the event of a Russian victory, it could not allow Poland to be destroyed. Not everyone agreed. Hankey thought that 'it is inevitable that sooner or later Russia gets a coterminous frontier with Germany'.[12] At the same time within the country, British labour formed 'Councils of Action' to resist any British intervention in the fighting. Many of the British leaders had not altered their views that the German–Polish boundary was one of the parts of the settlement which should be revised and the French treaty was therefore seen as a foolish encouragement of the Poles and a provocation to Germany. From the French point of view, one of the main weaknesses of their alliances was that they could not strengthen their containment of Germany in the east by the conclusion of an agreement between Poland and Czechoslovakia. Those two countries were divided by bitter disputes over the border district of Teschen and they were not brought together by a perception of having the same enemies. Poland might fear Germany and the Soviet Union, but at that stage Czechoslovakia believed that it had more to fear from revisionist Hungary.

### Reparations, Rapallo and the Ruhr

Over the issue of reparations Britain and France had to reach some agreement so that they could present their demands for a final sum to the Germans in May 1921. The British successfully fought for the relatively small figure of 132 milliard (billion) gold marks, a considerable reduction on previous projected demands. That amount was divided into two main parts. The first fifty milliard gold marks was to be paid within fifty years and only after that was complete would the payment of the remaining 82 milliard gold marks begin. While the financial experts may well have recognised that the second sum would never be paid, domestic pressures in Britain and France meant that that could not be publicly acknowledged. According to Schuker, what Germany was actually required to pay under a schedule of payments agreed to in London amounted to some 6 per cent of its national income.[13] Even Keynes referred to it as 'a signal triumph for the spirit of justice' and although he hoped that further downward revision of Germany's obligations would follow, he did not believe that it called on the Germans to do anything in the immediate future of which they were incapable.[14]

The Germans thought otherwise. None of the political leadership believed that Germany would or should meet the Allied demands but they were divided over tactics. Some thought that an attempt to fulfil the terms of the London schedule would prove that they were incapable of fulfilment and would therefore win sympathy and further concessions, especially from the British. Others believed that delaying and pleading inability to pay would leave time for Anglo-French differences to grow and would lead to the avoidance of payments altogether. In the summer of 1921, Germany made its first cash payment under the London schedule. At the same time the German minister of reconstruction, Rathenau, and his French counterpart, Loucheur, tried to arrange more direct Franco-German economic co-operation. In lieu of some reparation payments Germany would directly assist in the reconstruction of northern France. Little was achieved owing to the suspicion and opposition of both French and German industrialists and the critical response of the British, American and Belgian governments to the idea of a separate Franco-German agreement. After December 1921 Germany failed to meet in full its reparation payments either in cash or kind. The German government pleaded that the economic state of the country, and particularly the high rate of inflation, made payment impossible. The reason for that rate of inflation is another of the issues of the period which was vigorously debated amongst contemporaries: the debate has continued amongst historians.[15] It has been attributed to the cost of the war itself, the demands for reparations, the machinations of German big business to ensure its own profits, and the manipulation of the German government to avoid deflation with its likely accompaniment of unemployment and social unrest. While it might now appear that all these pressures played some part, at the time the French were convinced that the primary factor was the joint manipulation of big business and the German government and that their purpose was to avoid the payment of reparations. For them it was a question not of Germany's inability to pay but of its unwillingness to pay. If further evidence of German ill-will were required, it was seen in the conclusion of a separate Russo-German agreement in the middle of the international conference at Genoa in 1922, which had been called by Lloyd George to try to resolve the economic problems of Europe as a whole.

Support for closer relations between Germany and Russia had grown in both countries after the defeat of the Soviets by the Poles and the end of the Russian civil war. Germans and Russians were united in their antagonism to the new Polish state and believed closer ties would result in mutual political, military and particularly economic benefits. The Soviets wanted investments and technical expertise to help rebuild their country after the years of war but they did not wish to have terms imposed upon them by any consortium of the capitalist states. Germany seemed most likely to succumb to the temptation of a separate agreement. German heavy industry was especially enthusiastic about the possibilities of supplying industrial machinery and expertise to Russia. The German military had contacts with their Soviet counterparts from early 1921 and were seizing the opportunity to evade some of the military restrictions imposed by the treaty of Versailles by developing and testing prohibited weapons in the Soviet Union. The German political leadership, however, was not easily persuaded to make a separate agreement with the Soviets. The Socialists in particular had reservations. They remained unconvinced by Soviet government claims that the Comintern (the Communist International), which was based in Moscow and continued to support the communist party in Germany, was a separate organisation from the Soviet government. The German government under Wirth and Rathenau was not averse to the idea of taking part in a multinational economic agreement. It could enable Germany to improve its own economic position in the short term without further alienating the West and provide the opportunity to develop a position of dominance in eastern Europe in the future. The Soviets, however, were determined to avoid having to make an agreement with an international consortium. At the Genoa conference they fed German fears that they might come to terms with the West in exchange for demanding reparations from Germany. Apprehensive of such a development and also of losing a share of the potential Russian market, the Germans signed a separate agreement with the Soviets at Rapallo on 16 April 1922.

In some ways the Rapallo agreement could be seen as a new peace treaty between Germany and Russia as the treaty of Brest-Litovsk had been cancelled by the treaty of Versailles. Normal diplomatic relations between the two states were re-established. The USSR abandoned any claim to reparations from Germany and Germany relinquished any claim to former German property in Russia which the Soviets had nationalised. Both parties agreed to extend 'most favoured nation' status to the other and to give each other 'mutual assistance for the alleviation of their economic difficulties'. They further agreed that they would have preliminary discussion if there were further plans to deal with economic problems on an international basis.[16] The treaty therefore removed significant fears from both sides but Britain and France suspected that it did much more. They were apprehensive that there were further secret commercial and military clauses. The French in particular saw it as a threat to their ally Poland and therefore to their whole security system. While the idea of military collaboration with the Soviets against Poland was favourably discussed in German military circles, German diplomats and politicians contemplated no such use of force. For them the benefits of the treaty were economic, diplomatic and political. It satisfied the widespread domestic demand for a more active foreign policy and it was hoped it would give Germany more leverage in negotiating with the Western powers to obtain revisions of the treaty of Versailles.

Little was achieved at the main Genoa conference. Reparations were not even discussed. Numerous other conferences on reparations failed to procure Anglo-French agreement on how to cope with German delays and non-delivery. In August 1922 the British government expressed its willingness to forego any reparations and to agree to an all-round cancellation of war debts. If the latter could not be agreed upon they were prepared to collect from their former allies and from Germany only what they themselves had to pay to the United States. The French were unimpressed with the proposal. They perceived that unless Germany paid they themselves would have to pay more to the British. The Americans continued to refuse to acknowledge any link between war debts and reparations and would make no concessions. Historians are now inclined to believe that the British move was more of a public relations exercise to impress its own people than a serious effort to produce a general settlement. There is also now some speculation that a unilateral British cancellation of debt, which was what was consistently advised by the British Treasury, would have eased the French financial situation and engendered a great improvement in

Anglo-French relations. The British government did not follow that advice.[17] The French government was faced with a looming financial crisis, to a great extent the result of the need for debt repayment. At the same time Germany repeatedly defaulted in the payment of reparations in kind, especially timber and coal for which there was a desperate need in the French steel industry, an industry which had grown in Lorraine when that province was part of Germany and had had access to German coal. Slowly and reluctantly, the French government decided to use its one remaining weapon, military might, to seize reparations. In January 1923, with the support of Belgium, French troops occupied the Ruhr.[18]

The repercussions of the Ruhr occupation transformed the political scene in Europe. Encouraged by the British disapproval of the French action, the German government called for a policy of passive resistance. It was supported at home and sympathetically viewed abroad, but it fuelled hyper-inflation and by September 1923, the new German leader, Gustav Stresemann, the head of the German People's Party (DVP), had to compromise. Briefly, it appeared that France had gained a new ascendancy. It was beginning to gain economic benefit from the occupation and Germany was threatened with separatist and communist uprisings. Stresemann offered direct talks but Poincaré, the French leader, refused. Instead he pursued what seemed to be two contradictory policies. He accepted an American offer of a panel of experts to work out a new international agreement on reparations which for its success would need the rehabilitation of Germany but almost simultaneously, he backed a separatist movement in the Rhineland. Whatever the purpose behind this apparently inconsistent policy, the result was dismal. The separatist movement failed. The French franc plummeted and France itself desperately needed new American loans. The price of securing them was French withdrawal from the Ruhr and an international settlement that was in accord with Anglo-American views. The experts' report on reparations, the Dawes plan, recommended a smaller final sum, a graduated scale of payments rising from a very modest one to the maximum amount in the fifth and subsequent years and the stabilisation of the German economy by an injection of foreign loans. In return for the promise of these payments, the French agreed to evacuate the Ruhr within a year, to cease their exploitation of the area, to limit the powers of the Reparations Commission and to accept restrictions on future sanctions. The responsibility for the extent of these concessions has been placed on the shoulders of the new French prime minister, Eduard Herriot. He was inexperienced in diplomacy, judged 'incompetent' in financial matters and had a naïve optimism in his ability to promote 'peace, real peace, the good peace, peace with all'.[19] Admittedly he inherited a weak hand from Poincaré, but he was no match in the negotiations for the American bankers who wanted to ensure stability in Europe in the interests of their investors and for the British who supported them. If the 1924 agreement marked 'the end of French predominance', that predominance had always been precarious. It had depended upon the co-operation and support of Britain and the United States which had proved to be limited. It had also depended upon the enforcement of the constraints on German economic and military resurgence that were written into the treaty of Versailles and the means of exercising those constraints were significantly diminished.

The French received no consolation or reassurance about their security in the failure of two efforts to strengthen the League of Nations. Both failures were the result of British opposition to the proposed schemes. The Draft Treaty of Mutual Assistance made it obligatory for all members to go to the aid of the victims of aggression but limited the military obligations to the states of the particular continent in which the aggression took place. For the British with their worldwide possessions and responsibilities, that would have represented little limitation. The Dominions, increasingly adopting their own line on foreign policy, also objected. The alternative proposal, the Geneva Protocol, framed largely by Herriot and Ramsay MacDonald, the British Labour prime minister, abandoned the idea of regional arrangements but proposed making arbitration compulsory for all disputes and the imposition of sanctions compulsory against the designated aggressor. The Dominions still objected. Most importantly, the new Conservative government feared that such a protocol would add to British obligations, especially for the navy, at a time when the continuing need for economy demanded caution and restraint. The debate about ratification clearly highlighted the extent to which Britain's worldwide interests and imperial ties were a determining factor in its foreign policy even when crucial European interests were at stake. The British government rejected the protocol in September 1925.

Britain had a new foreign secretary, Austen Chamberlain, a self-confessed Francophile. France was a country he knew well and whose language he spoke with ease, an accomplishment which was revealingly described by one of his colleagues as 'a national misfortune'.[20] Chamberlain recognised and understood the French feeling of insecurity. He believed that unless its fears were allayed, France would feel impelled to continue the kind of policy which was alienating the British and feeding the resentment within Germany. Britain, he argued, should not withdraw from the situation and take the risk of finally being 'dragged along unwilling, impotent, protesting in the wake of France towards a new Armageddon' but should offer some security to France and play the role of moderator and reconciler between France and Germany.[21] His own preferred option was for a separate Anglo-French alliance but to that the cabinet would not agree. 'The anti-pactites', according to one of the group, Leo Amery, 'completely defeated the FO scheme (which captured Austen) for rushing the country (forgetting the Empire) into a definite commitment to defend France'.[22] Chamberlain therefore turned to a proposal which had earlier been made by Stresemann for a non-aggression pact between France and Germany which could be guaranteed by other powers.

### The Locarno agreements

Stresemann, who was chancellor from August to November 1923 and then foreign minister until his death in 1929, had been an outspoken exponent of German expansion during the 1914–18 war and a bitter opponent of the peace treaty. The trauma of 1923, however, had led to his adopting a more flexible approach to foreign policy. He questioned the wisdom of continuing hard-line resistance to the Western powers and developing too great a dependence on ties with the Soviet Union. While Soviet warnings to the Poles had reduced the possible threat of combined Franco-Polish pressure upon Germany during the Ruhr crisis, members of the Comintern had not hesitated to utilise the conditions to bring about a German communist revolution. Economically, too, the Soviet connection had its limitations. Germany had continued to extend its share of Soviet trade but the Soviet government had no means of helping Germany in the stabilisation of its currency and with the provision of loans. They could be provided only by the Western powers. What was more, Stresemann had come to the conclusion that it was only by diplomacy and some co-operation with the Western powers that Germany could obtain a further reduction in reparations, the withdrawal of the Allied Control Commission, and an early evacuation of the Rhineland. Like Chamberlain, he recognised that an increase in French confidence about their security was a necessary prerequisite to their granting such concessions.

After months of intense negotiations, a series of agreements were signed at Locarno in October 1925.[23] The treaty of Mutual Guarantee guaranteed Germany's western frontier including the demilitarised Rhineland. Germany, France and Belgium undertook not to make war on each other but to settle disputes by conciliation and arbitration. Britain and Italy agreed to go to the aid of any signatory which was the victim of a 'flagrant' act of 'unprovoked aggression'. The agreements relating to eastern Europe were more limited. Germany, Poland and Czechoslovakia promised to submit any disputes to arbitration but there was no guarantee of frontiers or any promise of assistance by the other powers for the victim of aggression. Germany was to be admitted to the League of Nations. At the time, the agreements were greeted with immense enthusiasm. Chamberlain, Stresemann and the French foreign minister, Aristide Briand, were all awarded the Nobel Peace prize. With a touch of exaggeration, Chamberlain was proud to claim that the Locarno agreement 'was mine in conception and still more mine in execution' although he did concede that it 'required for its full success both Stresemann & Briand, above all Briand'.[24] Many believed that Locarno marked the real end of the war and the beginning of a new era of understanding and peace.

With the benefit of hindsight, it is clear that these hopes were not fulfilled and that there was no lasting rapprochement amongst the powers. In some ways there were inherent problems from the beginning. Despite their goodwill and desire to negotiate compromise settlements, the three statesmen themselves had incompatible policy objectives.

The main reason for Chamberlain's delight at the settlement was his belief that he had given France a greater sense of security and had also taught Germany that its security lay 'in our friendship with France and not in dividing France and us'.[25] At the same time what he knew was crucial to its acceptance within his own country was that it had not extended British obligations beyond what was necessary for 'vital national interests'. In other words, there was no commitment to eastern Europe and, even in the West, the very nature of the guarantee meant that there were no embarrassing plans for military co-operation and assistance. The whole purpose of the guarantee was to act as a deterrent to the use of force. However great his sympathy for France, Chamberlain's aim was to provide the climate for more conciliatory and fruitful diplomacy between France and Germany without substantially increasing British commitments.

Stresemann's objectives have been the subject of considerable debate.[26] His reported frequent references to Germany's national interests, his emphasis on German economic expansion, his interest in Germans outside the German states, as well as his constant demands for the revision of Versailles, have led some historians to claim that he was pursuing a policy of expansionism that was little different from his wartime predecessors or even Hitler. According to more recent scholarship, Stresemann believed that there was a need to balance Germany's demands against those of European peace.[27] With support from the German foreign office Stresemann wished to restore Germany to its great power position not by confrontation or the use of force but by diplomacy and compromise. He recognised that the removal of all of Germany's grievances from Versailles could not be immediately achieved. The recovery of Germany's colonies and *Anschluss* with Austria, for example, would have to wait. For the rest Stresemann hoped that the increased security which the Locarno agreement had given France would lead to concessions about reparations, the early evacuation of the Rhineland, the end of the military control commission, the return of the Saar, and the opportunity of revision of the German–Polish border. The achievement of these limited goals, however, would have made Germany sufficiently powerful to be unacceptable to the French.

Briand, no less than his predecessors, was concerned about French security. There was no unanimous welcome for the Locarno agreements within France but a recognition that, in many ways, France had lost its previous freedom of action. It could no longer occupy the Ruhr if Germany failed in its reparation payments. If Poland were invaded by Germany, then France would have to wait for the latter to be pronounced the aggressor by the League before it could go to the aid of its ally. Briand and his supporters, however, believed that the Locarno agreements were the best protection which could be obtained for France at that time. Some guarantee from the British was better than nothing. Washington, the source of needed loans, continued to urge conciliation in Franco-German relations. A number of French industrialists hoped to use the new international climate and the advantages of a weak franc to consolidate their position in the German market. Briand, however, was not going to abandon lightly and easily the remaining power which France still had in its occupation of part of the Rhineland and the control of the Saar. He hoped to use the Locarno agreement to integrate Britain further into the French security system and impose some constraints on Germany.

At the same time, a change in French military thinking complemented the new stance in diplomacy. A move from an offensive to a defensive strategy had much to recommend it. The pressures about disarmament apart, it was difficult to envisage keeping the French army in Europe at its existing strength owing to financial stringency, the unpopularity of conscription and the demands for increasing military reinforcements to cope with the nationalist uprisings in Syria and North Africa. The building of a line of fortifications along the French north-east border was designed to make it easier to defend the country with a smaller army. The emphasis on defence, it was hoped, would not only undermine the continuing Anglo-American suspicions about French aggression but would also act as a powerful deterrent for any potential invader. 'Even victory' did not 'compensate for the disaster of invasion', said André Maginot, the war minister after whom the line of fortifications was named. France's main concern, stressed the president of the Chamber, was 'not to avoid defeat but to avoid war and invasion'.[28]

### From Locarno to the Depression

In the four years following the signing of the Locarno agreements there were some signs that the hopes of a new era in international relations were not without foundation. There was much more cordiality at the highest levels of diplomacy between Stresemann, Briand and Chamberlain. At that level too, the distrust which had hampered Anglo-French relations was at an end. The new emphasis on the peaceful resolution of disputes was reflected in the signing of the Kellogg–Briand pact by which nations agreed to renounce war as an instrument of policy. The participation of Kellogg, the American secretary of state, in this project aroused some hopes that the United States would begin to use its political as well as its economic weight to support international stability. The economic situation appeared to be transformed. The French rebuilt their northern territories and, having accepted the need to devalue the franc, experienced a period of economic prosperity in the late 1920s. Germany likewise, with the influx of American loans, made a rapid economic recovery. It also continued to obtain modifications of the treaty of Versailles. It was admitted to the League of Nations. The Allied Control Commission was withdrawn although not one of its reports had stated that Germany was totally fulfilling its disarmament obligations under the treaty. The Allies committed themselves to end the occupation of the Rhineland by June 1930 instead of 1935 and agreed to a further scaling down of reparations in what was known as the Young Plan. It could appear that a peaceful modification of the treaty was taking place, that Germany was in the process of being readmitted as an independent member of the European states system and that France was ensuring its security by other means.

Germany had not abandoned its links with the Soviet Union. A new Soviet–German treaty of non-aggression and neutrality was concluded in Berlin in 1926. Although Stresemann disliked the Soviets and had no desire to be dependent upon them, he recognised that the military and economic ties were too valuable to be lost. In the Soviet Union war material was manufactured and tested and German military personnel were trained in the use of weapons and equipment which were forbidden under the terms of the Versailles treaty. Germany made loans available to Russia and German heavy industry cultivated the Russian market. As a result by 1932 German exports to Russia equalled some 47 per cent of Russia's imports and large numbers of German technicians and engineers were employed under Russia's five year plans. The signing of the Berlin treaty, however, seems to have provoked less alarm in the West than the agreement at Rapallo. Germany was allowed to join the League of Nations with special reservations about its obligation to join in sanctions against the Soviet Union. For its part the USSR agreed to take part in the Disarmament Committee of the League and made moves to improve its relations with the French.

Fundamental causes of tension, however, had not evaporated. In many ways Franco-German relations remained a 'duel not a duet'.[29] German resentment about the treaty and the desire to further revise its terms remained strong. Despite his achievements, Stresemann himself was not content. There had been no magnanimous gesture from the French but instead every concession had had to be won by lengthy negotiations. The Young Plan was more burdensome than he had anticipated but he had had to accept it as the price for obtaining the early evacuation of the Rhineland. If Stresemann was disappointed at the pace of his achievements, his opponents within Germany were increasingly critical of his policy. He had had to struggle to keep the support of his own party, the DVP. The Nationalist Party or DNVP, which from 1925 to 1927 formed part of the governing coalition, split between those who were prepared to continue to support him and those who repudiated what they saw as his compliance in Germany's subordinate position. The latter group waged a particularly fierce battle against the Young Plan and in the process brought into national prominence its partner in the struggle, the National Socialist German Workers Party or NSDAP, known as the Nazis. Until then the NSDAP had been a relatively small, comparatively unknown party outside its Bavarian base. The appearance of the Nationalist – Nazi partnership added weight to what had been one of Stresemann's favourite arguments – that he needed concessions to strengthen his political situation and save Britain and France from dealing with a more difficult German government.

Within France, continuing fear and distrust of Germany militated against the making of major concessions. Briand, like Stresemann, could not ignore domestic political pressure. He may have been less extreme than those who, like Marshal Foch, believed that 'Germany only understood force' but he did not agree to the complete evacuation of the Rhineland until the construction of the Maginot Line was begun, the Young plan was negotiated and he was threatened with a unilateral withdrawal of their forces by the new British Labour government. The continuation of this hostility and suspicion within France and Germany was a serious obstacle to the proposals for some kind of European union which were mooted firstly by Herriot and later by Briand. The small amount of Franco-German economic co-operation which took place largely followed the improvement in political relations, but it was not pursued with vigour by either side. British lack of enthusiasm may have killed the 1930 so-called 'Briand plan' for European union but the Germans also had strong reservations. For any scheme to meet French requirements, it had to impose some constraints upon the benefits which Germany could derive from its own economic growth. The Germans knew that, if they could rid themselves of the remaining restrictions of the Versailles settlement, they could achieve predominance in Europe by reason of their superior resources. The French sought to delay that process by implementing the treaty and, even as late as 1929, anticipated that the Young Plan would provide a continuing drain on German wealth. The disappointment from the French point of view was the lack of support from Britain and the United States and their failure to perceive that the threat to European stability was likely to come from a resurgent Germany.

The frailty of the Anglo-French rapprochement was demonstrated by their differences over disarmament and by the reversion to old, more openly hostile attitudes once Chamberlain had ceased to be foreign secretary. Members of the new Labour government were critical of what they saw as French militarism and were prepared to renew the debate about the division of reparation payments. Ramsay MacDonald believed that France's 'mentality is purely militarist...war is the central fact of its mind'.[30] British bankers were jealous of France's increasing financial strength and its tendency to use it to forward French political ambitions in eastern Europe. The British economic recovery had not been impressive. Its overseas trade did not return to the 1913 level until the end of the 1920s and its financial predominance was not regained. Nor was Europe the main focus. British investment continued to be largely in the empire and South America and in the 1920s the trend towards increasing trade with the empire also began. Developments in India, China, Palestine and Egypt demanded British attention and the deployment of its resources. With Europe, Britain had 'a semi-detached relationship'.[31]

## Partial stabilisation

Other immediate post-war problems also remained unresolved. The Soviet Union remained an uncertain element in international affairs despite some normalisation of its relations with the main European states. Its agents were suspected of trying to stir up revolution throughout Europe, the British empire and the Far East. The threat was an ideological one as the Soviet state remained weak in economic and industrial terms, but by the end of the 1920s, under Stalin, it began its own major reconstruction programme, the Five Year Plan, designed to transform Russia into a modern industrialised state. The new eastern European states were not finding it easy to achieve political and economic stability. Nationalist passions continued to militate against economic co-operation between states and against internal harmony within states. Even if international investors had been prepared to provide more loans, most of the east European states would have been unable to service them. Largely dependent on agrarian economies, they were adversely affected by the fall in prices for primary products by 1928. Italian ambitions made for further uncertainty. The Fascists, who had come to power under Mussolini in 1923, had made the achievement of military greatness and territorial aggrandisement some of the major planks of their political platform. Franco-Italian relations had steadily deteriorated. They were vying for influence in the Balkans; they were in dispute over North Africa where Italy believed that it had been deprived of its share of the colonial spoils in 1919; and they were at odds over the French willingness to welcome the Italian political refugees from Mussolini's regime. Chamberlain, who prided himself on the good personal relationship which he had established with the Italian dictator, admitted that 'Mussolini is troublesome...any rag in Serbia, Germany and above all France can upset his temper and distort his policy'.[32]

The extent of the international stabilisation which had been achieved in Europe by the late 1920s has been described as 'partial, tentative and fragile' with many 'latent disaffections and unresolved conflicts'.[33] While acknowledging the existence of the latter, the achievement of a 'partial' stabilisation should also be recognised. Some easing of the major post-war tensions had occurred. Bolshevism had not spread into Europe. Moderation of the settlement with Germany had been achieved peacefully if by hard bargaining. There was some optimism that continuing economic prosperity would facilitate political stability in Germany. In the 1928 elections the more extreme parties – on the right the Nationalists and the Nazis and on the left the Communists – lost seats in the Reischstag. Whether continuing economic growth would have brought a stable enduring democratic government in Germany can only be a matter for speculation. Germany and the rest of Europe were soon to be deeply affected by the onset of the Great Depression.


## Japan and China

The counterpart of Versailles in the West was the Washington system in the East. The major threat to it in the 1920s arose from the inadequacy of the provisions for China. True, it envisaged change: the parties looked for the establishment there of 'an effective and stable government'. They envisaged a process by which, as that was established, the unequal treaties would be renegotiated, and over a period of time the special rights they conveyed given up. That was not likely to be sufficient for the Chinese nationalists. Could the powers accept a less gradualist approach? That was not at odds with the system itself, since it was built around the integrity of China and the Open Door. But the participating powers would have to accept the adjustment involved, the modification it required of the understandings on which they had endorsed the system, the implications for their interests.

Intellectuals in China had come to realise, particularly after 1919, that a more fundamental approach to reform was needed: the revolution had seemed but to bring about warlordism, civil war and continued foreign intervention. Some looked to Marxism, and in 1922 the Chinese Communist Party (CCP), prodded by the Comintern, approved an alliance with the nationalist Kuomintang (KMT) on the basis of joint opposition to warlordism and imperialism. In 1923 Sun Yat-sen's government in the south began to receive aid from Soviet emissaries, helping to reorganise the KMT, and developing a nationalist army on the model of the Red Army. In 1926 the Northern March began, designed to bring the northern warlords to heel. But its initial successes brought about tensions between the communists and nationalists, since the former seized the political opportunities that went along with military success. The climax came in 1927. The communists were expelled from the KMT, and in 1928 a purely KMT government was set up in Nanking headed by Chiang Kai-shek. The shift limited social revolution, while warlordism tended to be cloaked rather than displaced by nationalism. But the KMT–CCP break did not end anti-imperialism. Just because it had broken with the CCP, indeed, the KMT could not abandon that policy. The challenge to Washington's gradualism persisted.

The main foreign powers affected were Britain and Japan. In the course of the Northern March, crowds overran the British concessions at Hankow and Kiukiang, and in Nanking nationalist forces killed several foreigners. The British bore the brunt of the attacks in the mid-1920s, when the Northern March reached the central parts of China where their interests were entrenched. At first the British reacted violently, but, particularly with Austen Chamberlain's memorandum of 18 December 1926,[34] they became more ready to appease Chinese nationalism over the unequal treaties, and make concessions. Britain would stake its future in China on general co-operation with the Chinese rather than on retention of particular rights gained in the past. The process of accommodation would thus be rather less gradual than Washington envisaged, though in accord with its principles. Even so, the intransigence of Chinese nationalism did not make for easy negotiations. Some concessions – Hankow, Kiukiang, Chinkiang – were relinquished. An agreement on tariff autonomy was prepared. Negotiations on extraterritorial jurisdiction went more slowly.

Japan's line was conciliatory in the mid 1920s, more indeed than that of Britain. Washington had envisaged a conference on the tariff question, and the Tuan Chi-jui regime invited the powers to convene it in 1925 and to consider ending the unequal treaties. At the conference, Japan expressed sympathy for China's wish for tariff autonomy. It also refused to send troops to Shanghai when invited by the British to do so early in 1927.

At that time the Northern March was focused on central China, and Britain's interests were more in question than Japan's. But if the gradualist and conciliatory approach enjoined by Washington was always going to be challenged by the impatient nationalism of the Chinese, it would be even more difficult to sustain if the conflict reached Manchuria. Whatever the strength of Britain's interests in central China, they were less important to Britain than Japan's interests in the north were to Japan, and Tokyo might not be able to adopt the approach adopted in London by Austen Chamberlain. For Japan China was, of course, more significant than it was for other powers. In 1931 there were 250,000 Japanese in China, 70 per cent of the foreign population, and Japan took up about a quarter of its import and export trade.[35] China absorbed nearly 82 per cent of Japan's foreign investment, less than 6 per cent of Britain's, and less than 1.5 per cent of that of the USA.

Even so, there was a sense of unfulfilled promise, particularly in Manchuria and the north. Manchuria had yet to realise Japan's hopes of settling its population surplus or supplying its industries with raw materials but it was seen as vital to Japan's future economically, and also strategically. Japan's position, too, rested on treaty rights, acquired by the expenditure of blood and treasure. 'Manchuria and Mongolia are Japan's lifeline', an official of the Japanese-owned South Manchuria Railway (SMR) wrote in 1931. 'Every nation has a life-line that holds the key to its existence. As Gibraltar and Malta are to Great Britain and the Caribbean Sea to America, there definitely is an important point from which it is impossible to retreat if the nation expects to exist.'[36] Yet no new deal had been made by the time the Northern March reached Manchuria, and the young warlord, Chang Hsueh-liang, taking over from his assassinated father Chang Tso-lin, hoisted the KMT flag late in 1928.

The absence of the Soviet Union had weakened the Washington system. Again, however, Japan acted conciliatorily. Finally withdrawing from Siberia in 1922, it proceeded to recognise the Soviet regime in 1925, Japan's share of the Sakhalin oilfields being a main subject for negotiations.[37] But mistrust persisted. In 1926 the Soviet Union proposed a non-aggression pact, as it had to Germany, but the aim was to drive a wedge between Britain and Japan and prevent their intervention in China.[38] The Russians hoped thus to facilitate Borodin's work, and until the 1927 CCP/KMT break, the Comintern continued to support the Chinese revolution, as well as communist activities in Japan itself. At the same time, moreover, as it pursued the new ideology, Russia had sought to maintain its old privileges in Manchuria, and after the 1927 split it was particularly concerned to maintain control over the Chinese Eastern Railway (CER) in face of Chinese opposition. That did not make the Japanese less anxious about the objectives of the Russians, nor push them to compromise with the KMT.

The policies of the mid-1920s were endorsed by the Kato coalition, and largely carried through by its foreign minister, Shidehara Kijuro, a career diplomat. His vision of Japan was a democratic nation, with a developed commerce and industry, seeking and relying on overseas markets, but not through territorial expansion, which would destroy international co-operation.[39] It was thus compatible with the Washington settlement and its spirit. In regard to the mainland his policy was 'China friendship': he pursued a conciliatory line, rather than the opportunism that had prevailed at least since 1915.That would facilitate trade and avoid boycotts. 'Like England we must obtain our sustenance abroad and our products must go to overseas markets. China's markets and materials mean to other countries only more trade; to Japan they are vital necessities.' In his view the Open Door and equal opportunity in China meant 'economy, if not actual salvation, for Japan'.[40] But though patient, Shidehara was rigid, and his task was complicated by the interests of other powers. By the time the government fell in 1927, he had not succeeded in obtaining new tariff agreements or ending extraterritoriality. In Manchuria he was again conciliatory, but not disposed to surrender Japanese rights.

The government, led by Wakatsuki Reijiro since Kato's death, had been brought down by a domestic financial crisis: the privy council refused to sanction support for the Bank of Taiwan's loans. The Hankow incident had also suggested that Shidehara's foreign policy was bankrupt: a mob had attacked the Japanese concession. Under the new prime minister, Tanaka Giichi, Shidehara's policy, already criticised as weak-kneed, was displaced by 'positive policy' or 'autonomous diplomacy'. It aimed at the endorsement of 'legitimate' Chinese aspirations, offsetting that by a willingness to implement 'decisive' actions whenever Japanese lives or property were placed in jeopardy; and by a commitment to a 'vigorous' course of action designed to dissipate all anti Japanese movements on the mainland. Mongolia and Manchuria were seen, too, as of prime importance to the security and resources of the empire. 'If disturbances should spread to Manchuria and Mongolia and menace Japan's special position and interests in these regions, the Imperial government must be prepared to combat this menace, regardless of where the danger may originate.'[41]

How big a break with his predecessor's policy did Tanaka intend? The so-called Tanaka memorial – allegedly presented to the emperor in July 1927 and envisaging the conquest of Manchuria and then the conquest of China – may not have existed, though he could have entertained the idea. There was, however, a shift. Tanaka sent troops to Shantung, to Tsingtao in May 1927, and then on to Tsinan in July, provoking protests and boycott. Troops were sent again in April 1928, when Chiang Kai-shek resumed the Northern March. A clash followed in May: 3600 Chinese died. In Manchuria Tanaka's plan was to co-operate with the old warlord, Chang Tsolin, and he pushed through a railway agreement with him late in 1927. Chang was to be a kind of puppet, enabling Japan to limit the penetration of the KMT into Manchuria without a formal challenge to the integrity of China. That policy was undermined when Colonel Komoto Daisaku of the Japanese army in Manchuria, the Kwantung army, masterminded Chang's assassination in June 1928. Komoto shared Tanaka's concern over Manchuria, but believed his remedy was inadequate: Chang was a 'cancer' working against Japan,[42] which should get rid of him and set up a puppet regime under his son. To Tanaka the assassination was an 'unthinkable disaster'.[43] 'My life's work is finished', he allegedly declared.[44]

Indeed his policy was in ruins. He pressed Chang's son, Chang Hsuehliang, not to adhere to the KMT. But his pressure, and that of the KMT, brought about the young warlord's agreement with Chiang Kai-shek in December, and that could only make the Manchuria question more intractable. Tanaka's policy was also disastrous for trade. Boycotts following the Tsinan intervention reduced Japanese exports to north China by 10 per cent and to the rest of China by 25 per cent. Nor was the government even able to punish the assassin, and it fell in July 1929.

Shidehara returned to power in the new government, and reasserted the policy of 'China friendship'. He had criticised Tanaka's policy. It was, he said, designed to curry popular support by belligerence overseas: if such policies dominated foreign relations, 'we cannot but be apprehensive of the future of our country and of the peace of the world'.[45] Other powers, themselves not finding it easy to come to terms with Chinese nationalism, were unlikely to be wholly unsympathetic to the Japanese in Manchuria, provided their policy did not too openly breach the Washington principles. A populist policy might lead Japan beyond those limits, and a government that could not exert control over its agents might find itself being led by them.

### The background to Japan's foreign policy

The governments of the mid-1920s, though they were party governments impressed by the example of the democracies, were not populist. The leader of the coalition, Kato, had argued in 1919 that, while the power of the masses was increasing, they must have proper guidance 'in order to preserve the essence of *kokutai* [the national polity] and the majesty of the imperial family'.[46] In 1925 the government introduced universal manhood suffrage. But it also introduced, perhaps partly as a sop to conservatives fearful of rice-roots democracy, the peace preservation law, giving the government wide powers to put down radical, communist and subversive organisations – perhaps as well a counterpart to recognition of the Soviet treaty.

Indeed, whatever his commitment to democracy, Shidehara cannot have found the cautious approach to popular participation unwelcome, since the idea of popular participation, as Kato's own background showed, had tended to be associated with a vigorous, even violent, propagation of Japan's interests. But the current system of party politics was itself no guarantee of moderation. Tanaka, a former protégé of Yamagata, was the leader of the Seiyukai party, chosen shortly before it broke the coalition with Kato's Kenseikai. The goals of the two parties in China were not radically different. They differed chiefly about the means of realising them, 'and the Seiyukai used this variance to further its political fortunes',[47] exploiting Shidehara's difficulties and denouncing weakness and non-intervention.

There were more extreme politicians and military officers than Tanaka, as the genro Saionji Kinmochi recognised. In turn, indeed, Tanaka had been outbidden by military officers who defied the party political system itself. Indiscipline in the armed forces had increased following the death of Yamagata in 1922. But it had other sources, too.

The war had brought Japan considerable dislocation as well as considerable opportunity. The rice riots of 1918 had involved 700,000 people, but it was also the era of the narikin, the new rich. The pace of social change, speeded by wartime industrialisation, intensified: by 1925 one-sixth of the population was in cities of over 100,000. Post-war there was some recession, and then Japan was hit by a major natural disaster, the Kanto earthquake of September 1923, which destroyed 400,000 houses and killed or injured 1.5 million people. A reconstruction boom followed, in turn followed by deflation and the financial crisis of 1927. The economic storms were not on the scale of those in Weimar Germany but, like them, they tended to increase the power of those who could best survive them: the landlords in the countryside; the *zaibatsu* (the major combines) in industry – Mitsui, for instance, controlled 15 per cent of Japan's corporate wealth. Such elements were likely to accept the status quo: party politics at home, 'China friendship' abroad.

The great industrialists – flourishing in the war, surviving the post-war recession – supported the liberal politicians in reaction to the *dirigisme* of the Meiji period. The outcome of the Chinese revolution worried them, but the 'China friendship' policy of Kato and Shidehara seemed the most likely way to avoid boycotts and guarantee the market. The *zaibatsu* were indeed unlikely to favour more radical policies, unless conditions became far more severe: they might lose what they had gained and their hopes of building on that. But the connection with party politics was too close, and exposed the system to criticism, and with that the policies associated with it. The pitched battles in the Diet in March 1926 symbolised the low level of political life. Money counted more than speeches and campaign literature. Party politicians themselves lost confidence. 'You know the world of politics is like a town where frauds, thieves and pickpockets gather. That's where your father works,' Nagai Ryutaro was to tell his children.[48]

The economic storms affected the countryside even more than the cities. The 1920s are sometimes called the period of 'agrarian panic'.[49] Farm prices were low; domestic industry was destroyed; and villages were burdened by returning urban unemployed. The government's repressive measures were not merely an elitist inheritance, nor a political deal with the conservatives. They were intended to deal with the discontent that the recession fostered, which tended to express itself outside the system of party politics. The widening of the suffrage, to which Kato was committed, might change that in the long term, but not in the short. The discontent was also making itself felt in the armed forces.

Nationalist societies had long been a feature of Japan's political life, operating as pressure groups, provoking protests like those against the treaty of Portsmouth. They grew in the 1920s. Some drew on Kita Ikki's

*An Outline of the Reconstruction of Japan* (1919), published in Manchuria in 1923. He envisaged a coup by an enlightened few, who would rid Japan of army cliques, bureaucrats, corrupt industrialists and party politicians. That would clear the way for the redistribution of land and for the introduction of state ownership in industry. But there would also be a programme of military expansion. Indeed Kita Ikki's 'social democracy', like earlier popular rights reforms, was linked with, even just a prelude to, forceful expansion.[50] 'The British Empire is a millionaire possessing wealth all over the world; and Russia is a great landowner in occupation of the northern half of the globe. Japan with her scattered fringe of islands is one of the proletariat, and she has the right to declare war on the monopoly powers.... In the name of rational social democracy Japan claims possession of Australia and Siberia.'[51] Japan would be 'the leader of Asia'; it would ultimately emerge as 'a great revolutionary empire', a Tokugawa Shogun for all other nations. 'The second coming of Christ, prophesied in every country on earth, actually signifies the scripture and sword of Japan [as a new] Mohammed.'[52]

The ideas seem a mishmash. But they contained an idealism that might be sought in vain in the politics of the day, an idealism that echoed, albeit in an extravagant way, the kind of aspirations Japan developed at the time its isolation was challenged in the mid-nineteenth century. Old ideas were being put into new words. They were also being shared with new social groups, and in particular appealed to those affected by the economic storms of the 1920s. Those, too, were now strongly represented in the army. In its early years the army, relatively small, had been dominated by upper-class officers, often from the Choshu clan. The expansion of Japan's activities in East Asia had required the expansion of its army, and officers were increasingly drawn from the lower middle class, from shopkeeping, petty bureaucratic and petty landowning elements, those whose position the changes of the 1920s made most uncertain. Doctrines like Kita Ikki's responded to their impatience with a Japan ruled by the *zaibatsu*, the landlords and the politicians, apparently subordinating the needs of the state to their own. The accession of a new emperor in 1926 suggested that a 'Showa restoration' might parallel the Meiji restoration: like the feudal lords of an earlier generation, the parties and the industrialists should surrender their powers to the emperor as part of a campaign of purification.

Like Kita Ikki, the younger officers were impatient, too, with what they saw as Japan's undue caution in foreign affairs and its servility towards the Western powers. Following Yamagata's death, and with the army bitter over what seemed a purposeless war in Siberia, insubordination increased, though it expressed itself in terms of an allegiance to Japan's higher destiny. Extremism was strong in the Kwantung army, and the assassination of Chang Tso-lin was a glaring example of the growing defiance of discipline. Nor could Tanaka get it punished.

Army cliques were among Kita Ikki's targets, and the lesser officers were also critical of the 'top brass', who were collaborating with party politicians in their programme of armaments limitations and in their pacific approach to international affairs. A particular butt of criticism was the war minister, General Ugaki Issei. His policy was certainly one of efficiency and rationalisation. Like the military leaders in the Weimar Republic, however, he saw that as a means of strengthening the army, not weakening it: it was an opportunity to modernise and mechanise. But critics could say that he was displacing the army's traditional values by an unemotional technology, emasculating its fighting spirit at the dictate of the civilians, destroying the soul of the Japanese state and the guardians of the 'Imperial Way', *kodo*. Such criticism was popular with the younger officers, with reservist organisations, and with nationalist societies. It was picked up, too, by rival factions among the 'top brass', such as that identified with Araki Sadao. Like Ugaki, they too wanted a modern army, but they were prepared to turn nationalist rhetoric to account so as to undermine him. That at once diminished the prospect of punishing the younger officers and helped to articulate their nationalist rhetoric.

The Meiji oligarchs had enforced their will in domestic and in foreign policy, but not by creating a monolithic state. Their state was, as Duus puts it, a truncated Leviathan.[53] The emperor in whose name they ruled had, like the emperor in Tokugawa times, no power in practice. Power was shared by a number of agencies and institutions, the leaders of the house of peers, the privy council, the cabinet, the parties in the Diet, the bureaucracy, the high command of the army and navy. The latter had 'the right of supreme command', direct access to the emperor, and indeed the striking feature of the Meiji constitutional arrangements was their lack of co-ordination. In some systems such a gap is filled by a strong personality. In Meiji Japan, it was filled by the oligarchy: it was 'government by crony'. The genro had resolved differences and set priorities.[54] Now Yamagata was dead, and Saionji, last of the civilian oligarchs, born back in 1849, did not believe he was in a position to fill their former role. 'I have never possessed the ambition, or should I say desire or should I say courage, to break open new ground out of dissatisfaction with existing conditions, or to stem the tide of a violent trend.'[55] Yet there was no formal substitute for this informal role. The constitution was not amended: the parties simply tried to run it in a different way. While there was no crisis, they might be strong enough to prevail. But could they co-ordinate Japan's policy if a crisis came? That was more doubtful.

The Washington system relied on the continued adherence of its participants to the principles it endorsed and the ineffectiveness of its opponents. The Chinese were impatient with its gradualist approach. That put in question the adherence to it of the Japanese, for they hoped that the new arrangements would still enable them to advance their interests, albeit with an emphasis on economic rather than territorial expansion. Even those Japanese in favour of the new approach, like Shidehara, were cautious and rigid, while their critics saw them as submissive and ineffectual. The party government of the day was ill equipped to impose its control on the organs of the Japanese state, still less well equipped to compel it to continue a moderate foreign policy in a time of crisis. Indeed the army, or elements in the army, were already defying the government. In theory the power of the emperor, in whose name the state was administered, had the power to check it. But could invoking that power be risked when it might be shown to be merely theoretical? 'Should the Emperor express himself and the army disobey', as Saionji put it, 'it would seriously damage the Imperial character.'[56] Any chance of sustaining and developing a constitutional monarchy would vanish.

### The survival of the settlements

In East Asia Japan had accepted the settlement, and it had agreed to pursue the 'new diplomacy' as a means by which it might secure its interests. During the mid-1920s it pursued a 'China Friendship' policy, while the British also sought to accommodate a Chinese nationalism disappointed by Versailles and Washington. In the East as in the West, it seemed in the mid-1920s that the settlements would survive, because they had been modified, and also shown that they could be modified. But more clearly in the East than in the West, the settlement was breaking down even before the Depression of 1929.

'The Western Powers had taught the Japanese the game of poker... but after acquiring most of the chips', as Matsuoka Yosuke, a future foreign minister, put it, 'they pronounced the game immoral and took up contract bridge.'[57] Perhaps they did too little to help Japan to adjust and promote the 'China friendship' approach. 'Without any kind of alliance, without any kind of a Monroe Doctrine of the Far East', William J. Castle of the State Department wrote in October 1930, 'we ought to be willing to play pretty closely with Japan. It seems to me that, if Japan can feel that we are wholeheartedly her friend, she will be much more likely to play the kind of game we want played in China.'[58] Certainly the Western powers were not well placed to enforce the Washington system if Japan should come to defy it. The Depression precipitated the crisis.

*Chapter 4*

# The Depression

While the Wall Street crash of October 1929 has been seen as signalling the onset of the Great Depression, it is acknowledged that its causes were more long-standing and complex. There had been no major reconstruction of the whole international economy following its dislocation by the war, only piecemeal attempts to return to pre-war conditions. Many problems, whose origins lay in the pre-war period, were not recognised. In Britain, for instance, the need for the modernisation of its old staple industries, particularly shipbuilding and mining, was ignored. Several years before 1929 there was an overproduction of primary products with a consequent decline in prices. The rural parts of Germany, many of the east European states and the mainly primary producing British Dominions, as well as rural America, were already experiencing the adverse effects of this situation when the financial crash occurred. Much of the European economic recovery in the 1920s had been dependent on American loans, usually short-term ones. Germany had had something approaching $4 billion and Austria $3 billion. Prior to the 1929 crash, this flow of American capital abroad had been shrinking as investors were tempted by the boom in their own country, but after the crash, the flow became a mere trickle. Markets contracted, businesses failed, banks collapsed and millions faced unemployment throughout Europe.

The Depression was clearly a turning-point in economic history: it brought a setback in a long period of expansion, hitherto interrupted only by smaller cycles of recession. It affected the industrial countries, the USA, the UK and other European countries, and Japan; and it affected the countries outside Europe that produced food and raw materials for the industrial world – the Australasian dominions, Argentina, Indonesia, Burma and Malaya. It prompted governments to reappraise their economic policies. Some insisted on deflation, some resorted to inflation, some tried one, then the other. Protectionist measures were adopted even by countries that had generally avoided them, such as the British at home and the Dutch in Indonesia, while other governments, like that of Malaya, sought to limit production in order to sustain prices. Some sought a regional or group approach: at Ottawa the commonwealth countries agreed on a system of 'imperial preference'. In general the Depression prompted both theorists and practitioners to favour a greater degree of intervention in the working-out of economic trends, and to favour planning, sometimes in partial emulation of the five-year plans that Stalin had begun in the Soviet Union.

Despite the international nature of the crisis no one took the lead in suggesting that the remedy could lie in international planning and co-operation. Instead, the protection of national interests and the recovery of the national economy became the priority of most governments, with a corresponding growth of suspicion and antagonism towards other states.

However governments reacted to the Depression it was bound to have a major political impact, both on the situation within each country and on relations between countries. Nowhere did it occur in a political vacuum, and appraising its role in political change is thus a matter of judgement. How big a change did it help to bring about? Were the Depression years, as Boyce has claimed, 'the watershed between two wars – the point at which the post-war era gave way to another pre-war era'?[1]

Within Europe, almost all of the constraints upon Germany from the treaty of Versailles were removed. Reparations were ended; rearmament was taking place; the democratic form of government of the Weimar Republic was replaced by the Nazi dictatorship. Britain, shaken by the Depression, shocked by Japanese aggression in the East, became more preoccupied with protecting its imperial, commonwealth and other overseas interests. France, plunged into a delayed but long drawn-out financial and economic crisis and torn apart by bitter internal political divisions, had to abandon all ideas of retaining any shred of 'predominance' on the continent. In societies which had scarcely adjusted to the trauma of the war and its repercussions, the impact of the economic crisis was heightened and public support was given to those who advocated strongly nationalistic solutions. Fear and despair drove many to abandon their traditional political loyalties, even to question the value of the liberal democratic form of government and to turn to exponents of more radical solutions – whether of the left or right.

### The situation in Germany

This was particularly true in Germany, where people had experienced also the devastating effects of the astronomic inflation of the mid-1920s. With the system of proportional representation which had been established under the Weimar constitution, no one party obtained sufficient support to obtain a majority of seats in the Reischstag. All governments were therefore coalitions and usually short lived. Parties were divided into factions. They were associated with sectional and class interests and their leaders appeared to be afraid to compromise with other parties for fear of alienating their own supporters.

After the trauma of 1923 Stresemann hoped that a broader agreement on foreign policy and the achievement of some success in that field would help to lessen the importance of domestic conflicts amongst the main political parties. For a time there appeared some ground for optimism. The coalition government to which he belonged had members from the German Democratic Party (DDP), the Centre party, the DVP and, from 1925 to 1927 the right-wing DNVP. The Socialists (SPD), who did not join the coalition until 1928, usually supported Stresemann on foreign policy issues. His achievements, however, were not sufficient to satisfy an important sector of the DNVP which distanced itself from the party leadership which had supported the government. With Stresemann's death and the early signs of a new economic crisis, the fragility of the coalition became apparent. At different ends of the political spectrum the DVP and the SPD became increasingly nervous about losing supporters to more extreme parties. The DVP, with its strong ties to business interests, feared the appeal of the DNVP and the SPD that of the Communists, the KPD. Neither party therefore was willing to compromise in working out a policy to cope with the economic crisis for fear of alienating their traditional supporters. With potential stalemate in the Reichstag, Chancellor Brüning of the Centre party, who had headed a government for a few months only and had depended upon emergency powers granted by the president, decided to call new elections in September 1930. In those elections the Centre party and the SPD retained their support and the latter remained the largest party in the Reichstag with 143 seats. The moderate liberal parties, however, lost heavily and disturbingly large gains were made by the radical anti-parliamentary parties. The KPD increased their seats from 54 to 77 and the Nazis from 12 to 107.

A large literature exists on the complex and controversial question of who voted for the Nazis at this election and at the election in 1932.[2] Their nationalistic appeal and their assertions that Germany's problems stemmed from Versailles, and particularly from reparations in their continuing form of 'Young Slavery', 'Young Misery' and 'Young taxes' undoubtedly appealed to many.[3] It has to be acknowledged, however, that other parties, especially the Nationalists, exploited many of the same issues in their election campaigns but did not achieve similar success. One of the advantages of the Nazis was that they were not so closely associated with particular interest groups in German society as were many of the traditional parties. In the local elections of 1929, they had gained considerable support in the small towns and rural communities of north-west Germany where the

73

agricultural recession had brought distress and fears for the future to the small farmers, the shopkeepers and the craftsmen. Similar fears about the future spread to many other groups in German society in the next few years and the Nazis, untainted by previous failures in government, had a broad programme and a strong basic organisation to exploit the situation. They offered national unity, a solution to Germany's economic problems, strong leadership, a foreign policy which would restore Germany's pride and prestige and to many they offered the major alternative to communism.

The German government, which remained under the leadership of Brüning, proved unable to prevent a worsening economic situation despite following a policy which won plaudits from abroad for its attempts to balance the budget by tax increases and cuts in government spending. At first, he did not beat the anti-reparation drum too loudly for fear of doing further damage to Germany's external credit but, by mid-1931, he was under increasing pressure from the president and the political right to adopt a firmer stance towards other powers. It was a policy which to a great extent he himself favoured. He wanted a speedy end to reparations and more widespread disarmament as a preliminary to a complete removal of the restrictions of Versailles. And he was inclined to welcome domestic right-wing criticism as a means of inducing the Allies to make such concessions. His announcement that the limit of privations which could be imposed upon the German people had been reached and that Germany's precarious economic situation required the removal of the reparations burden was successful in obtaining the suspension of reparation payments for a year under the Hoover Moratorium of June 1931. At Lausanne a year later they were abolished altogether, apart from one final sum of 3 billion marks which was to be paid when the German economy recovered. That recovery did not come quickly. Confidence within Germany remained low. The government had increasing difficulty in organising short-term loans. The numbers of unemployed rose from 2.25 million in 1930 to over 6 million in 1932. The German government's attempt to achieve another foreign policy success by organising a customs union with Austria in 1931 failed, owing to the opposition of the other powers, particularly France. Brüning's hopes that the evidence of radical nationalist activity in Germany, which was certainly being supplied by the Nazis, would induce the other powers to make further dramatic concessions to his government failed. He had ruled largely by presidential decree to obtain the passage of much of his unpopular domestic legislation but in May 1932 President Hindenburg ceased to support him and replaced him with Franz von Papen, a conservative politician who could make no claim to large support within the Reichstag. His calling of elections in July 1932 to strengthen his position resulted in a 37 per cent vote for the Nazis, which made them the largest party in the Reichstag. That was insufficient to bring the Nazis to power and they lost some support at the elections of November 1932. Hitler finally came to power in January 1933 because of the machinations of some of the military leadership and the right-wing politicians who foolishly believed that they could control Hitler and use the mass support of the Nazis to forward their domestic interests and win further concessions for Germany in foreign policy.

It is impossible to know whether the Nazis would have come to power without the advent of the Depression. What is certain is that its advent and the policies which the German governments followed in trying to deal with it produced a situation where a considerable mass of the population and a significant number of people in positions of influence chose to support the Nazis. Whatever the reasons for their support, they brought to power a party that had a contempt for democracy, an avowed racist policy and an openly proclaimed intention of pursuing an aggressive and expansionist foreign policy far beyond the revision of the perceived injustices of the treaty of Versailles which had been pursued by their predecessors. Hitler's views on foreign policy had been published in his lengthy and turgid tome, *Mein Kampf,* and echoed in subsequent speeches. He made it clear that the union of all Germans in a Greater Germany was only the beginning of his ambitions. For Hitler, the history of mankind was a struggle between races for the control of land and resources. He saw no reason why the Germans, members of what he saw as the superior Aryan race, should be 'penned into an impossible area'. Germany needed more good agricultural land on which to settle its people and provide for their nourishment. This living space or *Lebensraum* was not to be found in overseas colonies but in 'the land in the east... Russia and her vassal border states'. The inferior Russian Slavs, he believed, would have little ability to resist as their former 'leading strata' of Germans had been replaced by 'the Jew' during the Bolshvik revolution. A reckoning with France would be necessary but he anticipated that an alliance could be formed with the disgruntled Italians and the anti-communist British. War would be necessary and desirable. He expected to win the land that he thought would be vital for the life of the German people by 'the might of a victorious sword'.[4]

It was not only within Germany that the effects of the Depression exacerbated existing domestic problems and frequently led to the end of democratic government. Within Czechoslovakia, the previously mild discontent of the Germans in the borderlands swelled as the Depression began to affect the prosperity of that industrialised area. In Yugoslavia, Croat opposition to what they saw as a Serbian-dominated state erupted into open revolt and parliamentary government gave way to royal dictatorship. In Austria, there was increasing unrest as right-wing nationalists and socialists struggled for supremacy and, from 1933, governments resorted to ruling by decree. The swing was definitely to the left in Bulgaria where the Communists won considerable successes at the national and local elections. Within Spain, the divisions between right and left became so extreme and violent that the country was plunged into civil war in 1936. The countries which survived without undue social or political upheaval were already under dictatorships, albeit of differing kinds – Russia under Stalin's brand of communism and Italy under Mussolini's fascism. To many it appeared that Europe was about to become a battleground not so much of nations as of ideologies, of left versus right, of communism versus fascism.

### Britain, France and the United States

In Britain and France, the effects of the Depression were profound but they did not result in the overthrow of the existing forms of government. A severe financial crisis developed in Britain in the summer of 1931 as a result of increasing balance of payment problems, deficit budgets and a seemingly panic withdrawal of foreign credits. The chancellor of the exchequer in Britain's second Labour government, Philip Snowden, hoped to stem the tide by the strictly conservative economic measures of cutting government spending, including unemployment pay. Such measures would have adversely affected Labour's traditional supporters and the Cabinet could not agree on such a policy. It resigned and was replaced by a National government, made up of some of the Labour party, the Conservatives and the Liberals. That government took the drastic step of abandoning the gold standard, which, in practice, meant that sterling was devalued. The immediate financial crisis came to an end but the economic recovery, based partly on a greater competitiveness in international markets, was to be slow. Most importantly, the new government, strengthened by an overwhelming victory at the polls, believed that its main purpose was to fulfil the tellingly described 'doctor's mandate' of nursing Britain back to economic health. Strongly influenced by the cautious views of the Treasury, the government believed that it could not countenance increased spending on defence. Neville Chamberlain, the new chancellor of the exchequer, warned his colleagues in January 1933 that 'financial and economic risks are by far the most serious that the country has to face and that other risks have to be run until the country has had time and opportunity to recuperate and our financial situation to improve'.[5] In those circumstances, and unable to ignore a growing crisis in the Far East, the British government was confirmed in its unwillingness to undertake further commitments on the continent or to co-ordinate plans with the French to stand up to the new regime which had come to power in Germany.

In France, the impact of the Depression was delayed. The country was cushioned by the devaluation of the franc in 1928 and by the strength of its domestic market. By 1933, however, the Depression was beginning to bite and French governments, coalitions largely dominated by the Radicals (a broad-based centre–left party), administered the traditional medicine of retrenchment and an attempt to balance the budgets. This financial ortho-doxy and a refusal to devalue the franc again helped to perpetuate the effects of the Depression. Social unrest and support for alternative forms of government grew. On the left the Communists continued to advocate a revolutionary overthrow of the bourgeois republic. On the right a number of the paramilitary leagues, some of which closely resembled fascist move-ments, were also all opposed to the existing republican regime. The eco-nomic conditions and a growing number of rumours and scandals about members of the ruling parties led to considerable support for anti-govern-ment riots led by the leagues in Paris in February 1934. They are now not seen as having posed any serious threat to the republican regime, but at the time there was less certainty and they fuelled the fears as well as the anger of the left and helped to pave the way for the formation of the Popular Front, a union of the Radicals, Socialists and Communists. This was a significant change. The Communists and Socialists had previously seen each other as bitter opponents vying for the support of the working classes. The Socialists had frequently formed electoral alliances with the Radicals but they had refused to join them in government. The Popular Front triumphed at the polls in 1936 and formed a government, but that did little to reduce social unrest or to ease the bitter and violent divisions of political life. In this financially weak and deeply divided state, France faced a resurgent Ger-many which had begun to climb out of the trough of the Depression by 1933.

Internationally, France's position also deteriorated in the early 1930s. Both Britain and the United States were alienated by their perceptions of French policy. They were particularly estranged by the negotiations over the end of reparations, the proposed Austro-German Customs Union and the Disarmament Conference. President Hoover's proposal of a year-long mora-torium on all inter-government debts in June 1931 was made public with-out prior consultation with the French. The British, who had consistently supported a revisionist policy on war debts and reparations and who, like the Americans, wished to protect the interests of their nationals who had loans and investments in Germany, supported the proposal. France hesi-tated. From its point of view, the proposal had two main disadvantages. There was no specific preservation of the principle of reparations nor any protection from an American demand for the resumption of war debt payments from France and Britain. French suspicions had some validity. The precipitate nature of the proposal and the limited extent of the mora-torium seem to have resulted from a desire to pre-empt a general discussion of the war debts issue and to reassure the American voters that they would not be deprived of their rightful dues for too long. Some, like Keynes in Britain, believed that the whole proposal was flawed in that a year was insufficient time for a recovery, but many more believed that it was the French delay in accepting it which destroyed the expected benefit of a major restoration of confidence in the German mark. What was more, the British financial crisis of 1931 followed almost immediately and members of the British cabinet and leading bankers were convinced that the French had organised the run on the pound to put pressure on the British government to give them their political support. While it is now recognised that this was a total misreading of the situation, the fuelling of anti-French sentiment in Britain was intense. The French, according to Neville Chamberlain, were 'anxious to get their hands on our throats as they have on the Germans'.[6] There was an equally strong reaction in the United States when a run on their gold reserves in September 1931 was laid at the door of the French.

French acquiescence in the Lausanne agreement came at the end of long drawn-out negotiations and as a result of considerable British pressure and a greater willingness to compromise by the new centre-left government of Edouard Herriot. The power that did not compromise was the United States. At the end of 1932 it demanded a further instalment of war debt payments. Suspicious of each other, Britain and France did not co-ordinate their response. Too proud to default on their debt despite, or perhaps because of, their financial situation, the British paid. The French, in a far healthier financial situation, did not. The extent of anti-French sentiment in the United States was reflected in the comment of President Herbert Hoover, 'France always goes through this cycle. After she is done and begins to recuperate ... she gets rich, militaristic and cocky: and nobody can get on with her until she has to be thrashed again.'[7]

The proposal for an Austro-German customs union was announced in March 1931 without any preliminary discussions with other powers. While the Germans claimed that it was part of a general movement towards European federation and economic co-operation, the French were suspicious immediately that it was the preliminary to a political union between the Austria and Germany and designed to appeal to the growing nationalist fervour within Germany.[8] France immediately initiated moves to have the proposal blocked in the League of Nations Council and referred to the International Court of Justice at The Hague on the grounds that it violated the treaty of St Germain. The decision of the Court was against the proposed union but before that announcement was made, the French government chose to exercise its financial muscle by making much-needed loans to Austria dependent upon the abandonment of the customs union. The British deplored such methods. Vansittart, the permanent under-secretary of state at the foreign office, compared them to 'a stronger man making conditions with a weaker one while the latter's house was on fire'.[9] As French action over the Ruhr in 1923 had been seen as an improper use of its military strength, so France's behaviour during the early years of the Depression was seen as an improper use of its financial strength.

Throughout 1932 and 1933, other economic issues continued to bring increasing tension between the major democratic powers.[10] The British decision at the Ottawa Conference in 1932 to establish imperial preference brought a very adverse reaction from the United States. The Americans believed that it was a hostile discriminatory measure, specifically designed to exclude them from a large part of the world market. As the United States already had protectionist tariffs, the British viewed such complaints as impertinent hypocrisy. The question of war debts remained a source of acrimony. Britain and France had some hopes of a change in American policy with the advent of the new president, Franklin Roosevelt, in March 1933, but once he was in office he made it clear that he had no interest in cancelling or modifying war debts. The British made two token payments in 1933 and were then mortified and angry to learn in February 1934 that they, with other defaulters, would be excluded from future access to American capital markets under a bill before Congress. In June 1934, the British government decided not to pay its sixth monthly instalment to 'this untrustworthy race'.[11] Roosevelt also proved a disappointment to Britain and France in his attitude towards the issue of international currency stabilisation. With little warning, and with what many believed no great necessity, he took the dollar off the gold standard in March 1933 and in July ensured the failure of a world economic conference by announcing his unwillingness to take part in any scheme to stabilise the exchange rate. With the franc coming under pressure the French were dismayed at the outcome of the conference and, although there were mutual recriminations between themselves and the British, the major condemnation from both states was directed at Washington. On the American side, they attributed the Depression to their involvement in Europe, based their assessment of British policy on an overestimation of the wealth and strength of Britain, and were critical not only of French financial policy but also of what they saw as continuing French militarism.

On the matter of disarmament, the British and the Americans expected the French to make concessions over land and naval armaments. They themselves, however, had been involved in lengthy and at times acrimonious discussions before they had agreed on an acceptable formula over battleships at the Washington conference and over smaller warships at the London naval conference of 1930. At Washington, the French had agreed to accept parity with the Italians over battleships, but at London they would not accede to a similar agreement over other warships. The French argument was that, unlike Italy which was solely a Mediterranean power, France had to be able to defend itself in the North Sea and the Atlantic as well as the Mediterranean. The tonnage of cruisers and smaller vessels which it claimed would be necessary for this task led the British prime minister, MacDonald, to declare that acceptance of the French view would mean it was 'a Military not a

Disarmament Conference'.[12] No accommodation between France and Italy was reached.

The major disarmament conference, which had been years in the planning, opened at Geneva in the inauspicious circumstances of February 1932. Whatever the technicalities that were raised, the real issue was the balance of armaments between France and Germany. Germany made the seemingly reasonable case that other powers should disarm to its level or Germany should be allowed to rearm without restriction. The problem for France was that either course would undermine its security. Without other guarantees France would be vulnerable from a Germany which had demographic superiority, a potentially stronger economic base and fewer overseas commitments. Its efforts to obtain that security through regional League pacts and an international peace-keeping force foundered on British opposition. Direct Franco-German negotiations failed. A complicated American scheme designed to differentiate between weapons of defence and weapons of aggression made no progress. The British persevered with proposals in the belief that some agreed limitation on German armaments was better than none and, after Hitler had come to power, the French made some small concessions. By that stage, if not earlier, the discussions were irrelevant. It was an open secret that the Germans were proceeding with rearmament and in October 1933 they felt sufficiently confident to leave the conference and the League. The legacy of the conference was not merely that Germany was unrestrained by any new international agreement on its rearmament but also that it had added to the bitterness and recriminations in Anglo/French/ American relations. The French were critical of the limited understanding and support which they had received from Britain and the United States and the latter blamed the French for the ultimate failure because of their unwillingness to make concessions at an earlier stage of the negotiations.

The coming to power of the Nazis in Germany is now seen as one of the most significant developments of the Depression years but at the time it did not arouse universal concern. Some, like the prescient British ambassador Sir Horace Rumbold, expressed great apprehension. 'I have the impression that the persons directing the policy of the Hitler Government are not normal. Many of us, indeed, have a feeling that we are living in a country where fanatics, hooligans and eccentrics have got the upper hand'. He did not think that there was any immediate danger of war but warned 'that Hitlerism will ultimately lead to war is a contingency which cannot be ruled out. . . . The glorification of militarism, the incessant celebration of anniversaries, the return of the heroic ideal, all point in one direction'.[13] Others, however, were more sanguine. The most optimistic believed that Nazism was a temporary phenomenon. Others hoped that, however extreme Hitler's pronouncements had been in the past, his policy would be modified under the responsibilities of office. In France, some of the leaders consoled themselves that the spectacle of 'mediocrities and fanatics' in power in Germany would 'unite Europe in fear and common interest'.[14] Other developments of the Depression years had made that an unlikely prophecy. States were divided by stronger nationalistic sentiments and extreme ideologies. The leading democratic powers in Europe, Britain and France, and the United States were alienated from each other and were more firmly focused on national concerns than they had been in the 1920s. French statesmen were becoming 'almost wholly absorbed in the fight to save the franc and the search for economic recovery'.[15] The United States was preoccupied with implementing the measures for its own economic recovery which were set out in the New Deal and wished to further distance itself from European affairs. The Americans, according to the somewhat jaundiced view of Neville Chamberlain, were 'chiefly anxious to convince their people that they are not going to be drawn into doing anything helpful to the rest of the world'.[16] The British were not only absorbed in the task of economic recovery but also in working out a new relationship with their Dominions, framing a new constitution for India and coming to terms with the threat to their interests in the Far East from Japan.

## The Manchuria Incident

Japan's policy was already changing before it was hit by the Depression. Undoubtedly, however, the Depression helped to precipitate the Manchuria incident of 1931. Was that in turn decisive in changing the way in which Japan's politics were conducted after 1931? And how far did the crisis in Manchuria weaken the Washington system and the approach to international relations that it represented?

At the time the Depression struck, indeed, the Tanaka government had been displaced, discredited by its failure to punish the assassins of Chang Tso-lin, and a government dominated by the Minseito party, heirs to the Kato tradition, was in power, led by Hamaguchi Yukō, and with Shidehara again foreign minister. He still projected 'economic diplomacy', stressing collaboration with China and renegotiation of the unequal treaties. By May 1930, he had negotiated tariff autonomy, and early in 1931 he was still prepared to see KMT policies as following a 'trail once blazed by Japan in her struggle to emerge from a position of international inequality'.[17] China had, however, to undertake constructive reforms, of the kind Japan had implemented earlier. It must, too, recognise the complementary needs of China and Japan. Shidehara sought in fact some type of confirmation of Japan's rights in southern Manchuria. Not even he could entertain the idea that the KMT should be permitted to construct a competitive railway system in Manchuria, which would compromise the position of the Japanese based on the South Manchuria Railway, and if need be, he would invoke a 1905 protocol that prohibited it. Shidehara stuck in essence to the Washington principles. He was too rigid to satisfy the Chinese, while at the same time his policy was criticised in army circles in Japan and by Seiyukai spokesmen as supine and unproductive. He could not eliminate the possibility of a crisis. But something more was needed to produce one.

Shidehara's negotiations with the Western powers at the London naval conference of 1930 also exposed him to criticism at home. The Washington conference had reached an agreement over the ratios of capital shipbuilding, but it had not covered other ships, cruisers, submarines and destroyers, partly because the USA and the UK could not agree on what would constitute parity in these categories. The British were anxious for an agreement. In the interim, Japan had been free to build ships in these categories. Now it was prepared to accept a 10 : 10 : 6 ratio. That would involve a great change in the actual ratio – Japan had 12 cruisers, the USA 1 – but it would still guarantee the security of Japan, the fundamental basis of the Washington agreement. The USA, however, wanted to apply the same 10 : 10 : 6 ratio to cruisers as to capital ships. Though that had a tidy logic, it would in fact diminish Japan's security: the US navy would be able not simply to defend Hawaii, but to carry a war to Japan's home islands. The Minseito government finally agreed to the Reed–Matsudaira compromise, which agreed on 10 : 10 : 6 in principle, but deferred its implementation.

Then the government had to win its case at home. The ratification of the London treaty was driven through, despite opposition Seiyukai protests that the chief of the naval general staff had been denied the right of supreme command – direct access to the emperor – a rather paradoxical argument for a political party to adopt. Nationalist unrest increased, involving, among other episodes, the founding of the Cherry Society by general staff officers increasingly discontented with Shidehara diplomacy. More long-term results were the attempted assassination of Hamaguchi in November 1930 and the attempted *coup d'etat* in March 1931, suppressed because of Ugaki's objections. Even within the ministry of foreign affairs, Shidehara was not supported. But by this time, the Depression was clearly having an effect. That further eroded the position of the government and gave its opponents new opportunities for challenging it.

The American market had taken 40 per cent of Japan's goods in the 1920s. Now it had slumped. The exports of 1931 were only slightly over half the value of those of 1929. High unemployment ensued – 2.4–2.6 million in 1930 – but the Minseito cabinet stuck to a deflationary policy. Japan, its critics argued, needed a bolder policy on the mainland to make up for its losses elsewhere. The *zaibatsu*, hoping to ride out this storm, like the storms of the early 1920s, still preferred the status quo. Hesitating to accept the arguments for a change of policy, Dan Takuma, the Mitsui executive, supported Shidehara, himself married into the family that owned Mitsubishi. But the Depression stimulated more radical views. Its impact on Japan and on Japanese attitudes was all the greater because of the dramatic changes since the war in the economic, social and political spheres, and the cultural as well. Once more Japan had opened itself to 'the latest styles from America and Western Europe'.[18] The Depression seemed to put a premium on those who claimed to reassert old values and end what they saw as the moral decay of the 1920s.

The Manchuria incident of 1931 was an initiative of the Kwantung army, like the assassination of Chang Tso-lin in 1928. By contrast to the 1928 initiative, however, the 1931 initiative appears to have had some preliminary backing in Tokyo. Certainly, once begun, it produced quite a different reaction there. The difference offers some measure of the impact of the Depression, though not a perfect one. In the interim Shidehara had gone through a frustrating naval negotiation and an only partially successful renegotiation of the unequal treaties, themselves episodes on which indeed the Depression had made an impact. Overall it is perhaps safe to conclude that the Depression turned a potential crisis into an actual crisis.

Within the army there were factions and differences of perspective and opinion, but over Manchuria there was, as Crowley has argued,[19] substantial consensus. In the operations division of the general staff, Araki had pointed to the augmentation of the Red Army in the maritime provinces of the Soviet Union as a reason for military action that would ensure a strategic advantage for Japan. The intelligence division was concerned over the rise of Chinese nationalism, stimulated rather than blunted by the assassination. The war ministry put more stress on concepts of total war, general mobilisation and internal army reorganisation – concepts developed by men like Nagata Tetsu-zan as a result of their appreciation of German achievements in the First World War[20] – but recognised the importance of the resources of Manchuria.

The Kwantung army drafted a plan of operations that would enable it to move beyond protecting Japanese property and nationals and to seize control. It was approved by General Honjo Shigeru, commanding officer in Manchuria, and submitted to General Tatekawa Yoshitsugu, Araki's successor. A number of incidents in Manchuria prompted the Seiyukai and the nationalist societies to demand retaliation. Wakatsuki and Shidehara preferred a pacific settlement. Their concern was allayed by the war minister's decision to send Tatekawa to confer with Honjo. In fact Tatekawa gave advance notice of his arrival, seen by the Kwantung conspirators as an invitation to act quickly.[21] A mysterious bomb explosion in Mukden led to a skirmish and the Kwantung troops proceeded to seize control of Mukden and Kirin: they hoped to realize 'the paradise of coexistence and co-prosperity for the 30 millions residing in Manchuria and Mongolia'.[22] The general staff were in favour of the action and the war ministry unwilling to oppose. The army ruled in favour of an aggressive approach to the Manchurian problem.

The Minseito cabinet was unable to regain control. Shidehara and the finance minister, Inoue Junnosuke, argued against the aggressive approach, and Wakatsuki ruled that the crisis should be localised and settled promptly. This decision was undermined by the army's invocation of the right of supreme command and by the despatch of vague and discretionary instructions to Manchuria. Public opinion had responded favourably to the army's initiative. 'Any action they [the cabinet] may take to defend her [Japan's] interests in Manchuria will receive unanimous public support', reported Sir Francis Lindley.[23] At the League of Nations, to which China appealed, the Chinese spokesman insisted that Japan must draw back its troops into the railway zone before negotiations could begin. As Shidehara told Lindley, he could not secure that. The Seiyukai, moreover, criticised his 'spineless' posture, while a dissident wing emerged in the Minseito, and the home minister himself announced a personal boycott of cabinet meetings in protest at the Shidehara policies. Shidehara persuaded the cabinet to accept a League of Nations enquiry into Sino-Japanese relations, but that was as far as he could get. The cabinet resigned on 12 December.

Not only could the cabinet not restrain the army: the cabinet system itself disintegrated in face of the nationalist predisposition of party politicians. The nomination of a new premier still lay with the senior statesman, Saionji, and he searched for as moderate a man as he could find, significantly avoiding the head of the Seiyukai. He settled on Inukai Ki, a Seiyukai man indeed, who had berated Shidehara and defended the right of supreme command in 1930, but who, more moderate than many, had not endorsed the pressure for an 'independent' Manchuria that was building up. Saionji also conveyed the Emperor's views to Inukai: 'The meddling of the army in domestic and foreign affairs is something which, for the welfare of the nation, must be viewed with apprehension. Be mindful of my anxiety...'[24] But it was not thought that imperial constraint could go further. Intervention, if ineffectual, would erode confidence in the imperial institution.

What Inukai tried to do was to conciliate the army by permitting reinforcement in Manchuria, but also to negotiate a settlement with the Chinese government that would preserve at least a fiction of Chinese sovereignty over Manchuria. He told the foreign minister: 'if the situation develops towards the formation of an independent country, we shall have serious trouble with the Nine Power Treaty nations. For this reason, I am actively trying to achieve our national purpose in Manchuria within the existing forms of political power'.[25] But the attempt to reconcile Japanese rights and Chinese sovereignty, pursued for twenty years in one form or another, had little chance of success at this juncture, and the chance of avoiding a breach with the Washington powers was diminishing. The question rather was how deep and enduring it might be.

By late February Inukai had already abandoned his hopes. In part that resulted from army policy: it pushed ahead with setting up local political structures in Manchuria. The atmosphere was also worsened by the Shanghai incident. Following an intensification of anti-Japanese boycotts, that was a clash, instigated by a Japanese military aide, between some Chinese workers and local Japanese. It developed into a clash between Japanese marines intended to defend the Japanese sector of the international settlement in Shanghai and the KMT's 19th Route Army, and led to a Japanese aerial bombardment of part of the Chinese suburb of Chapei. Inukai sought to settle the dispute. But it destroyed any hope of a settlement in Manchuria. In March his cabinet authorised the creation of a separate Manchurian government with Pu Yi, the claimant to the Manchu throne in China, as head of state.

Even so, Inukai was assassinated by an extremist in May. Saionji again avoided giving the prime ministership to a Seiyukai leader. Instead he resorted to a bureaucratic cabinet headed by Admiral Saito Makoto. Again the concept of parliamentary responsibility was diminished in the hope of a moderate foreign policy, but bureaucratic cabinets did not guarantee that. The Saito cabinet recognised the new state of Manchukuo in August, its foreign minister, Uchida Shinya, telling the Diet that it was his 'fervent hope that the day is not far distant when Japan, Manchukuo, and China, as three independent Powers closely linked together by a bond of cultural and racial affinities, will come to cooperate hand in hand for the maintenance and advancement of the peace and prosperity of the Far East'.[26] Matsuoka led the Japanese delegation out of the League of Nations when it adopted the substance of the Lytton report, which recommended the formation of a new administrative arrangement for Manchuria that would protect Japan's special rights and interests and be consistent with the principle of Chinese sovereignty over Manchuria, and one month later Japan left the organisation entirely.

As Uchida's remarks suggest, Japan's experiment was placed to some extent in a framework of principle and rhetoric that borrowed from an earlier pan-Asianism. Perhaps that was designed to make it more acceptable. Pan-Asian idealism had, however, been eroded in the decades of opportunism and realism. It was certainly going to be difficult to give it credibility in China. At the same time it might alarm the Western powers, to the extent that it was successful in expanding the threat to their interests by claiming some kind of Asian leadership for Japan.

### Extremism

The creation of Manchukuo was itself a considerable breach in the Washington system created at the beginning of the previous decade, and leaving the League put a further gulf between Japan and the Western powers. But to see these steps as a 'turning-point' may still be the result of hindsight. The Western powers had seen Manchuria as something of a special case and, if Japan were satisfied with its achievement there, the Washington system might not be fatally undermined. Further analysis of the reasons why the Manchuria incident developed in the way it did between 1931 and 1933 may assist in making a judgement. Is 1933 a 'turning-point' in Asia as in Europe?

Within Japan there had been no coup of the kind Kita Ikki had envisaged. After the Mukden incident, the Kwantung extremists were reported to have boasted: 'We have succeeded. Therefore when we return to the homeland this time we shall carry out the *coup d'etat* and do away with the political party system of government. Then we shall establish a nation of National Socialism with the Emperor as the centre. We shall abolish capitalists like Mitsui and Mitsubishi and carry out an even distribution of wealth'.[27] But that did not occur. Instead once more Japan changed, not its institutions, but the way it worked them. The army leadership, having condoned the Kwantung initiative, took advantage of it to destroy the influence of the Minseito cabinet and increase their control of policy making. But Araki did not respond to the extremists in the Cherry Society who wanted to carry out Kita's plan. Indeed the conspirators were rounded up and the Society dissolved.

In subsequent months extremists were active in Japan. The assassination of Inukai in May 1932 was preceded in February by that of Inoue and of Dan Takuma, the Mitsui leader. This was the work of a radical army movement, whose prophet was Gondo Seikyo. Known later as the National Principle School, it believed in purifying Japanese life by killing the iniquitous. Again they had no backing from the top brass and were rounded up. There was certainly no connivance as in the Mukden incident. Once having used that to increase their power, the army chiefs did not support the revolutionising of Japan. What the extremists of the period did was to intensity the atmosphere of crisis, and to increase the currency of nationalist rhetoric. Of those the top brass might take advantage.

There was no revolution in Japan, but the incident in Manchuria encouraged the tendency to channel radicalism abroad. Would that process continue? The malaise among the lower officers was still very evident. Would their acts of insubordination undermine the control of their superiors and lead to further initiatives in foreign policy that did not enjoy advance support but would be difficult to retreat from? If the checks within the army were still effective, the checks upon the army were much less so. The two-year crisis had shown the inability of the political parties to sustain a system of cabinet responsibility. In the absence of constitutional provision, the oligarchs had depended on cronyism. Saionji felt he could do little. His answer was to instal bureaucratic cabinets, but they could not prioritise.

## Manchuria in international relations

The analysis must cover not only domestic but also external factors. China's failure to offer Shidehara a more positive response clearly weakened his cause and encouraged Japan's resort to force. The setting up of Manchukuo did not make it easier to bring about a deal with the KMT that would have revived the prospects of an economic diplomacy and put Japan's expansion on an economic basis, even if Depression conditions had allowed it. The rhetoric of Japanese expansionism reformulated pan-Asianism. But even though the KMT's fear of communism grew, it could not accept the emphasis on Japan's leadership that pan-Asianism now involved.

In the 1920s the other powers had done little to promote an all-round agreement on the unequal treaties that would have helped Shidehara. In the Manchuria crisis they did little to promote a settlement. Such might have assisted those in Japan who wanted to check the ambitions of the military and revert to a more pacific diplomacy. It might, however, also have been seen as encouraging those who resorted to violence. If one breach of Washington was allowed, why not another? Was the system better preserved by accepting some compromise or by rejecting compromise altogether? Nor, of course, was it clear, particularly in the midst of the Depression, that the powers, even if they resolved on compromise, could do much to bring China and Japan to accept it.

Japan's actions in Manchuria, as Lytton was to put it, were not 'a simple case of the violation of one country by the armed force of a neighbouring country, because in Manchuria there are many features without any exact parallel in other parts of the world'.[28] In the West there was considerable sympathy with Japan, particularly given the growth of Soviet power in the Far East. In London some had argued that Japan should be allowed to expand in Manchuria, since it could not expand elsewhere. The Depression led to measures in other countries that affected Japan's trade, such as the US tariff of 1931, the Ottawa agreements of 1932, and later the Dutch shift to protection in the Indies – allowing the Japanese to argue, as George Sansom put it, 'that the very Powers which reproach them for their conduct in Manchuria are forcing them to desperate measures by closing their markets against them'.[29]

In Manchuria the Japanese had 'a great deal of right on their side', Sir John Pratt wrote. 'By their corruption, incapacity and blind conceit [the Chinese] were reducing to ruin one of the wealthiest regions in the world.... They ignored both Japan's treaty rights and the historical justification for Japan's position in Manchuria'.[30] 'The Chinese have consistently attempted to undermine [the] Japanese position', though it rested largely on treaty rights. Wilson's doctrine of self-determination and the League, Lindley suggested, had given 'such backward countries as China ... the idea that they can make themselves as intolerable as they like without suffering any of the consequences which would have followed such behaviour before 1914'.[31]

These ambivalent attitudes argued against forceful measures to stop Japan, but other arguments were stronger. Sanctions against Japan were unlikely to work – 'sticking pins in tigers', as President Hoover put it[32] – and imposing them might lead to war. Continued isolationism, naval weakness, the ravages of the Depression, were set against that risk in Washington. Ten years earlier the secretary of state had insisted that the USA would not intervene in China. Now the president declared that 'neither our obligations to China, nor our own interests, nor our dignity require us to go to war over these questions'.[33] As Sir R. Lindsay, the British ambassador in Washington, put it, the president would 'very effectually check anything he thought likely to lead to more than an exchange of notes'.[34] Britain could not coerce Japan alone; the USA would not assist, nor would the Soviet Union, even if its assistance were acceptable. Sanctions were out of the question.

Nor could Japan be pushed into a settlement, even if ambivalence suggested it. For that to be feasible, China, too, would have to compromise, and that would require a push too. How far could the USA sacrifice its concept of the integrity of China? Could Britain risk losing the China market in the midst of Depression? Instead of attempting to stop Japan, or making efforts to bring about a settlement, the League went along with the policy of 'non-recognition', which secretary of state Stimson enunciated early in l932. This, developed initially in regard to Manchuria, and reiterated after the Shanghai episode, declined to recognise any agreement impairing the integrity of China or the Open Door or brought about by means contrary to the Kellogg pact outlawing war. The Washington system was upheld in words, but not in deeds. It was, says Thorne, a 'satisfying but as yet unproductive answer' to the challenge it faced.[35]

In the shorter term, such a declaration obviously had no deterrent effect. In the longer term, it would reaffirm the framework within which any negotiations involving China and Japan would have to be considered: Manchuria could not be treated as an exception. No doubt it was, or came to be, the hope of the USA that restating the Washington principles would give them a strength in the future that they did not possess currently. It was indeed an encouragement to the Chinese not to make a deal in other terms, though an encouragement they thought far from sufficient. It was also, less realistically, seen as a discouragement to the Japanese. That notion was built on the long-standing perception of Japan's weakness, which its normal caution in international affairs had encouraged the Western powers to conceive.

The passivity of the powers in 1931–3 is hard to criticise, but the idea that the verbal protest with which it was coupled would contribute to a settlement was more clearly an error of judgement. Contemporaries were too optimistic. 'The fact is that Japan [has] bitten off more than she can chew', Lytton wrote in 1932,

> and if left alone circumstances will be too strong for her. With a hostile China boycotting her trade, with a hostile and resentful population in Manchuria and continual guerrilla warfare, the drain on her resources will be terrific and already her economic position is on the verge of collapse. If resisted her people will unite and suffer any amount of hardship and privation, but if left alone – disgraced, humiliated, but unchallenged – with no fruits to show for their violence, liberal opinion in Japan will begin to assert itself and the military party will be criticised for the mess they have got the country into.[36]

Some of the commission were hopeful that after, say, a couple of years, Japan would decide to drop Manchukuo and accept the plan of settlement, wrote George Bladeslee, an American adviser to Lytton. 'Japan is not in a financial position to support for too long the luxury of an expensive foreign military enterprise and is even thought by some to be in danger of an economic catastrophe in the near future'.[37]

That was too sanguine a view of the future so far as the Western powers were concerned: that the KMT would continue to resist the Japanese with not much more than the verbal encouragement that non-recognition offered; and among the Japanese, unable to sustain the conflict and facing non-recognition, something called liberal opinion would reassert itself. Such an appraisal was surely to make too much of Japan's weakness and of its tradition of deference to Western powers. It was to mistake the nationalist nature of 'liberal opinion' in Japan and to downplay the influence that the political system and the Depression had now given the army. Non-recognition might indeed be spur rather than restraint. Lindley pointed out that the German emperor's telegram to Kruger had eliminated criticism in Britain of the 1895 Jameson raid that prompted it. Similarly foreign condemnation 'merely served to strengthen the Military party in Japan'.[38] In any case, whatever they said in disapproval, the Western powers had not acted to stop Japan. There was no parallel to another event of 1895, the Triple Intervention.

The Western powers had not been able to stop Japan in Manchuria, nor to achieve a deal between China and Japan. It was easier to resort to a policy of non-recognition because it was felt that in the longer term China and Japan would be more equally matched than in the short term and Japan would have to abandon the policy it adopted in 1931. That might suggest a future deal. The non-recognition doctrine would, however, set bounds to that or make it more difficult to realise by reasserting the Washington principles and applying those of the Kellogg pact. The chances that Manchuria could be treated as 'exceptional', as in the days of the old diplomacy, were further reduced. The invocation of principle had completed the dramatisation of the conflict that Japanese violence had begun. The Western powers had not stopped Japan. They did not envisage a short-term settlement that Japan might accept. They rather dismissed the possibility that this might lead Japan to seek her own yet more radical solution.

There was a sense, as Ian Nish has suggested, that Lytton and his colleagues had 'deliberately pulled their punches in the interests of a future conciliated settlement'.[39] At the British Foreign Office Sir Victor Wellesley thought that Japan had indeed bitten off more than it could chew. Time was needed for that feeling to mature, but also it was necessary 'to build a bridge for her over which to retreat'.[40] Sir John Simon, the Foreign Secretary, wanted to avoid a pledge of perpetual non-recognition.[41] 'Non-recognition', another British official later wrote, 'was a peculiarly American technique...wholly out of harmony with the British tradition in international affairs'.[42] Some Americans were, however, also uneasy. 'A declaration of non-recognition means that eventually one side or another will find itself in a position where it must "eat crow"',[43] as Hugh Wilson of the State Department put it. Newton D. Baker, a former secretary of war, thought the USA could have found more ways of helping Japan escape from its difficulties. 'I cannot forget that Japan was the one Oriental Power with largeness of mind enough to remodel its own civilization in order to live collaboratively and helpfully with the nations of the Western World'.[44]

The Manchuria episode certainly marked a change in Japan's policy and in the way it was made, 'an explicit turning point', says Ogata, 'for it was taken deliberately as the course preferred over international cooperation'.[45] It also made it clear that outside Japan the opposition to more radical policies was ineffectual. The handling of the crisis, furthermore, tended against a settlement based on the exceptionality of Manchuria. The further pursuit of radical policies was therefore possible. It was not, however, certain. It may be that the undeclared war with China was a more significant 'turning-point', if one is to be found, and for that other explanations have to be added. Neither that, still less war with the Western powers, seemed likely in 1933.

## The impact of Manchuria

'[T]he pathway to the beaches of Dunkirk lay through the waste of Manchuria', declared Sir G. Mander.[46] That judgement may be informed with too much hindsight. East and West certainly acted on each other, perhaps more than the historians of one or the other have recognised, but there was no direct 'pathway' to Dunkirk, on, or on to which, Manchuria was a turning-point. The failure of the League to take action in this case, Sumner

Welles of the State Department, wrote, was 'the chief cause for Mussolini's aggression against Ethiopia; for the triumph of Fascism in Spain; and for Hitler to proceed with the creation by force of his "Greater Germany" '.[47] No doubt Manchuria weakened the League – 'any loss of confidence in the application of the principles of the Covenant and the Pact of Paris in any part of the world diminishes the value and efficacy of those principles everywhere', as Lytton put it[48] – and no doubt it encouraged the Duce. But it is not clear that taking action would have stopped aggression. Nor is it necessarily sensible to view all crises as major crises. What can be criticised is the insufficiency of the new diplomacy.

In the West the Depression had promoted major political changes. The crisis in the East worsened, if not prompted, by the Depression, intensified the crisis in Europe, particularly for Britain. But the way the two crises were handled differed significantly. Both Versailles and Washington were challenged. But though the East Asia settlement was not undermined to the same extent as that in the West, the approach of the Western powers was more comminatory. What happened in Europe might be disapproved. What happened in the East was not 'recognised'. The USA and the League had not applied sanctions but they had invoked the new diplomacy to the extent not only of disapproving Japan's methods, but of not 'recognising' their outcome. That was to stand in the way of a settlement such as might have been effected by the old diplomacy, protagonists of which, like Yoshida Shigeru, indeed hoped that the West would come to accept Manchuria as a *fait accompli*.[49] In turn it affected the policies of the UK and the USA: the latter could not accept a compromise, and the former could not promote one. The Japanese were not dealt with, nor were they encouraged to make a deal. The crisis in the East weakened Britain in the West, and Japan's action invited emulation, with a chance, too, that the other powers would not extend the non-recognition doctrine that, underestimating Japan, they thought would deter it.

# Chapter 5

# The End of Collective Security

The hopes at the end of the First World War for a new era in international relations and an end to war had been based on the concept of 'collective security', of which the twin pillars were disarmament and the League of Nations. The developments of the first few years of the 1930s seriously undermined these hopes. The long-awaited Disarmament Conference had failed to reach an agreement on land armaments limitation. Despite the Washington and London conferences, agreement on naval limitation was by no means complete. Germany was firmly under the control of a regime which had openly expansionist aims and was blatantly rearming. The messages emanating from the other major fascist state, Italy, were somewhat confusing, but Mussolini's constant incitement of the Italians to warlike attitudes, his glorying in the instruments of war, the savage nature of the Italian reprisals on the rebels against their rule in Libya and their fomenting of discord in Yugoslavia led some foreign diplomats to see Mussolini as 'one of the chief existing dangers to European peace'.[1] While the hopes for disarmament and for a growing commitment to peace were disappointed in Europe, the League had also failed to curb Japanese aggression in Manchuria.

Many British and French politicians and military leaders were confirmed in their existing scepticism about the League. For the British and French public, however, and particularly the former, much of their faith and hope in the League persisted. Taking a Eurocentric point of view, they believed the Manchurian crisis had not been a true test. The distance from Europe, the prevailing state of confusion in China, the uncertainty about the precise nature of the early developments and the difficulty in obtaining information all led to the optimistic conclusion that the outcome would be different if a crisis developed nearer to Europe. The sanguine belief that public opinion in all countries favoured peace and that governments would bow to the pressure of that opinion remained strong. The chairman of the

League of Nations Union in Britain, Professor Gilbert Murray, expressed the optimistic view in 1933 that Germany 'possibly imagines that by leaving the League she gains some kind of freedom; but she does not... She does not escape from the control of European public opinion or even of European diplomatic action'.[2] Supporters of the League, therefore, often continued to call for disarmament within their own countries. The so-called Peace Ballot, organised by the League of Nations Union in Britain in mid-1935, showed that even those who supported the use of military sanctions against an aggressor could still favour national disarmament.

Developments in 1934 and the first half of 1935 provided some support for the optimists who believed that the Nazis, once they had the responsibility of government, would moderate their policies and that, in any case, their mere presence would create a greater unity amongst the other European states. Hitler continued to give signals that he was interested in negotiation and peaceful change. In January 1934, in what appeared a reversal of the previous German regime's relentless hostility towards Poland, Hitler concluded a ten-year non-aggression pact with the Poles. He kept open the possibility of returning to the League, negotiating about disarmament and even considering proposals for a Locarno-style pact of guarantee for eastern Europe. The Nazis also received warnings that they needed to proceed with caution. In Austria, the local Nazis, who had been receiving encouragement and support from Germany, attempted to seize power in July 1934. Although the Austrian chancellor, Dollfuss, was killed, the attempted coup was a failure and Mussolini indicated his firm intention of supporting Austrian independence by rushing troops to the Austro-Italian border. With Italy in possession of the largely German-speaking South Tyrol, Mussolini had little taste for a powerful Germany taking control of Austria. Hitler chose to disclaim all responsibility for the activities of the Austrian Nazis.

Italy responded favourably to the overtures of Louis Barthou, the French foreign minister who, in 1934, attempted to revive the idea of increasing security through League-sponsored regional and bilateral pacts. An energetic, resourceful and determined man, Barthou unfortunately only had a few months in office before he was assassinated in October 1934 by a Croatian nationalist during a state visit to France by the king of Yugoslavia. Little had been achieved in the way of regional agreements but French relations with Italy and with the Soviet Union were greatly improved. The work of strengthening Franco-Italian contacts was continued by Barthou's successor, Pierre Laval, with the strong support of the French military who perceived Italy as a much-needed potential European ally. The benefits of improving relationships with Italy were demonstrated in April 1935 when, in the face of the German announcement that they were reintroducing conscription, France, Italy and Britain met at Stresa to reaffirm their commitments under the League and the Locarno agreements.

The Soviet Union also began to make new moves in foreign policy once it was clear that the Nazis did not wish to continue the special relationship and the secret military co-operation of the Weimar period. Although they did not break all contacts with Germany, the Soviets established diplomatic relations with the United States, joined the League of Nations in September 1934 and, after several months of negotiations, signed treaties of mutual assistance with France and Czechoslovakia in May 1935. The former was admittedly a much less binding agreement than had been proposed originally by Barthou but the pressure for modification had come from the French side. Laval and many of his colleagues were anti-communist, suspicious of Russian motives, and believed that the main benefit of a Franco-Soviet agreement lay in preventing the renewal of Russo-German co-operation. The treaty therefore was carefully subordinated to the appropriate League procedures and was not accompanied by any proposal for a military convention. The Soviet–Czech agreement was equally constrained and had the additional proviso that any assistance to whichever party might be the victim of aggression was dependent upon prior assistance being offered by the French. Despite these restrictions, the whole effect of the improvement in Franco-Italian relations and the closer involvement of the Soviet Union in European affairs seemed to be a strengthening of the League and the beginnings of an effective coalition against Germany.

### The Anglo-German naval agreement

Two developments blighted these hopes. The first was the conclusion of an Anglo-German naval agreement in June 1935 and the second, and more serious one, was Mussolini's pursuit of his ambitions to conquer Abyssinia. The British decision to act unilaterally and to agree to a modification of the naval restrictions of the treaty of Versailles, without even the mere courtesy of keeping the French informed of the state of the negotiations, confirmed traditional French views about 'perfidious Albion'. By the naval agreement, Germany could build up to 35 per cent of the tonnage of British capital ships and, with notification, up to 100 per cent of submarines. The benefits from the German point of view were clear. They had removed another of the 'shackles' of Versailles; they had sown dissension amongst the Stresa partners; and their apparent concession of accepting some constraint on their naval building was an illusion as they had had no plans to build beyond the negotiated limits in the foreseeable future. What is more difficult to understand, and particularly with the benefit of hindsight, is why there was so much enthusiasm for the agreement in government and service circles in Britain in 1935. The answer seems to lie in a combination of fear, faulty calculations and misplaced hopes. Above all, the British, in their then economic state, feared a naval race reminiscent of the one before the First World War. They overestimated Germany's immediate interest in initiating such a race and its capacity to do so. They hoped, as Sir Eric Phipps (the British ambassador in Berlin) expressed it, that Hitler's 'signature once given will bind his people as no other could'.[3] The French were unimpressed with the British explanations and sought some reassurance and greater security for their own position by concluding a military convention with Italy.

## Abyssinia and the League

The increasing French desire for Italian friendship suited Mussolini's purpose. He had decided to conquer Abyssinia and begin the creation of a new Roman empire. Abyssinia, which had inflicted a humiliating defeat upon an Italian army in 1896, was one of the few remaining parts of Africa that was not occupied by a European power. It was surrounded by Italian, British and French territory. Mussolini wished to be able to carry out his conquest without interference from the other two European powers who had interests in the area. During the 1920s, Italy had sponsored Abyssinia's membership of the League of Nations and had developed its economic interests and a privileged position in that country through co-operation with the Abyssinian emperor. As early as 1925, however, Mussolini was making preparations for a full-scale military invasion of Abyssinia when the European situation seemed opportune. In 1934 he believed that time had arrived. Economically Italy was not escaping from the flow-on effects of the Depression and Mussolini's rhetoric about greatness and glory for the Italians needed to be matched by some achievements. He wanted and expected a quick victory in Africa before he had to deal with the political challenge of Germany to Italian interests in central and eastern Europe. The Japanese success in Manchuria was admired and was to be emulated. 'In the Japanese fashion there will be no need whatever officially for a declaration of war...*No one in Europe would raise any difficulties provided the prosecution of operations resulted rapidly in an accomplished fact*', Mussolini declared.[4] The Italians had begun a deliberate policy of infiltrating into Abyssinia along the poorly delineated Italo-Abyssinian border and as a result there was a serious clash between Italian and Abyssinian troops in November 1934. Abyssinia referred the matter to the League.

Italy, in the meanwhile, had been trying to prepare the ground diplomatically with France and Britain. The response from Laval seemed favourable. He visited Rome in January 1935 and concluded a series of agreements with Mussolini. The secret ones dealt with Abyssinia. France and Italy agreed to share the development and the profits of the Jibuti–Addis Ababa railway and France promised not to pursue any other economic interests in

Abyssinia but to leave Italy 'a free hand'. What was meant by this last phrase became a matter for dispute. There were no witnesses to the negotiations between the two leaders. Laval later maintained that he had intended the phrase to apply to economic matters alone while Mussolini claimed that there had been no such restriction.

The British government would enter no agreement about Abyssinia and, in what might be regarded as the classic tactic of procrastination, announced that it was establishing a commission to decide on the extent of its own interests in the area. Despite the undisguised build-up of Italian troops in Africa the British statesmen who went to the Stresa meeting chose not to raise the matter with Mussolini. That silence has been criticised on the grounds that it encouraged Mussolini to believe that Britain would turn a blind eye to his whole venture.[5] British officials at the Stresa meeting, however, did discuss the matter with their Italian counterparts. At that level it was made plain that Britain could not condone the use of force, and that, were it to be used, the extent of the outcry from the British public was likely to be sufficient on its own to prevent any sympathetic policy towards Italy from the British government. The Italian officials, for their part, confirmed that preparations for the use of force were in progress.

Britain and France realised that a serious international crisis and a new challenge to the League were imminent but they did not formulate a common policy to deal with the situation. Mutually suspicious, each government followed a policy which it believed would best preserve its own major interests. For France, the prime concern was to try to preserve its newly found friendship with Italy. Laval's own predilection was for a rapprochement with Berlin as well as Rome; if the former were not forthcoming then the latter was even more necessary. He had no desire to be mainly reliant upon the Soviet Union or upon a Britain which would not undertake specific commitments in Europe. The French military leadership strongly endorsed the pro-Italian line. Italy was not only prepared to offer to send troops to France itself but would also provide a passageway for French troops to reach central and eastern Europe. The latter provision was most important to Gamelin, the French commander-in-chief. If war had to come, his major aim was to avoid a repetition of the First World War and to fight the war away from French soil. He wrote that 'the interest for us is in a conflict beginning in Central Europe so that we would act as a secondary force against a Germany already engaged in that region with its principal forces'.[6] For France to be able to reach and collaborate with the forces of its allies in eastern Europe and to be able to plan to make use of Austrian territory, Italian co-operation was vital. Whole-hearted support for Italy over Abyssinia, however, was not a political option. Many of the Radicals, on whom Laval relied to preserve his coalition government, were supporters of the League. They would expect some measures to be taken by the League and supported by France against a blatant aggressor. These considerations led Laval along a tortuous path. He tried to find a compromise that would be acceptable to Mussolini; he felt compelled to support the proposals for economic sanctions against Italy at the League; and he did his utmost to thwart the imposition of what could well have been a highly effective oil sanction.

In practice the policy which the British followed deviated very little from that of the French but tension arose in arriving at this common policy. What the British government most desired was to avoid the development of a crisis at all. They feared that if the Italian attack went ahead, then the League would call for sanctions and the British would be expected to use their navy to implement them. Public support for the League was much more vocal in Britain than in France, and in the 1935 Peace Ballot there was a large vote in favour of the League and of the use of economic sanctions against an aggressor. That result had a considerable influence upon a government that was preparing to fight an election before the end of the year.[7] It needed to be seen to be working through the League to resolve the clearly developing crisis but at the same time it was receiving the most dire warnings from the chiefs of staff about the military implications of Britain's becoming involved in the conflict as an agent of the League. What they stressed were the dangers in Britain's global position. Japanese expansionism was a threat and Germany had already been identified as the main potential enemy in Europe. Britain, they argued, could not afford to become involved in a Mediterranean imbroglio. They did not fear that the Mediterranean fleet would be defeated by a 'mad dog' act of retaliation by Mussolini but that it would be so weakened that Britain would not have the naval resources to cope with Japan in the future. Any air force losses would adversely affect Britain's efforts to match the growth of German air power. Hitler had claimed in March 1935 that Germany had reached parity with Britain in the air – a claim which was believed at the time although it is now known to have been untrue. The unwillingness of France to make any firm commitment of assistance in the event of a conflict with Italy served to increase the nervous warnings of the chiefs of staff. The fact that 'the men on the spot', the commanders in the Mediterranean, did not share their seniors' apprehension made no difference to the formulation of British policy; it was the Chiefs of Staff – privately described by Samuel Hoare, the British foreign secretary, as 'the worst pacifists and defeatists in the country' – who, in 1935, had the ear of the government.[8]

Faced with the conflicting pressures of the domestic political scene and military advice, the British government tried to ward off the impending crisis. In June 1935 they had attempted to 'buy off' the Italians as Vansittart, the senior civil servant at the Foreign Office, bluntly admitted. Anthony Eden, the minister for League affairs, had been sent on a special mission to Rome to offer British assistance in negotiating a deal between Italy and Abyssinia. Britain would give up the port of Zeila to Abyssinia in return for the latter ceding its southern territory of the Ogaden to Italy. Mussolini scornfully rejected the proposal. Equally unsuccessful were Britain's last-minute efforts to deter Mussolini from taking action by making a parade of British support for the League and by strengthening the fleet in the Mediterranean. Hoare's famous speech at the League Assembly on 10 September 1935, where he pledged British support for the League, had no effect upon Mussolini's plans. Elsewhere, however, there was a widespread belief that Britain had pledged unlimited support for the League and a failure to notice that Hoare had carefully added that British support would be exercised 'with others'. In practice this meant that Britain would not act without French backing and over the imposition of a potentially telling oil sanction, the French employed endless delaying tactics. In the meanwhile, the two powers privately continued a search for a compromise agreement, which, once it had been accepted by the two parties, could be presented to the world through the League. The outcome was the Hoare–Laval agreement of December 1935. It was the culmination of weeks of negotiation but the final details were hastily and unexpectedly worked out at a meeting between Hoare and Laval in Paris. Italy was to obtain a large part of Abyssinia either outright or for economic exploitation and, in return, the rump Abyssinian state was to receive access to the sea through British territory. There is some evidence that Mussolini would have received the proposal favourably but, before it could be presented to either party, it was leaked to the press. Howls of outrage greeted its publication in Britain. The League of Nations Union orchestrated a campaign of protest. 'A corridor for camels' was how *The Times* derisively and damningly described the concession to Abyssinia. The agreement was seen as a betrayal of Abyssinia, a betrayal of the League and a demonstration of the total hypocrisy of the politicians who had fought the election a few months earlier on a platform of support for the League. The majority of the government decided that they could not support the proposal although they had previously agreed to very similar terms for negotiation. Hoare resigned and a few weeks later Laval, who had faced less of an uproar in France, also left office. The moral indignation of the public may have been assuaged but the dilemma for the two governments of how to deal with the Abyssinian situation remained.

Public expectations in Britain were high. The new foreign secretary, Anthony Eden, was thought to be pro-League and was expected to lead a 'common front against aggression' and to 'find a means of ending an unwarranted and disastrous war by a peaceful settlement'.[9] It was a tall order as the Hoare–Laval fiasco had neither made France more willing to agree to an oil sanction nor reduced the nervousness of the British government about acting on its own. The one encouraging development for both governments in January and early February 1936 was that militarily the Italians were faltering. There was reason to hope that the Abyssinians would be able to hold out until the rains in April and that then Mussolini could be persuaded to go to the negotiating table. Such hopes were shattered by a dramatic improvement in the Italian military position in mid-February. The British government reluctantly accepted that an oil sanction would have to be imposed. Two prime influences in this were the pressures of public opinion, inflamed by reports of the Italian use of mustard gas, and the hope that the prestige of the League could be restored. Eden was particularly conscious of the attitude of the United States. Although American suppliers were benefiting from the situation to increase their export of oil to Italy he believed the imposition of the oil sanction could influence 'American opinion in favour of the collective peace system'.[10] The French were not moved by Eden's argument. They remained reluctant to take a step which would totally alienate Italy and jeopardise the Franco-Italian military agreement of June 1935. In response to British persistence, they required alternative security, a British guarantee of support for the demilitarised Rhineland. Over that, it was the British turn to procrastinate. While they were doing so, the whole issue of the Rhineland was brought to the fore of international relations, and Abyssinia was almost forgotten. Germany marched its troops into the demilitarised Rhineland on 7 March 1936.

### The Rhineland

Britain and France had recognised that Germany would soon raise the issue of the existing status of the Rhineland but they had not anticipated the exact timing and nature of the German action. It was Hitler's decision to take this bold move in the face of the nervous caution of his generals. The international disarray caused by the Abyssinian crisis made the timing appropriate. Economic, strategic and political considerations were also important. The full potential of the Rhineland, and especially the Ruhr, could not be utilised for rearmament while the area was undefended from potential attack. Improved defences in the west were thought to be desirable in the face of the Soviet agreements with France and Czechoslovakia. While Hitler's popularity at home remained high, that of the Nazi party did not. An international triumph would further boost his power and prestige and counteract some of the growing domestic discontent and disillusionment with other aspects of the regime. It was the army and not the military wing of the party which marched into the demilitarised zone, so that it was seen as a national and not as a party triumph. The numbers who marched were limited so that it could not be interpreted as an immediate threat to France. But it was no mock move. If the French had retaliated the Germans were under orders to conduct a fighting withdrawal.

The French took no counter military action. The government was weak, recognised as a 'caretaker' one until the elections in April. Britain offered no material support and urged restraint. The French military leadership, which had ceased to regard the Rhineland as vital in its strategic planning, had no preparations for immediate countermeasures. The British had equally abandoned the Rhineland in their thinking. There was some sympathy for the view that it was a residual grievance from Versailles which was being rightfully remedied. 'It is the *inevitable* result of trying to keep down a virile population of 70 million', wrote Henry Pownall, the assistant military secretary to the Committee of Imperial Defence.[11] The British had hoped, however, that the status of the Rhineland could be used as a negotiating point in working out a more general settlement with Germany which would be 'honourable and safe' and 'lessen the increasing tension in Europe caused by the growth of Germany's strength and ambitions'.[12] What they particularly had in mind was an air pact, an agreed limitation on the growth of the air forces of the major European powers. The German move into the Rhineland torpedoed the British proposals. The continuing German procrastination about entering into serious negotiations for a further settlement, despite Hitler's offer to do so, was Britain's major regret and frustration about the crisis.

By mid-1936 Mussolini and Hitler appeared triumphant, and their success had boosted their respective power and popularity in their own countries. Italian troops had continued to advance and had taken the capital of Abyssinia. The king of Italy had been proclaimed emperor of that country in the place of Haile Selassie who had fled. Mussolini had defied the League and won. The economic sanctions which had been in place were quickly withdrawn. Faith in the ability of the League to resolve serious disputes or to protect the victim of aggression was irrevocably shaken. None of the excuses for its failure over Manchuria applied. 'It does mean the final end of the League', wrote Harold Nicolson, who had been a keen supporter.[13] It was evident that the effectiveness of the League depended on the will and effectiveness of its main members and, in this case, Britain and France had clearly been found wanting. Mussolini not only did not forgive their failure to accord him outright support but he also despised their weakness. His ambitions correspondingly increased. Control of the Mediterranean now seemed attainable and from 1937 plans for a war against Britain to achieve it began to be made on the supposition that Britain would have to maintain considerable forces in East Asia to face Japan. Mussolini also withdrew from the firm stance against Germany which he had adopted in 1934 over Austria and at the Stresa meeting. Prior to the German move in March, he intimated that he would no longer oppose German intervention in Austria and that he would not support Britain and France should they take action against a German remilitarisation of the Rhineland. Whether Mussolini was then firmly committed to working with Germany, or whether he believed that Italy could balance between France and Britain on the one side and Germany on the other and act as a 'decisive weight' in Europe, is a matter of debate amongst historians.[14]

In Germany the victory of Italy and its own success over the Rhineland led to increased confidence. Hitler openly acknowledged to Eric Phipps, the British ambassador: 'with dictators, nothing succeeds like success'.[15] German diplomats and generals acknowledged Hitler's skill in reading the international situation and gave him more respect. There appeared much less need for caution and conciliation than had been the case in the past. Britain and France had hesitated to use such power as they still possessed to defend the League or their own interests. There was clearly no close working relationship between them. Germany's strategic position was greatly strengthened. It could now build fortifications on the Franco-German border, fully utilise the Ruhr for armament production and release troops from defensive duties in the west for service elsewhere. Germany was much freer to plan aggression in the east should it decide to do so.

France salvaged little from the two crises. The loss of one of the last vestiges of Versailles and the violation of the Locarno agreement were a serious blow to French morale and pride. Their attempt to use the crisis to induce the British to make a firm commitment of future assistance was unsuccessful. Although the change in the Rhineland itself made little difference to French military planning, the subsequent Belgian declaration of neutrality was a serious blow. It undermined France's own previous plans for defence and it raised the difficult question of whether or not to extend the Maginot Line along the Belgian frontier. France's failure to defend the Rhineland further undermined its relationship with its eastern European allies. Was it likely that France would risk abandoning the security of its own defences to send forces to eastern Europe?

The Abyssinian and Rhineland crises have been seen as decisive in determining the course of future developments in Europe. The Abyssinian crisis alone, according to Bell, was 'a turning point in European affairs and the turn was towards war'. Eden certainly quickly came to regret 'the missed opportunity afforded by Abyssinia of pulling him [Mussolini] up'.[16] Wholehearted support for the League and a preparedness by Britain to risk using its naval strength against Italy could have thwarted Mussolini, weakened his power in Italy, curtailed Italian ambitions and at least made Germany and Japan pause in the pursuit of their aggressive designs. The Rhineland, too, has been seen as decisive, as the last opportunity to stop Hitler without war.[17] Such a view assumed that a military response by Britain and France would have brought an immediate German retreat. As we now know, Germany planned no such retreat. France would have had to engage in some serious fighting to expel the Germans. It is possible that Allied resistance would have been a major blow to Hitler's prestige and undermined his position in Germany. It is equally possible that it would have intensified the German sense of grievance which had been so widespread since Versailles. In any case the perception that this was a missed opportunity came later. In 1936 neither Britain nor France were prepared to become involved in a fight . For the French who were most affected, the defences of the Maginot Line were seen as a replacement for the security which they had previously enjoyed through their control over the status of the Rhineland.[18]

In Britain, there was a mixed response to the two crises. The military leaders and the government fully acknowledged the deterioration in Britain's strategic position with the addition of Italy to Japan and Germany as potential enemies. The government introduced some rearmament measures but they were not enough to satisfy Churchill and his supporters, who believed that 'Britain's efforts were still on a minute scale' and that much more needed to be done to educate the public on 'the true position about foreign armaments' and to impose a certain quota of war production upon British industry.[19] Such arguments won little support within the government and the Labour opposition, two days after the remilitarisation of the Rhineland, opposed the government's modest proposals for increased defence spending on the grounds that they would be provocative and would contribute to international tension and unrest. The Labour stance in fact changed little with the crises. They continued to advocate a policy of support for the League and the promotion of disarmament. It can be only speculation that their attitude towards rearmament would have changed had the government shown itself more wholehearted in support of the League during the Abyssinian crisis. While Mussolini's blatant aggression produced the growth of widespread antagonism towards Italy, the Rhineland remilitarisation had less effect upon the attitudes of hostility towards France and sympathy for Germany which were deeply entrenched in many sections of British society. 'The French are almost impossible and cry for the moon,' wrote Pownall. The crises strengthened the belief of a 'rare lot of people' that Britain should rely upon its diplomacy and pursue a wide-ranging agreement with Germany.[20] A more limited number supported the view that, once 'the African business' had been settled, friendly relations could and should be restored with Italy. There the crucial concern was the security of British communications through the Mediterranean to the Middle and Far East. Churchill might believe that 'our communications cannot be left at the mercy of so unreliable a thing as Italian friendship' but others thought that 'our only hope of maintaining our Empire is to have Italy as an ally'.[21]

### Japanese objectives

The growing ambitions of the Japanese had been a factor in Britain's policy. No plan is evident: a 'pathway' is discerned, if at all, only in retrospect. The striking feature of Japan's policy, however, is that, without realising its objectives, it continued to expand them. Even in 1934 Japan enunciated a

'Monroe doctrine' for East Asia, and by 1936 the rhetoric is about 'co-prosperity and coexistence' in a more aggressive vein than Yamagata's in 1915. The explanation must take account of events outside Japan as well as inside.

During 1933 the Saito government sought to hammer out a foreign policy following the setting-up of Manchukuo. It had to take account of the rise of Chinese nationalism; the development of the Soviet Union in the Far East under the Five-Year Plans; and the non-recognition doctrine of the USA and the UK. In October the foreign ministry drafted a policy. Japan must rely on diplomacy in dealing with the Western countries and meanwhile build up its defences so as to be able to deal with any potential threat. It must develop Manchuria, respect the Open Door, eradicate Chinese boy-cotts of Japanese goods, and be circumspect with regard to the Soviet Union. The policy recognised that Japan must rely on its own strength, but be moderate in regard to China and the other powers. But, as a result of amendments by the service ministries, the policy the cabinet adopted in November lost some of that moderation. It emphasised the formation of local governments in northern China, and anticipated a crisis with the Western powers when the naval treaties came up for revision in 1936. 'The security of East Asia has come to depend entirely on the actual power of the Empire.'[22] Though Manchukuo was still in its early stages and the West declined to recognise it, Japan now sought to dominate north-ern China and to exclude the influence of others. At the foreign ministry's suggestion, the government did, however, agree to improve relations with the USA and the UK before naval negotiations started.

An explanation of Japan's policy by Amo Eiji, press officer to the foreign ministry, undermined those relations, however. In April 1934 he declared that Japan opposed financial aid to China; it might threaten peace in Asia, which, with China, Japan was responsible for maintaining.[23] That produced British and American protests. In May, when the Japanese sug-gested that the USA should be regarded as the stabilising power in the East Pacific and the Japanese in the West, the American secretary of state, Cordell Hull, declared that the USA had 'a special interest in preserving peace and order in China'.[24] In August, at the instance of the navy, the Japanese government announced that it would abrogate the agreements on naval building. The foreign ministry sought at least to do this in co-operation with other powers, rather than by unilateral action. Parity, the aim, might be reached in stages. Talks preceding the second London naval conference got nowhere, however, and on 30 December Japan announced abrogation. At the conference itself, Japan sought parity with the USA. Not obtaining it, it withdrew.

Apprehensive about the creation of local governments under Japanese patronage, the KMT government sought a friendship agreement with Japan in 1935. The foreign ministry argued that Japan should avoid a commitment to a comprehensive treaty, but attempt to settle issues one by one, 'scolding' the Chinese government into acknowledging the pre-eminent position of the Japanese government.[25] But the military wanted much more, and a consensus among the ministries produced the policy of 4 August: friendly relations with China, though any Japan–China treaty would have to involve the cessation of anti-Japanese movements in China; Chinese recognition of Manchukuo; and a military pact against the Bolshevik menace in Outer Mongolia – the so-called three principles of Hirota. That was not the end of the matter, however. A new war minister and the field armies secured a more unaccommodating approach. Concerned about his Communist foes, Chiang Kai-shek was ready to offer de facto recognition of Manchukuo in return for Japanese support for the KMT in China. But the Inner Cabinet (28 September, 4 October) adopted the policy of making five provinces of northern China independent.

In 1936 the priority of the army general staff was consolidation rather than further advance: it wanted a long-term build-up, based on mobilising the resources on Japan and Manchukuo, and on a planned economy, the aim being to counter the build-up of the Soviet Union in the Far East. The navy accepted moderation in China, but wanted peaceful penetration of the 'southern seas'. Oil was in mind.[26] Japan depended on imports brought across the US-dominated Pacific, mainly from the USA. It wanted to be certain of other sources, and the largest then known in East Asia were in Netherlands India. Japan's moderation in China, coupled with Britain's difficulties in Europe, might make the British government more amenable, and its client, the Netherlands, more compliant. With the resources of South-east Asia, including the oil of Borneo and Sumatra, Japan could face any constraint imposed by the American fleet, as well as the Soviet army, and so enhance the prospect of dominating the mainland.

The objectives came, as Crowley shows, to form the basis of the Fundamental Principles of National Policy of August 1936. The army must be able to deal with the Far Eastern forces of the Soviet Union; the navy must be able to command the Western Pacific against the US navy. The Inner Cabinet's principles thus included 'the frustration of Soviet aggression in East Asia' and 'the acquisition of naval power sufficient to ensure naval command of the Western Pacific'. The latter required access to the 'south seas', and 'footsteps' were to be taken discreetly, lest they 'stimulate the powers concerned'.[27] Japan thus undertook additional commitments: to national planning and to 'footsteps' in the south. New language was employed, too: not that of the Monroe doctrine, Western-style; but that of the 'principle of co-prosperity and coexistence based upon the Imperial Way'.[28]

The new policies did not envisage the renewal of aggression, at least in the short term. The navy developed its building programme and organised ostensibly private business organisations to promote investment in South-east Asia. The army expanded its Kwantung forces and its build-up of

Manchukuo. The other steps taken were diplomatic rather than military. The chief of them was the Anti-Comintern Pact, which the Hirota government concluded with Nazi Germany late in 1936. The published treaty provided for exchange of information about the Comintern. The secret agreement provided that, if one party were attacked by the Soviet Union, the other would not relieve the latter, but would consult its partner on measures to preserve their common interests. Neither party was to make treaties with the Soviet Union that did not conform to the spirit of the agreement without the consent of the other.[29] The drawing together of Germany and Japan was far from an alliance, but was designed to make their opponents more apprehensive and thus more yielding. The Japanese army saw the pact as a device for reducing the possibility of a conflict with the Soviet Union in the Far East, since the Soviet Union would be more concerned about Nazi Germany. The navy hoped that worsening the situation for the democracies in Western Europe would make it more likely that Britain would facilitate access to the resources of the southern seas. The foreign ministry regarded the Pact as a counter-thrust to Soviet penetration into Outer Mongolia and Comintern activities in China. The policy, however, brought no obvious success. By contrast, after Chiang Kai-shek was kidnapped on 7 December at Sian by the Manchurian warlord, who wanted him to be more active against the Japanese, he dropped his concentration on attacking the Chinese communists. 'So long as Japanese pressure on China continues', the British ambassador commented, 'so long will the Communists be able to make a specious appeal to the patriotic sentiments of the population.'[30]

### Radicals and factions in Japan

Part of the explanation for Japan's policy in this phase lay, of course, in domestic affairs. One feature still was the continued malaise among the military officers, and the radical opinions to which that contributed. The actions included further assassinations, including that of Nagata. The climax was the mutiny of February 1936. On 16 February small groups of soldiers from the First Imperial Division murdered various prominent officials, including the former premier Admiral Saito (inflicting forty-seven bullet wounds)[31] though they missed Saionji and also Premier Okada, who hid in the maids' quarters and then escaped disguised as one of his own mourners.[32] Leading newspaper offices were bombed, and Captain Nonaka proclaimed the Manifesto of the Righteous Army of Restoration:[33] senior statesmen, financial magnates, government officials, army factions trespassed on the emperor's prerogatives; they were traitors who had to be destroyed.

105

These movements gave additional currency to the radical ideas they expressed, but did not contribute directly to the further radicalisation of Japan's foreign policy that took place in these years. There was no clear parallel with the Manchuria incident itself, when the top brass had connived at an initiative from the lesser officers. Never favouring revolution at home, the former used the Manchuria incident to expand their own influence and so transform the way Japan's institutions were run. Now they used army radicalism in a different way. Araki's 'Imperial Way' faction, with its emphasis on nationalist rhetoric, had more appeal among the lower officers than the ideas of the rival 'Control Faction', which stressed planning and mobilisation. The two factions did not in fact greatly differ: they both wanted to combine the traditional fighting spirit and modernisation. Araki, however, could use his *kodo* rhetoric to embarrass his opponents in the faction struggle. Indeed, he made some contact with the National Principle leaders. But that was to embarrass him. The Control Faction now seized on the mutiny to discredit and displace many of its Imperial Way rivals.

Public opinion, affected by the Depression, readily went along with the active foreign policy Japan pursued. The proletarian parties, for what little they were worth, had themselves supported the Manchurian adventure.[34] Japan continued to externalise its problems, and to focus not on internal revolution, nationalist or otherwise, but on the injustice with which others appeared to treat Japan, the abiding sense of inequality unredeemed, the pride that helped to power the Meiji restoration and that made the concept of a Showa restoration a powerful one, too.

Other factors that help to explain Japan's policy after 1933 replicate those that operated between 1931 and 1933. Civilian control over the military had been rejected in 1931. Though it was no guarantee of moderation it was in any case impossible to reassert it in an atmosphere of threat and conflict. Yet more significant, perhaps, was a practice initiated during the 1931–3 years after the collapse of the Minseito cabinet and the assassination of Inukai. Seeking means of exerting some restraint in the absence of oligarchy, Saionji created bureaucratic cabinets. His device did not succeed. Such cabinets tended to be unable to impose prioritisation or moderation. Japan now hammered out its policies by agreed statements of principle and formulae agreed among the ministries. The result was that it tended to cumulate objectives, rather than to rank them, to do as much as possible of everything.

### External factors in policy making

Policy making was also affected by events outside Japan and by Japan's perception of them. On all sides perceptions and misperceptions were significant. In part as a result of the Manchuria crisis, the Japanese had a low estimate of the KMT regime, and conceived that it would lead only to the Bolshevisation of China. That encouraged them to reject the understanding that Chiang offered in 1935, when he had driven his communist rivals into the interior. But, whatever the weakness of the regime, Chinese nationalism was strong and, stressing the former, the Japanese tended to depreciate the latter. Under their pressure, indeed, the KMT had to concentrate on the national cause. That helped the communists to survive, so that Japanese policy might produce the very outcome it was intended to avoid.

The Western powers, as again the Manchuria crisis showed, tended to underestimate Japan's determination and to depreciate its capacity, economic and military, despite evidence to the contrary given at least since 1904–5. The deference to the other powers that Japan had often shown gave them exaggerated expectations of their non-recognition policy. Of the capacity of the Chinese to resist, under whatever regime, they had a more realistic view, though they perhaps gave the nature of that regime too little attention. The general conclusion was that Japan could not long persist with an expansive policy: it was a passing phase. Even without much outside assistance, China would prove too resistant to the Japanese.

That assistance seemed more significant in the eyes of the Japanese. How else, with their preconceptions, could they explain the continued obstinacy of the Chinese leaders? They became more determined to insulate China from the outside powers so as to ensure their own dominance. But their main conclusion was that, while the West disapproved of their actions in words, those words were not backed by deeds. The words were seen as an irritant rather than an inhibition. Beset by their own problems, the Western powers had not intervened effectively when the Manchukuo episode breached the Washington settlement. Would they do more when also having to confront an expansionist Italy and a reviving Germany?

The Singapore base was incomplete, and the Singapore strategy increasingly doubtful. In April 1931 the First Sea Lord had declared: 'The number of [our] capital ships is now so reduced that should the protection of our interests render it necessary to move our Fleet to the East, insufficient vessels of this type could be left in Home waters to insure the security of our trade and territory in the event of any dispute arising with a European Power.'[35] The extent of the threat to Britain's interests in the East had been apparent in the Manchuria crisis, and the Dutch were apprehensive of a seizure of their oil wells. The rise of the Nazis increased the threat in Europe and the deterioration of relations with Italy was to pose a naval challenge in the Mediterranean as well.

These threats encouraged some British leaders, including the Defence Requirements Committee and particularly Neville Chamberlain at the Treasury, to urge a deal with Japan, rather than await its exhaustion. A deal, however, could not be merely bilateral in its impact. It might restrain the expansion of Japan's policy, but only if it offered some advantages to Japan. Those must, in whole or part, be at China's expense, and thus be the concern, not only of China itself, but of the USA, the other main Washington signatory. By promoting a deal, Britain would run the risk of alienating the Americans without securing an accommodation with the Japanese.

In March 1934 Chamberlain suggested a non-aggression pact. That, his colleague Simon said, would have a bad effect on China, on Russia, on the League: it would only be useful if it encouraged the Japanese to drop their attempt to undo the Washington naval arrangements. This, it was clear, they would not do. The chances of a deal were further reduced by the Amo episode. Even so the idea of a pact re-emerged late in 1934. It might make the Japanese more tractable over naval ratios. But, as the Foreign Office pointed out, it might also give Japan added confidence in expansion and hamper Britain's opposition to it. Japan could decide to attack the Soviet Union and so reduce its value as a potential check on Germany, and, if Japan were victorious, it could then move south. Finally, after the Amo declaration, it appeared impossible to include safeguards for China in the treaty. In November, in any case, the Japanese offered a negative response. The idea surfaced again in the 1935 naval negotiations, but even if a pact had been made, it is doubtful that the Japanese would have abandoned their search for parity. A further effort at rapprochement was made by the new Japanese ambassador in London, Yoshida Shigeru, in October 1936. Yet again the obstacles were apparent. Britain, as the Foreign Office saw it, could not offend opinion at home or in the USA or in the world in general by appearing as Japan's abettor in China; Japan would not protect Britain's interests in China in any case; China would in the long run prove 'too big a nut for the Japanese to crack'; and British co-operation with Japan would antagonise Russia and weaken it over against Nazi Germany.[36]

'If Great Britain is to retain her position and prestige in the Far East she must endeavour to gain and keep the friendship and goodwill of China', it was argued at the Foreign Office in 1934.[37] But the potential sacrifice of the China trade, or even the loss of prestige Britain would suffer in abandoning its long-standing policy on China, were not the final arguments against a deal with Japan. A deal might encourage the Japanese, rather than restrain them, and that the Foreign Office recognised. What counted above all, however, was the attitude of the USA. Condoning a weakening of the Washington system, and undermining the diplomatic principles stated in the Stimson declaration, might alienate the USA. Its support was not certain, but it might be needed, in Europe as well as Asia, and those in the Treasury, like Warren Fisher, who contemplated a break with the USA, were not supported. Nor was Chamberlain's argument that Britain should tell Japan 'we had not linked ourselves with America'.[38] Britain's position in the world at large meant that the USA must not be alienated, even if it could not be won over. The very weakness that made Chamberlain look to a deal with Japan also made it impossible. The limited aid Britain gave China, though viewed with suspicion by Japan, had been designed with the hope of promoting a Sino-Japanese agreement. Now it was likely to become what the Japanese suspected, a means of keeping China's resistance going.

Unsure of American support, Britain was unable to disregard American susceptibilities. Unsure of effective US opposition, Japan was increasingly disposed to do so. American policy was crucial, but it was also ambivalent. There was no commitment to fight for China, the economic interests of the USA were limited, and the Depression riveted American attention. There was, however, something of a moral commitment, arising from the missionary connexion with China, and from the hope that the new diplomacy might be demonstrated there. The Roosevelt administration after 1933 on the whole stuck to the Hoover–Stimson policy of non-recognition: the USA had no vital interests at stake by way of trade or investment, but it was concerned with the sanctity of the peace structure. Non-recognition, indicating sympathy with China, was coupled, as in Britain, with the belief that China would win through. 'China carried the burden of sustaining the paper treaties by rendering any Japanese infringement of the status quo painful and finally hopeless.'[39] Early in 1937, for example, Hull thought that Japan 'may break financially at an early date, which will render her impotent as to us...Japan had already discovered that she did not have the money to carry out her ambitious plans with respect to China.'[40] In the naval talks the USA had stood against parity, but its own building was in the event modest.

The Japanese took the Soviet Union into account as well as the USA. The Manchuria incident had turned the Soviet Union's lingering mistrust of Japan into apprehension: Japanese troops were back in striking distance of Siberia, some ten years after their withdrawal. The strengthening of the Soviet Union in the Far East, by contrast, was a strong element in Japan's calculations. The KMT–CCP alliance had collapsed in 1927, but the Japanese saw their action in China as defending it from the Bolsheviks, even though it tended to produce the reverse effect. Both army and foreign ministry were anxious to constrain the Soviet Union. The chances that the Soviet Union could work with the Western powers were limited, given its ideological threat to them and to their empires, but after September 1934 its apprehension of Germany had led it to change its policy. The Japanese were, however, already seeking closer relations with the Nazi regime, designed to inhibit both Russia and the Western powers.

Indeed, the relationship dated back to the Manchuria crisis. After leading Japan out of the League, Matsuoka had told the German press in March 1933 that Germany was 'the one and only country the history of which shows many parallels with that of Japan and which also fights for recognition and its place in the eyes of the world'.[41] Germany was indeed soon to leave the League as well. The German foreign ministry suggested in July 1933 that Japan would 'be able by her attitude, particularly where the Soviet Union is concerned, to exercise a strong influence on international affairs, and thus on Germany's political situation'.[42] Its rearmament, on the other hand, 'must have been most welcome' to Japan as it made France and Britain more anxious.[43] The 7th Comintern congress gave an excuse for the deepening of a rapprochement already in progress. Ribbentrop had been exploring the idea of an anti-Russian pact with the Japanese general staff. The outbreak of the Spanish civil war helped the Japanese army arouse anti-communist sentiment. Discussed at Wahnfried during the Wagner festival,[44] the pact was initialled in Berlin in October and signed in November.

Foreign minister Arita stressed that it was an anti-Comintern pact, not an anti-Soviet pact, taking Stalin at his word that there was no connection.[45] Nor was the tie now established between Germany and Japan a close one. It was, as Hitler told Ciano, the Italian foreign minister, a piece of bluff. It would constrain the Soviet army in the Far East, and so help Japan. It would prompt Britain to 'seek means of agreement',[46] benefiting both Germany and Japan. The two powers that wished further to change the settlements of the 1920s might be more effective in conjunction, but they were not in alliance. Germany, too, still had military advisers in China, called in by Chiang when he cut his links with the Russians, and affording the Reichswehr useful experience.

Within Japan bureaucratic cabinets failed to provide a substitute for oligarchy in managing Japan's policy making. Indeed the new process tended to bring about a cumulation of aims rather than prioritisation among them. Outside Japan it became more apparent that the Western powers would neither actively uphold the Washington system nor endorse the changes that Japan had brought about by other than peaceful means. The Western leaders believed that Japan would have to relinquish its forward policy in face of continued Chinese resistance. The Japanese believed that China would have to meet their demands if they succeeded in severing the outside links that they believed kept resistance alive. Beset by problems elsewhere, the West did enough to encourage the Chinese to resist, but no more.

Britain had contemplated a more active policy. Increasingly threatened in Europe, it had considered a deal with Japan that would have removed a concurrent threat in Asia. That could not be done, just because there was a link between Europe and the Far East closer than mere concurrence. What Japan did in China was of concern to the USA. Britain could not make a deal at China's expense lest that alienated the Americans, whose support would be needed if it came to a war in Europe. Europe was the core of Britain's concern. But that in fact foiled attempts to reduce the threat in East Asia.

The interests of Britain in the Far East were more exposed to the Japanese, after Italy began to challenge them in the Mediterranean in 1935. They did not adopt a policy of 'appeasement' in Asia but the continued threat of the Japanese contributed to the adoption of appeasement in Europe. At the same time Japan and Germany moved closer together, presenting a challenge not only to Britain and the USA, but also to the other major power with interests in Europe and Asia, the Soviet Union.

# Chapter 6

# Appeasement

Post-war discussions of international developments in the 1930s were inevitably influenced by the knowledge that a major war did break out in Europe in 1939 and in Asia in 1941 and that in the early years of the fighting the Germans and the Japanese won massive military victories. As far as Europe was concerned, it was assumed that Hitler had planned and prepared for the war which came. The statesmen of Britain and France who had made concessions to Italy and Germany until the eve of war and allowed them to extend their control over much of continental Europe were roundly condemned. Appeasement, which had been seen as an honourable policy of seeking to reduce strife and achieve a general pacification amongst nations, was now viewed as a weak dishonourable policy of simply giving way to demands. If negotiations had been designed to buy time for the democracies to further their own military preparations, why, it was asked, were they so apparently unprepared for the German onslaught when it came?[1] With the passage of time and with greater historical research, there have been a variety of answers to this question and a reassessment of the policies of all the major powers.

The view of Hitler as the master planner was dramatically challenged by A. J. P. Taylor in his *Origins of the Second World War*, first published in 1961, which claimed that Hitler had had no detailed plan of aggression and had not intended to embark on a major war in 1939. A vigorous debate followed this attack upon the then orthodoxy.[2] The extreme views of seeing Hitler as a master planner or as a supreme opportunist gradually gave way to a more balanced interpretation of his role. It was acknowledged that the precise order of developments which Hitler had outlined in *Mein Kampf* did not eventuate, but that did not mean that he had deviated from his broad goals of the domination of Europe and the conquest of *Lebensraum*. He reacted to events, exploited situations and used every opportunity to achieve them. This 'intentionalist' view, which continues to stress the importance of

Hitler, has been challenged by the so-called 'functionalist' or 'structuralist' historians who question whether Hitler remained free to exercise so much power. For them, the pressures from within as well as from outside the state limited Hitler's freedom of choice. He was subject to the influence of other Nazi leaders. He could not disappoint the expectations which had been aroused amongst the party followers and the population at large. He could not ignore the economic pressures generated by the extent of the rearmament programme. Hitler's 'intentions and impersonal structures are both indispensable components of any interpretation of the course of German politics in the Nazi state', according to Ian Kershaw.[3]

The modifications in the perception of Hitler's role called for a reassessment of the actions of other statesmen. If Hitler had not followed a precise plan, had there been more scope for others to determine the course which he would take? The opening of government archives in Britain and France in the 1960s and 1970s meant that a wealth of new material became available for consideration. Both governments were shown to have been beset by so many economic, social, political and military problems that their decision to try to avoid war by negotiating with Hitler and Mussolini appeared totally understandable. Many of these problems were unresolved in 1939, yet Britain and France, with little change in their leadership, chose to go to war. It would appear that the extent of their problems does not provide a complete explanation for the policy which British and French statesmen pursued towards Germany and Italy in the 1930s. Influenced by their personal beliefs, prejudices and assumptions, statesmen still had to make choices and take decisions.

### German preparations for war

In 1936, no European statesman had the certain knowledge that war was going to begin three years later, although there were growing signs that Germany was increasing its military preparations . Goering, the head of the German air force, boasted to subordinates, 'We are already at war; only the shooting has not yet started.'[4] The Four Year Plan, which was announced in September 1936, proposed to increase the scale and tempo of rearmament and to prepare the German economy as well as the armed forces for war. It was introduced against the advice of Schacht, the president of the Reichsbank, who had masterminded the finding of the credit necessary for Germany's existing rearmament and reconstruction. His warning that its implementation could produce a major balance of payments problem was ignored and Goering was appointed to head the Plan. There has been a lengthy and intense debate amongst historians as to the main purpose of the Plan. Following the work in the 1960s of Alan Milward and Bernice Carroll on the pre-war and wartime German economy, it became widely accepted that the Plan was a temporary expedient to enable Germany to prepare for short sharp wars of conquest, the gains from which would provide the ultimate solutions to Germany's economic problems.[5] More recently this view has been challenged, especially by Richard Overy.[6] He has argued that Germany's economic preparations were not limited, designed merely to furnish the requirements of a short, *Blitzkrieg*-type warfare but were massive and long term – designed to prepare Germany to fight a major war no earlier than 1943. Whichever interpretation one favours, there is no question that the purpose of the Plan was preparation for a war. Its introduction and the attempt to implement it represented a triumph for Hitler and the Party over the more conservative economic establishment which had supported him in his early days in office. Their solution to Germany's problems was to try to integrate fully into the international capitalist economy and greatly to reduce spending on raw materials designed for rearmament and heavy industry. That was totally unacceptable to Hitler.

The power and influence of the more traditional members of the foreign office and the military leadership was also being curtailed. At a meeting with his military leaders in November 1937, Hitler, according to the report of his adjutant, Hossbach, expounded his views on Germany's need for the future acquisition of *Lebensraum*, and the consequent necessity of preparing for war. Such expositions were not new, but on that occasion, Hitler also made it plain that the pace of rearmament would not slacken and that he was prepared to use any suitable opportunity to attack Czechoslovakia and Austria even at the risk of war. Such a war, he assured his hearers, would be short and would not involve the major powers. His senior army officers were less certain and advised caution. A few months later, the war minister, Blomberg, and the commander-in-chief of the army, Fritsch, were forced to resign. Generals who were thought to be unenthusiastic in their support of the Nazis were also removed. At the foreign office, the minister, Neurath, whom the Nazis had inherited from the previous regime, was replaced by an ardent Nazi, Ribbentrop, and the diplomatic staff was also purged. Blomberg was not replaced but Hitler himself became supreme commander of the armed forces and Fritsch was replaced by a general who was less critical of Hitler's plans.

### The Spanish civil war

France and Britain were still pursuing a policy of seeking diplomatic solutions to international tension combined with a modest increase in their rearmament when the European powers were confronted with the outbreak of the civil war in Spain in July 1936. Spain had long been torn apart by political, social and regional divisions and subjected to violence from extremists of the left and of the right. A combination of left-wing groups, known as the Popular Front, narrowly won the elections of February 1936 in Spain but they were divided amongst themselves and unable to control much of the lawlessness and violence of some of their own supporters. Faced with what they believed to be an impending revolution and fearful for their own positions, some of the army leaders planned a coup. It was only partially successful as about half of the army and much of the airforce and the navy remained loyal to the elected government. In that situation, General Franco, the leader of the rebel forces, the Nationalists, appealed to Germany and Italy for assistance. In both countries, the decision to intervene was taken by the respective leaders, Hitler and Mussolini, and for the same main ideological reason: to prevent 'the danger of the Red Peril's overwhelming Europe'.[7] Hitler himself later maintained that without the ideological perspective he would not have acted but there were additional factors associated with Germany's economic and strategic position which favoured intervention. While Hitler may have intervened against the advice of his foreign office, he had the support of Goering and Blomberg. The former coveted the raw materials vital to the rearmament programme which could be obtained from Spain, while the latter appreciated the strategic importance of depriving France of a friendly southern neighbour and of a bridge to its North African possessions. With an eye to the future, Hitler also hoped that 'in the final conflict for the reorganisation of Europe...Spain would not be in the camp of Germany's enemies but most likely the friend of Germany.'[8] For Mussolini also strategic considerations were a supplementary factor. A successful intervention in Spain could provide Italy with naval and air bases on the Balearic Islands and a considerable strengthening of its position in the Mediterranean at the expense of Britain and France.

Despite their knowledge of the German and Italian assistance to the Nationalists, the response of the French and British governments was to try to isolate the Spanish conflict. They initiated a non-intervention agreement in August 1936, which was also signed by Germany, Italy and the Soviet Union. For both countries the main consideration was to avoid the escalation of the Spanish conflict into a major war, but in other respects they approached the conflict from different points of view. The French Popular Front government naturally sympathised with its Spanish counterpart. Its initial response had been to agree to the Spanish government's request for assistance but the fear of a right-wing backlash, further violence and even civil war in their own deeply divided country suggested the need for caution. Clear signals that Britain intended to pursue a strictly neutral policy reinforced this decision. The sympathies of the majority of the British governing elite were more pro-Nationalist than pro-Republican. They feared that the triumph of the left in Spain would mean the triumph

115

of communism and its possible expansion into France. Not all were as extreme as Hankey, who declared: 'In the present state of Europe, with France and Spain menaced by Bolshevism, it is not inconceivable that before long it might pay us to throw in our lot with Italy and Germany.'[9] His more cautious superiors believed that they could not actively help rebels against an elected government; they hoped that their non-intervention policy would be a sufficient protection for British economic interests which lay within the Nationalist-controlled part of Spain and for the future safety of Gibraltar.

The civil war was not the short one that Germany and Italy had anticipated at the beginning. Instead it lasted until the spring of 1939. The farce of the non-intervention agreement was maintained although the Nationalists continued to receive military personnel and war *matériel* from Germany and larger numbers of men and more substantial quantities of *matériel* from Italy. In addition to the volunteers in the International Brigades, the Republican side received extensive assistance from the Soviet Union, and more covert assistance from France in the provision of financial assistance to purchase arms and in the intermittent opening of the Franco-Spanish border to facilitate their transport. Apart from a brief period in 1937 when British patrols in the Mediterranean hampered Italian submarine attacks on shipping going to Republican ports, British neutrality mainly favoured the Nationalist side. In 1937, Britain went so far as to give de facto recognition to the Nationalists and to exchange special representatives with them.

At the popular level, Spain was the focus of a great deal of attention within Britain and France and the war assumed something of the significance of an apocalyptic struggle between left and right. None of the major powers wished that to happen but the on-going conflict had a significant effect upon their relationships. The maintenance of a common front between Britain and France was not easy when France succumbed to its desire to help the Republicans and when the British pursued a general agreement with Italy despite its flagrant intervention on the Nationalist side. Spain was also an obstacle to the improvement of relations between the Soviet Union and the two democracies. While Britain and France were suspicious that Soviet aid to the Republicans was designed to convert Spain to communism, the Soviets began to despair of the success of a policy of collective security against fascism when Britain and France responded so feebly to Italian and German aggression. The growing Italian commitment to Franco, whose success Mussolini equated with the success of fascism and his own prestige, consolidated the Rome–Berlin axis. It made any rapprochement between France and Italy almost impossible and it hindered the negotiation of an agreement with Italy which the British sought. The Spanish conflict also provided the Axis powers with benefits in their preparation for war. It gave them a training ground for their military personnel, and an opportunity to test some of their weapons, and it rewarded Germany with raw materials vital for its rearmament programme.

### Chamberlain and Eden

The British, and to a lesser extent the French, continued to try to ease international tension by negotiating general agreements with Italy and Germany. After Neville Chamberlain became prime minister in May 1937 and the Far Eastern situation became more threatening with the development of full-scale hostilities between Japan and China, the British pursued this policy with more vigour. An agreement with Italy became particularly urgent, according to Chamberlain, because 'the Japs were growing more and more insolent and brutal'.[10] An agreement with Italy would reduce the number of Britain's potential enemies and in particular would ease the threat to communications through the Mediterranean. At best, it could lead to an Anglo-German agreement as Hitler might be more prepared to negotiate if Italy were less firmly tied to him. Chamberlain was particularly committed to an Italian agreement despite the caution of his foreign secretary, Anthony Eden, who wished to extract actual withdrawals of Italian troops from Spain in return for the recognition of Italian control of Abyssinia. Chamberlain by passed the Foreign Office, corresponded with Mussolini through his sister-in-law and conducted negotiations himself with the Italian ambassador in London.

In February 1938, Eden resigned. Humiliated about the Italian negotiations, frustrated by Chamberlain's lukewarm response to a rare American initiative about a possible participation in a world conference, Eden recognised that he had lost the battle with the prime minister for the control of British foreign policy. The majority of the cabinet supported Chamberlain. Eden was not as strong an anti-appeaser as he later portrayed himself. His latest biographer, David Dutton, has accepted the view that Eden and Chamberlain 'agreed wholeheartedly on the most important issue in foreign policy: that Britain could and should avoid war with Germany'.[11] His resignation, however, brought delight in Germany and Italy and the expectation amongst ardent pro-appeasers that it had greatly improved the chances of success for their policy. Hankey admitted that Eden's resignation gave him 'a strange feeling of relief' and a hope that now 'there was just a possibility of peace', and Nevile Henderson, the ambassador in Berlin, equally expressed relief because he believed that 'it was unlikely that any understanding with Germany was possible as long as Eden was secretary of state'.[12] An Anglo-Italian agreement was signed after Eden's departure, but it brought little change to the international situation. Britain promised to promote recognition of Italy's conquest of Abyssinia at the League of

Nations once Italian 'volunteers' had been withdrawn from Spain, but that withdrawal was not forthcoming.

An agreement with Germany, however, was what Chamberlain most desired. 'If only we could get on terms with the Germans, I would not care a rap about Musso', he wrote in July 1937.[13] The British tried to obtain from Germany a clear indication of all its demands so that a general settlement could be discussed, instead of enduring the tension-producing uncertainty of waiting for one German demand after another to be made. To procure such a settlement they realised that sacrifices would have to be made. They discussed the possibility of colonial concessions in Africa, at the expense of other colonial powers rather more than of themselves. They offered economic concessions in the hope of luring Germany away from its autarkic policies and back into the mainstream of the international economy. Gladwyn Jebb, the economic adviser to the Foreign Office, argued that the cancerous symptoms of Nazism would respond 'to the radio-active treatment of increased international trade'.[14] The Germans were prepared to have some economic discussions, talk vaguely of the need for colonial adjustments , indicate that there would have to be changes in eastern Europe but they would not be drawn into a comprehensive agreement.

### Anschluss and Munich

In March 1938, Germany again took unilateral action to alter the political map of Europe. It occupied and annexed Austria. After the failure of the attempted Nazi coup in 1934, German policy towards Austria had been cautious. They had encouraged the Austrian Nazis to build up their strength, infiltrate the government and slowly reduce Austria to the status of a German satellite state. With the acquiescence of Italy, this policy had had considerable success but in February 1938 the Austrian chancellor, Schuschnigg, was summoned to meet Hitler and bullied into making further very far-reaching concessions. Recognising that the independence of Austria was now at stake, Schuschnigg returned home and announced a plebiscite in which the people would be asked to vote for 'a free and German, independent and social, for a Christian and united Austria'.[15] Hitler was not prepared to risk the result. The decision to occupy Austria was an opportunistic reaction to this new situation. The army was caught by surprise and had no adequate contingency plans for such a move, not even appropriate maps and refuelling provisions for their motorised vehicles. Goering, however, was most enthusiastic. He was anxious to secure Austria's financial assets and wanted to avoid the possible damage a long crisis would cause to Germany's own economy. The Austrians offered no military resistance and the German army and Hitler himself were received with flowers and cheers by crowds of people. Hitler decided to take the further step of declaring a complete union of Germany and Austria. The German gains from the union, or *Anschluss*, were manifold. Hitler had increased his popularity at home, eased Germany's financial situation, opened up the way for further economic and political penetration of eastern Europe, and greatly improved Germany's strategic position. While the exact timing of this advantageous move was largely the result of an opportunistic reactive response to an unexpected development, it took place as the result of a crisis which Hitler had precipitated by his pressure on Schuschnigg and in an atmosphere where he had been preparing his subordinates for some new move on the Austrian question.

Britain and France made some ineffectual protests at what Halifax described as 'the exhibition of naked force'.[16] Failing to enlist British support for a earlier warning to Hitler that they could not 'tolerate any *coup de main* or act of war likely to bring into question the status quo of Central Europe', some of the French leadership were resigning themselves to the possibility that 'central and eastern Europe would slip into the hands of Germany without war'.[17] France, in any case, was without a government when the actual occupation took place. For the British government the avoidance of war was crucial. They believed that they could not intervene and that it would be 'criminal' to encourage Schuschnigg to resist when they could offer him no assistance to do so. The fate of Austria did not deter the British prime minister from the main lines of his previous policy. He pressed on with the negotiations with Italy and believed that 'some day' it might be possible to 'start peace talks again with the Germans'.[18]

The immediate question was whether Hitler was planning to use the unrest among the German minority in Czechoslovakia to stage another violent coup. Unrest amongst the Germans, who lived mainly in the Sudeten area, was not new. They resented their minority status in a Czech-dominated state and the privations of the Depression years heightened their sense of grievance. A strongly nationalist party, the German National Front, led by Konrad Henlein, had been supported, encouraged and incited by a variety of Nazi groups, some of whom had been admonished by Hitler for their excessive zeal in the mid-1930s. In 1938, Hitler was prepared to exploit the situation. Henlein, who had been seeking better conditions for the Germans within Czechoslovakia, was pressured by the Nazis and his own extremists to go on raising his demands to the point where the Czechs could not grant them and maintain the integrity of the state. Hitler had already made it plain to Keitel, the chief of the high command of the armed services, that he intended to destroy Czechoslovakia and occupy the old, mainly German, provinces of Bohemia and Moravia at the first opportunity. The grievances of the Sudeten Germans could provide 'the moral justification for military measures in the eyes of at least a portion of world opinion'.[19]

Developments at the end of May 1938 brought a new intensity to the crisis. Rumours of German military preparations near the Czech border resulted in a partial Czech mobilisation and British and French warnings to the German government. Halifax went so far as to say that if France felt compelled 'to intervene by virtue of her obligations to Czechoslovakia', the British government 'could not guarantee that they would not be forced by circumstances to become involved also'.[20] Hitler, who had not intended to attack at that juncture, was angered at the intervention, announced his intention 'to smash Czechoslovakia by military action in the near future' and ordered his generals to make the necessary preparations for its execution before 1 October 1938.[21] Ignorant of this directive, the British nevertheless feared that such a plan was in the offing. They sought by all means to achieve a negotiated settlement that would prevent its implementation. What they most feared was that a German attack on Czechoslovakia would result in France honouring its treaty obligations and declaring war on Germany. If France were then to experience difficulties, the pressure upon Britain to become involved in another continental war would be immense. 'It was impossible to contemplate France with her back to the wall and three million young men in this country in plain clothes', thought Duff Cooper, the first lord of the admiralty.[22] Horrified at such a prospect, Chamberlain and the majority of his colleagues sought to restrain the French and coerce the Czechs into making concessions to their German subjects. The French were warned that in the event of war arising out of the Czech situation, there was no absolute guarantee of British assistance and that, in any case, British military assistance could only be very limited. The French were not unwilling to join with Britain in urging the Czech government to make concessions. Nervous about their own military situation, especially in the air, and uncertain of Soviet support, the French did not wish to stand alone with their Czech allies against Germany. They equally did not wish to take the main responsibility of abandoning an ally. The lead which the British were taking in the negotiations was emphasised by their sending a mediator to Czechoslovakia and, when that failed, by Chamberlain's flying twice to Germany to meet Hitler before he was joined by representatives of the French government at the final meeting at Munich. The Czech leaders, unrepresented at Munich, had to accept the proposed cession of the Sudetenland to Germany and the division of the rest of their state or fight in a very uneven struggle with the remote possibility of aid from the Soviets. They capitulated.

The Munich settlement appeared to be a major German success. The Czechoslovak state was destroyed. Its natural and constructed defences were overrun and major industrial plant had passed into German hands. Hitler, however, was less than triumphant. He had been deflected from his policy of seizing Czechoslovakia by force. He was irritated by what he saw as Chamberlain's persistent interference in an area which was of no British concern. He had reluctantly agreed to a diplomatic settlement because of the pressure from Mussolini who was unprepared to face another war; because of the last-minute threat of the possibility of a major conflict which was implicit in both the French call-up of reservists and the British mobilisation of the fleet; and, above all, because of the alarming signs of the lack of a warlike spirit amongst the German people. They had greeted with silence a military parade in Berlin, but cheered the peace-seeking missions of Chamberlain and welcomed the settlement which had been achieved without war.

In Britain and France, the immediate relief at avoiding war was immense but it was not long before there were a growing number who were asking whether the price had been too high and whether the pursuit of appeasement for so long had been the right policy. Those questions remain a matter of intense debate to the present. Critics of the appeasement policy have dealt harshly with the leadership in both France and Britain while its apologists have excused both governments on the grounds that their choices were severely circumscribed by the economic, social and political pressures which they faced.

## France and appeasement

Studies of appeasement which were written in the first two post war decades paid little attention to what happened in France. It was believed that 'the key to French policy lay in the final analysis in London'.[23] The view that Britain was the driving force behind the appeasement policy, which it had bullied France to follow, had been put forward by French diplomats and politicians and was accepted by French as well as British historians. In addition, French foreign policy in the 1930s, like the French defeat in 1940, was seen as a reflection of the whole social and political disintegration of a deeply divided society.[24] More recently, the actions of the political and military leaders have been subject to greater scrutiny and it has been argued that neither the state of French society nor British policy totally removed their freedom of action. They chose appeasement and the defensive military strategy which was associated with it.[25] On the other hand, no one denies that their problems were manifold. Economically, they were faced with the delayed effects of the Depression at the very time when the threat from the Nazis was becoming manifest. Their reactions, like those of most of their contemporaries elsewhere, were determined by the predominant economic theories of the day. With a devaluation of the franc as recently as 1928, governments were reluctant to resort to another devaluation and did so only in 1936, which proved insufficient and had to be followed by others in 1937 and 1938. They tried to balance budgets, which meant that there

121

had to be limits on social spending and rearmament – something which was particularly difficult for the Popular Front governments after coming to power in 1936. Capital drained out of the country in the mid-1930s, either because investors simply sought greater profits or, as some would maintain, to exert political pressure on the Popular Front.[26] Whatever the reason, the effect on governments was much the same. They had to resort to borrowing, convinced that they had to make the restoration of economic confidence a priority. One of the lessons of the First World War, they believed, was that economic strength would be vital to the winning of another war if they had to face one.

Economic problems exacerbated the political and social divisions within the country. Workers, who were discontented with the gains from the Popular Front, resorted to demonstrations and strikes which not only affected some rearmament programmes, but also fed the fears of the middle and upper classes that they were faced with revolution and communism. Developments in Spain contributed to these apprehensions. Internal polit-ical divisions, particularly when governments always had to be coalitions, circumscribed choices in foreign policy. While the left could not counten-ance closer ties with fascist Italy, the right and many of the centre opposed any strengthening of the alliance with the Soviet Union. Closer links with Moscow, it must be admitted, had few supporters. Many of the Socialists could not forgive the Moscow-inspired communist opposition to them in pre-Popular Front days and many of the military were suspicious that the Soviets wished to 'force France into a confrontation with Germany' with a view to becoming 'the arbiter in an exhausted Europe'.[27] Above all, the right wished to avoid any commitment that would involve France in a war. The communists, they believed, 'would profit from these complications and declare civil war to overthrow capitalism and crush the bourgeoisie so that they could be replaced with the dictatorship of the proletariat and by socialism'.[28]

The French high command was also against a policy of risking a conflict with Germany. Throughout the early 1930s continued expense on the Maginot Line was acceptable domestically and could be defended internationally as a defensive measure. Other military expenditure, how-ever, was drastically cut as part of the financial restraints that the state of the French economy was thought to require. While it was recognised in 1936 that more money would have to be spent on rearmament, French finances were still in a poor condition to meet the demands of all three services. Believing what are now known to have been the exaggerated Ger-man claims of their military preparations, and conscious of their own weaknesses, the French high command was unwilling to depart from its main defensive strategy. There was no question of recommending an offen-sive to help defend Austria or even France's ally, Czechoslovakia. The main concern, and to some extent an understandable one, was whether France was adequately prepared to defend itself. At the time of Munich, the air force chief of staff, Vuillemin, warned that, in the event of war against Germany, the French fighter force would be destroyed in a fortnight.[29]

When faced with so many internal pressures and military pessimism, it is not surprising that French leadership was, as Delbos, the foreign minister 1936–39, admitted of himself, 'at his wits end to devise a method of meeting the problems which have now arisen'.[30] French statesmen, however, had to make choices and their choices were influenced greatly by their desperate desire to avoid another war. They were very conscious of the extent of French losses in the 1914–18 war. Bonnet, the foreign minister, who pursued a strong pro-appeasement line in 1938 and 1939, has been described as having a 'visceral horror' of war. Daladier, the prime minister, defended the concessions which he had made at Munich on the grounds that France should 'not sacrifice another million or two million peasants'.[31] French statesmen were aware that their own aversion to war was shared by many of their compatriots. In September 1938, the main agricultural union, war veterans, associations, the leading teachers, union and many business circles supported the government's policy because they did not wish to face another war.[32] The governing elite, however, made little or no effort to lead public opinion in another direction and mobilise it for a firmer line against Germany. Their own desire to avoid war may well have contributed to a false optimism about the possibilities of a Franco-German settlement. Like the British, they nursed vain and naïve hopes that the Germans would be attracted by economic and colonial concessions and were even prepared to offer an 'evolutionary extension of German influence in Austria ... or in Czechoslovakia'. Daladier convinced himself, or at least tried to convince the Radical Party Congress in 1938, that 'between the French and German peoples ... there are strong ties of mutual respect which should lead to loyal collaboration'.[33]

Ambivalence not certainty, however, was the main feature of the French leaders, response to their situation. They were not sure that they could avoid war but believed that in the meantime it had to be postponed. Time was needed for the franc to stabilise, for the economy to recover and for further rearmament, especially in the air. 'If I had had a 1000 bombers behind me, I would have been in a much stronger position at Munich to resist Hitler's demands', said Daladier. If war was going to come, then France would have to be prepared for a long struggle. It needed a major committed ally. Recent research may be suggesting that the Soviets were serious in their desire for a united front against fascism and even in their preparations to help Czechoslovakia in 1938, but the French were not sure of that at the time. The Soviet military preparations during the Czech crisis were secret and made known to the French only after they and the British had made their major capitulation to the Germans over the Sudetenland.[34] The French, however, had not previously reassured the Soviets nor sought to strengthen the Soviet alliance. A firm commitment from Britain was what the French most desired. In September 1938, Britain agreed to hold more formalised Anglo-French staff talks and to share in the guarantee of the rump Czech state. These commitments were, according to Robert Young, 'the one thing which Daladier was really after'.[35]

### Britain and appeasement

Britain had refused previously to undertake any guarantees in eastern Europe or to extend its commitment to French security beyond its obligations under Locarno. There were no firm military undertakings. British statesmen felt burdened by the existing extent of the country's commitments, as Anthony Eden made clear in a speech to his constituents in 1936. He explained that Britain had 'definite obligations' to fight 'in our own defence and in defence of the territories of the British Commonwealth of Nations ... in the defence of France and Belgium against unprovoked aggression in accordance with our existing obligations', and to uphold 'our treaty of alliance with Iraq and our projected treaty with Egypt'.[36] In the 1914–18 war, Britain, starting from a much greater position of economic strength than she had in the 1930s, had not been able to finance its war effort. How could it afford to make the necessary preparations to fulfil all its obligations when there was a possibility that it would be attacked simultaneously by Germany in Europe, by Italy in the Mediterranean and by Japan in the Far East? While some present-day historians may argue that Britain's power in the 1930s has been seriously underestimated and that its commonwealth and imperial possessions made it a truly world power, the British leadership at the time was much more conscious of its weakness and of the vulnerability of its possessions.[37] In 1914, the imperial possessions had not been seriously at risk and the empire had provided a great deal of additional manpower for the European war. In the 1930s, not only were major imperial possessions directly threatened but also two of the main powers of the commonwealth, Canada and South Africa, would not commit themselves to imperial co-operation on defence and would give no guarantee of assistance if Britain became involved in another European war. Chamberlain might have agreed that the British still had a 'very rich Empire' but what concerned him was that it was 'vulnerable' and that there were plenty of 'adventurers not very far away who look on us with hungry eyes'.[38]

The British, like the French, believed that the lesson of the 1914–18 war was that economic strength was essential for victory in any future conflict. The economy was the fourth arm of defence. Rearmament, therefore, could not be carried out at a pace which would jeopardise long-term economic recovery or interfere with the normal course of trade. Excessive borrowing was thought to be inflationary and increased taxation a danger to business confidence. If rearmament had to be limited, then choices had to be made between the requirements of the other three arms of defence – the navy, the army and the air force. The air force steadily increased its share of the funding. Widespread fears of Britain's own vulnerability to air attack, which had been fed by the news coverage of the bombing in the fighting in China and Spain, combined with an overestimation of German air strength, won support for the major spending on rearmament to be allocated to air defence. Ironically, the air force itself would have preferred to focus on a more offensive strategy. Naval rearmament up to 1936 had been limited not only by financial constraints but also by the arms limitation agreements of 1921 and 1930. Naval leaders were inclined to see Japan rather than Germany as the major enemy and their ideal would have allowed them to build enough capital ships to oppose Germany and Japan simultaneously To that the Treasury, which had considerable influence on the allocation of resources for rearmament, would not agree. While the lords of the admiralty were not entirely deterred from their ultimate goal, they recognised that the building of capital ships took time. They therefore were the most insistent of all the military leaders that Britain in the meantime should use diplomacy to reduce the number of its potential enemies. The army fared least well in the allocation of funds. Under a policy that was known as 'limited liability', Britain would try to provide for its own air and sea defence but there was to be no provision for any major expeditionary force to continental Europe. One difficulty was the uncertainty whether a force would be required in Europe or elsewhere and while the army remained inadequately prepared for any eventuality, its advice was inevitably against any policy that might precipitate war.

It is widely recognised that military leaders paint a gloomy picture to persuade their governments to give them more resources. The British chiefs of staff in the 1930s were no exception. They were haunted by the danger of war against Germany, Japan and Italy at the same time when even the 'defence measures at home, both active and passive, are very far from complete'.[39] Their pessimism was fuelled by the information which they received from intelligence sources. According to Wesley Wark, the intelligence authorities between 1936 and 1938 'failed to provide a balanced reading of German strengths and weaknesses under the impact of cumulative worst case scenarios'. Instead, they depicted 'the near and medium-term military balance as "perilous" '.[40] From their point of view, the chiefs of staff could not stress sufficiently to the government that 'the problem we have to envisage is not that of a limited European war only but that of a world war'.[41]

Britain's fears about the possible extent of a future war were not eased by contemplating its potential allies. There was no deep trust in

Anglo-French relations. The British were concerned about the instability of French politics and the effects of their economic and industrial problems upon their preparations for war. Although they always recognised that they could never stand aside and allow France to be defeated, the British had no wish to make a commitment that could encourage the French to pursue a more confrontational policy.

As far as the United States was concerned, British leaders recognised the desirability of American support in international affairs but feared that no practical assistance would be forthcoming. In an effort to ease the Anglo-American tensions that had developed over the imperial preference system, the British made considerable concessions in the negotiations which led to the Anglo-American trade agreement in 1938. The Foreign Office admitted that it was the political implications of the agreement which were important. 'It is recognised that the fact of an agreement being reached between the two countries...is likely to have a very great effect on the international situation, and may be of special importance in view of the present position in Europe and in the Far East'.[42] A stronger expression of Britain's need to placate the United States was written by Oliver Harvey, Eden's private secretary, in January 1938, 'The only fatal risk for us is to antagonise Roosevelt and America: without his backing we might be overwhelmed in a war'.[43] For that reason Harvey, and Eden himself, were dismayed at Chamberlain's lukewarm response to Roosevelt's vague suggestion for an international conference to discuss the causes of the tension in international relations. They had no hope, however, that Roosevelt 'would accept any definite commitment to help us in Europe'.[44] It was recognised that isolationist opinion within the United States remained strong. Despite the backing of the president, the proposal that the United States should become a member of the World Court had been opposed on the grounds that it could push the country down the road to war, and the Neutrality Acts of 1935, 1936 and 1937 had denied belligerents the right to purchase arms and ammunition or obtain American credit for such purposes. Domestic political pressures may not have been the only constraints upon the American president. A recent analyst of his foreign policy, Barbara Farnham, has suggested that he did not know how to reconcile his two main aims of preventing the drift to war and avoiding American participation in it should it nevertheless eventuate. His initiatives were therefore experimental and tentative. His uncertainty may have been fuelled by 'his doubts about British policy' but British doubts about American policy certainly fuelled appeasement. Chamberlain would not be deterred from seeking his own agreements with Italy and Germany while he believed that 'The Power that had the greatest strength was the United States of America, but he would be a rash man who based his calculations for help from that quarter'.[45]

With regard to the Soviet Union, Britain both disliked its ideology and distrusted its intentions. Long suspicious of the imperial ambitions of pre-communist Russia, British fears of the new regime were heightened by knowledge of Russian contacts with the nationalist opponents of British rule in India. Planning for a major war with Russia over Afghanistan was only abandoned when it was acknowledged in 1938 that the combined hostility of Japan and Italy was a greater threat to India. Suspicion of Russian policy in Europe increased. It was 'stealthily and cunningly pulling all the strings behind the scenes to get us involved in a war with Germany', wrote Chamberlain in March 1938.[46] The purges of the mid-1930s in Russia, which removed much of the military leadership, fed the distaste for the communist regime, kept alive fears of Soviet–German contacts, and led to a questioning of Russia's military capability, whatever its trustworthiness as an ally. The news of a border clash between the Soviets and the Japanese on the Siberia–Manchukuo border in July 1938 seemed to the British Foreign Office to confirm 'previous reports about the inefficiency of Soviet troops' which was 'all the more significant when it is remembered that the Far Eastern Army is seen as a cut above the Red Army as a whole'. The Russian troops were to have a major success against the Japanese in 1939 but in the meantime the British remained convinced that the Soviets would be incapable of mounting any offensive operations in Europe.

Economic weakness and the consequent lack of military preparedness, fear for the safety of the commonwealth and the perception that there was no dependable ally, all favoured a policy of trying to avoid war. The decision to do so by seeking agreements with Germany and Italy was also supported by other considerations and assumptions. Britain had an established policy of 'settling international quarrels ... by admitting and satisfying grievances through rational negotiation and compromise'.[47] At the turn of the century, it had sought to reduce the number of its potential enemies by reaching agreements with France, Russia and the United States. The policy survived the First World War. After the signing of the Versailles treaty, Britain had accepted that the Germans had some grievances and they had attempted to remove them by negotiation and concession. It was believed that such concessions would strengthen the hands of the political moderates in Germany and that belief was not greatly weakened by the change in government. The reports of all three British ambassadors to Germany during the 1930s contributed to the view that some of the Nazi leaders were more 'undesirable' than others. Eric Phipps in particular perpetuated the view that Hitler might be one of the more reasonable. After the Night of the Long Knives in June 1934, when the leaders of the *Sturmabteilung* (SA) and other opponents of Hitler had been murdered, Phipps could write: 'The whole regime has been modified; Goebbels has been practically silenced; the wild men have been shot.'[48]

Whatever their fears and suspicions of Hitler's ultimate intentions, British leaders recognised that Hitler's demands until 1938, including those about Austria and the Sudetenland, could be seen as no more than seeking to redress German grievances arising from the Versailles settlement. Given the popular acceptance of the right of peoples to national self-determination and the signs of welcome for the Germans in their new acquisitions, the British leaders questioned whether these were issues over which they could ask their people to fight. Revulsion at the idea of another war and fear of its consequences were widespread. While a military man like Pownall could describe war as 'a foolish and terrible thing', Chamberlain more forcefully described it as 'not only the cruellest but the most senseless method of settling international disputes' where there 'are no winners but all are losers'.[49] There was not only the terrible cost in terms of death and suffering; there was also the cost in terms of its effects upon Britain's economic position and upon the long-term development of its society. The British leaders rightly foresaw that war would change the Britain they knew and profoundly affect its place in the world. Such a risk, they thought, could only be taken as a very last resort. In one respect, too, they believed that they had the moral high ground. If the worst happened and war occurred, then Britain could show that it had done all that it could to avert it. The clear responsibility for beginning a war would lie elsewhere. Halifax later defended their Munich policy: 'one fact remains dominant and unchallengeable. When war did come a year later it found a country and Commonwealth wholly united within itself, convinced to the foundations of soul and conscience that every conceivable effort had been made to find the way of sparing Europe the ordeal of war, and that no alternative remained.'[50] In the meantime, while peace was maintained, the British could indulge in the Micawber-like hope that 'something would turn up' and that war postponed could become war averted. 'It *may* not be better later but anything may happen', wrote Cadogan in March 1938.[51]

Appeasement was pursued for so long because it was deemed necessary from so many points of view – from the optimistic belief that a long-term general settlement was possible to the more pessimistic calculation that time was needed to prepare more adequately for war. The policy seemed to have massive public approval but it is now clear that to maintain that approval Chamberlain and his closest associates put pressure upon the press and the radio not to publish material which might lead to a greater questioning of their policy.[52]

The military advantages of buying time in September 1938 have also been questioned. Britain may have been less adequately prepared for its air defence in 1938 than it was in 1939 but from the overall military point of view, the retrospective judgement of the secretary to the Committee of Imperial Defence, Lord Ismay, that 'it would have paid us to go to war in 1938', has won a great deal of support. By abandoning the Sudetenland, Britain and France deprived themselves of the support of the well equipped and well trained Czech army and air force, and strengthened Germany by handing over vital military equipment and industrial plant. Even without

128

Soviet aid, which it is now believed could have been forthcoming had Britain and France resisted Germany, there is a strongly held view that 'the defence of Czechoslovakia was far from being a desperate undertaking'.[53]

Such views are part of the new questioning of whether appeasement was the only practicable policy for Britain to follow. The role of Chamberlain in particular has been the subject of renewed critical scrutiny.[54] His horror of war, it is argued, blinded him to the fact that the dictators did not share his views and led to his misunderstanding the true nature of the fascist regimes. His search for a general settlement, therefore, was unrealistic from the beginning and was pursued for far too long and with too little consideration of an alternative policy. In particular he rejected the calls for greater rearmament and for the creation of what Churchill called a 'grand alliance' to resist the dictators. Such a course, however, would have been contrary not only to his obstinate belief in his own judgement and ability to negotiate a settlement but would also have been contrary to the advice of most of his professional economic and diplomatic advisers. While the vigour with which appeasement was pursued after 1937 owed much to the particular character and beliefs of the prime minister, there was only limited criticism of that policy until 1939.

The pursuit of an alternative policy to that of appeasement would have required a change in both Britain and France. The policy of one reinforced that of the other. Britain's reluctance to make firm commitments and its failure to plan for a continental expeditionary force or to have serious staff talks with the French until after Munich served to weaken French confidence and resolve. Its preparedness to take the lead in negotiations with Germany provided a cover under which French proponents of appeasement could work. On the other hand, French unwillingness to take a lead in standing up to Germany, even when it was in the stronger military situation in 1936 or when the fate of an ally was at stake in 1938, put no pressure on Britain to change its stance. In the face of their many problems, and apprehensive of what war would bring, the leadership of both countries chose to try to avoid it. The major difference between them lay in their reaction to the situation in the Far East. Although France had its possessions in Indo-China, it devoted comparatively little attention and resources to the problem of Japanese ambitions. After 1937 the French military assumed that Japan would be occupied fully in the conquest of China for a considerable time. What happened in Europe and the Mediterranean was their main concern and they consoled themselves that as long as they were victorious there they could make 'good later on any temporary defeat... in the Far East'.[55] For the British the situation was different. They were under pressure from the Dominions, Australia and New Zealand, which were concerned for their own safety, and they were mindful of the importance of their possessions in South-east Asia. With insufficient resources to divide between

Europe, the Mediterranean and the Far East they were haunted by the nightmare of a war against three enemies at the same time. What policy were they to pursue towards Japan in the hope of reducing that danger?

## The undeclared war

An incident between Japanese and Chinese troops at the Marco Polo bridge not far from Peking on 7 July 1937 escalated into the 'undeclared war' between Japan and China. The incident had been followed by bitter fighting, Chiang Kai-shek declaring on 30 July: 'The only course open to us now is to lead the masses of the nation, under a single national plan, to struggle to the last'.[56] The Chinese bombed the Japanese naval installation at Shanghai on 14 August. That meant that the conflict could not be localised.

Further escalation was much more the work of the Japanese than the Chinese. Initial successes, and public statements by the prime minister, Prince Konoe, committed Japan to a policy of chastising China, presumably not to be set aside, as Crowley argues, until it accepted the three principles of Hirota.[57] By 1 October, indeed, the objectives adopted by the Konoe cabinet were further extended: de facto recognition of Manchukuo; accession to the Anti-Comintern pact; suppression of anti-Japanese movements in China; enlargement of the demilitarised zone in Shanghai; recognition of a new regime in Inner Mongolia; payment of an indemnity. Chiang Kai-shek declined to negotiate, as proposed through German intermediaries, unless the Japanese restored the status quo before the incident at the bridge. On 1 December the Japanese general staff authorised an advance on Nanking, the Chinese capital, achieving a triumph amid an excess of violence that has remained controversial.

Chiang sought terms. But now the price was higher. Indeed, Prince Konoe had written off accommodation with Chiang Kai-shek, and aspired to replace him with some kind of puppet regime after the Manchuria model. The policy of 11 January 1938 required China's recognition of Manchukuo; renunciation of anti-Japanese policies; neutral zones in North China and Inner Mongolia; new political organs in northern China; autonomous government in Inner Mongolia; co-operation with Japan against the Soviet Union; agreement to co-operate in occupied zones in central China; economic agreements among China, Manchukuo and Japan; reparations. And all this with a 72-hour deadline. Indeed, the terms were designed to be unacceptable, and were apparently never even presented. At a press conference on 16 January, Konoe committed Japan not to deal with the Nationalist regime: it would co-operate with 'a new Chinese regime'.[58]

Within less than a year, Konoe had redefined Japan's aims in terms of building 'a new order which will ensure the permanent stability of East

Asia', its foundation being the tripartite relationship of Japan, Manchukuo and China.[59] 'Is it possible to put into effect a plan which calls simultaneously for long-term hostilities, military preparations against Russia, and the expansion of the navy?' asked the Emperor.[60] But by November Konoe was declaring: 'It is the establishment of a new order that will enable us to maintain [the] permanent peace of East Asia that the Empire seeks. This is really the ultimate object of the present expedition.'[61] The conditions for terminating the China Incident were defined anew; the Asia Development Board was set up; and Wang Ching-wei, Chiang's rival, was induced to organise a new Chinese government as the legal entity with which Japan intended to reach a settlement of the Incident.

The striking feature of Japan's policies is expansion of objectives. Unable in 1931–3 to get the Chinese or the West to accept a modification of the Washington arrangements, they had sought in 1933–6 to exert sufficient pressure to secure China's endorsement of Manchukuo and of Japan's control in northern China. That, too, had failed. But their answer was to adopt a still more ambitious strategy, to force China to accept Japanese dominance, even a Manchukuo style government. That was clearly not the result of a long-prepared plan. Nor, however, does it appear to be simply the result of a replication of factors that led to the earlier shifts in Japan's policy. There were indeed some significant differences.

Present still was the nationalist current in public opinion, stimulated by the words and deeds of the younger officers, and 'Imperial Way' rhetoric prevailed. There was, however, no Manchuria-style connivance on the part of the top brass. The army general staff, having adopted a policy of consolidation that was designed to mobilise the resources of Japan and Manchukuo, wished to avoid incidents meanwhile, and indeed made positive efforts to localise the Marco Polo bridge incident rather than escalate it. Nor was the faction struggle significant, as Konoe endeavoured to argue at the end of the war. In his presentation, then largely accepted, the two factions among the top brass, 'Imperial Way' and 'Control', were dedicated respectively to Japanese virtues and to fascism, one anticipating conflict with the Soviet Union, one concerned with China and the south. Following the mutiny, the argument went, the Control faction came out on top and led Japan to fascism and to deeper involvement in China. In fact, though there were personnel changes in the leadership of the army in 1936, its policy did not greatly change. It was opposed to a major struggle at that point.

There was another significant difference. The displacement of the Minseito cabinet at the end of 1931, and the failure of its successor, had led Saionji to instal bureaucratic cabinets, though they had not moderated Japan's policy as he had hoped. Konoe was a politician, not a bureaucrat. Indeed he had a political mission. The commitments into which Japan had entered required, it was believed, a high degree of state economic planning, so that the relatively limited resources available to Japan might be effectively mobilised. The last obstacle to this was the *zaibatsu*. The great firms had reservations over the radical turn in Japanese policy and over the amount of state intervention involved. Indeed, army patronage encouraged the creation of new *zaibatsu*, like Nissan. Given the opposition of the old, neither the Hirota cabinet nor the Hayashi cabinet was able to secure the assent of the Diet to the far-reaching legislation needed as a result of the adoption of the 1936 principles of national policy. The aim of Konoe's appointment in mid-June 1937 was to win political support for it. His method was to escalate the China Incident beyond the level of August 1937. 'The Government takes the view that we should utilise the China Incident as an opportunity to make another decisive stride in Japan's industry and economy', declared Yoshino Shinji, the Minister of Commerce and Industry, in December.[62] The incident became a Great Patriotic Endeavour, gratifying the cabinet, the bulk of the armed forces, public opinion. Cabinet approved the National Mobilisation bill in February 1938. Initially the parties in the Diet, seldom critical of foreign policy since Manchuria, were opposed, but the bill was finally passed unanimously. Safeguarding *zaibatsu* interests, it secured their co-operation.

Whatever the position in Germany, mobilising Japan's resources had been a long-term strategy. To secure formal backing for it and to enlist the zaibatsu, Konoe had given Japan a far larger and more defined objective, the military domination of China and the creation of a puppet regime. Mobilisation, as the general staff had seen it, had required a relatively quiescent policy for the time being, whatever its ultimate intention. Konoe indeed outwitted General Tada Shun and the general staff, who questioned his policy, by his announcement of January 1938. 'This electrifying declaration was as much an instrument to obtain approval for sweeping reform legislation – as much a continuation of Konoe's gamble – as it was an indication of the end of patience with Chiang Kai-shek.'[63] Konoe was himself at that time optimistic about promptly ending the incident.[64] He was, however, taking a gamble in foreign affairs in order to secure his objective at home. His irresponsible act committed Japan to an undertaking well beyond its resources, and well before they were mobilised. In April 1938 he realised his error, but his interest in negotiations was short-lived. The compromise on 'national unity' did not allow compromise in foreign policy. From November the 'New Order' defined Japan's purpose.

### Britain and the Sino-Japanese war

Other powers had a role in the expansion of Japan's objectives. China itself had contributed to the initial escalation of the Marco Polo bridge incident. To Chiang Kai-shek it may have seemed more like the Manchuria incident than in fact it was: he feared a repetition, even though the Japanese army's policy was at the time quiescent, and the top brass was not conniving at radicalism in the field armies. The importance of resisting Japan had, moreover, been recently underlined by the kidnapping of Chiang late in 1936. For those reasons he saw the incident as the occasion for a national struggle, and that prevented a prompt settlement. Konoe then escalated the war, and moved beyond the earlier attempts to browbeat Chiang into compliance.

Not in a position to stop Japan – Chamberlain thought it would be 'suicidal' to pick a quarrel, of which the dictator states might take advantage[65] – Britain had contemplated a deal with Japan. The opening of the 'undeclared war' put paid to the Yoshida initiatives, and the limited aid Britain gave China was now designed to encourage it to resist rather than to put it into a position to negotiate. 'The seizure of Manchuria was bad enough', wrote Sir John Pratt, 'but had Japan been content to remain on the other side of the Great Wall an uneasy modus vivendi might have been patched up. Now that Japan has intruded into China proper relations between Japan and China can consist of nothing but a series of clashes.'[66] Britain's concern was increased when fighting spread to the Shanghai region and its ambassador was wounded when travelling by car from Nanking. Faced with mounting crisis in Europe, the British found it easier to take a harder line with Japan. China must win, after all: nothing more should be sacrificed to secure Japan's goodwill. Many thought Japan was going to its 1812, as Eden put it: Britain's role was 'to do what we cautiously can to make it possible'.[67] Appeasing Japan was not necessary, nor was it desirable. It would discourage the Chinese, whose resistance would help to sustain the rest of the Washington status quo, and thus the security of Britain's interests in South-east Asia and Australasia which would be important in a European war. It would alienate the USA, whose support would be vital in a European war. A deal that accepted Japan's special position in northern China could be seen as an Asian Hoare–Laval.[68]

Only Sir Robert Craigie, the British ambassador in Tokyo, argued for appeasing Japan. He believed a conciliatory policy would strengthen the civilian moderates in Japan, and he urged mediation. Japan, he thought, would win the China war: Britain should try to end it, not play for time.[69] But though such an approach was not unlike the approach in Europe, not even Chamberlain agreed with Craigie. 'So far as the Chinese are concerned, though militarily weak they are racially strong and endowed with an enormous capacity for passive resistance to foreign encroachment both physical and in the realm of ideas', Sir John Brenan argued at the Foreign Office in London. 'In the long run they will be more than a match for the Japanese.'[70] Japan, it was still believed, would ultimately have to give up. Meanwhile China could be given some assistance, and the all-weather Burma Road, authorised at the beginning of 1938, was completed by the end of the year. 'Believing that Japan was getting bogged down on the Asian mainland', the British cabinet felt 'that they could outlast her, without being forced to fight a war or to make damaging concessions'.[71] Conciliating Japan would only help it in China, and then it might turn south. Britain's interests were linked with China's independence. 'We must leave the Chinese to fight their battles – or ours for us – and give them such assistance as we can.'[72]

From May 1938, when Konoe displayed a temporary interest in negotiations, the foreign minister, Ugaki Kazushige, had attempted to reduce Anglo-Japanese friction. Craigie argued for co-operation, even at the risk of alienating the USA, and suggested that it would help to keep Germany and Japan apart. The Foreign Office preferred a stalemate in the talks. That would avoid antagonising the USA and dropping Chiang Kai-shek; and, the British officials in London thought, a closer alliance between the Japanese and the Germans would not make much difference to the way they acted. Talks, begun in July, were deadlocked by September. By then, indeed, the Japanese were waiting to see the outcome of the Munich crisis: 'we shall get nothing out of the Japanese now.'[73] With it came the resignation of Ugaki and the return of the hard-liners. In the European crisis the British had to keep the Japanese in mind: they might take advantage of it. But there was no Munich in East Asia. Shortly after Munich, however, the Japanese attacked Canton, and in November Konoe made his call for a New Order.

### The USA and the Sino-Japanese war

US policy had not changed even with the Marco Polo bridge incident. On 16 July Hull had indeed generalised the Stimson principles:

> We advocate abstinence by all nations from use of force in pursuit of policy and from interference in the internal affairs of other nations. We advocate adjustment of problems in international relations by processes of peaceful negotiation and agreement. We advocate faithful observance of international agreements. Upholding the principle of the sanctity of treaties, we believe in the modification of provisions of treaties, when need therefor arises, by orderly processes carried out in a spirit of mutual helpfulness and accommodation.[74]

C. T. Wang said China wanted action, not words.[75] In October Roosevelt made his 'quarantine' speech,[76] suggesting international 'quarantine' of those nations 'that may be tempted to violate their agreements and the rights of others'.[77] Chamberlain found the analogy lacking: 'patients suffering from epidemic diseases do not usually go about fully armed'.[78] Indeed the president insisted that it did not imply economic sanctions against aggressor nations, and it was never given real formulation as a policy: it was a moral attitude. Even so it provoked the isolationists.

The League of Nations invitation that the nine powers hold a conference in Brussels again confronted the USA with a gulf between principle and practice, aim and action. Roosevelt would accept neither sanctions against Japan, nor a settlement that might infringe the sovereignty of China. He saw Brussels as a forum for the expression of international opinion. Norman Davis, his emissary, told Eden that much of the American public thought that Britain, in seeking action, was seeking to involve the USA in defending UK interests.[79] Confused by Davis's 'thinking aloud',[80] the conference accomplished nothing save to antagonise the Japanese. The Panay incident of 12 December 1937 – Japanese planes bombed the USS *Panay* just above Nanking – prompted Roosevelt to suggest staff conversations, and Captain Royal E. Ingersoll went to Britain early in 1938. Leaks, however, caused a 'furore' in Congress.[81] Three American cruisers visited Singapore for the opening of the graving dock on 14 February. But Britain's anxiety over its naval weakness contributed to its attempts to appease Italy and Germany in 1938.

Neither the USA nor, partly as a result, the UK would actively oppose Japan, and that was of course a factor in expanding its objectives. Nor did either favour a deal with Japan which would have recognised some of its objectives, and possibly as a result have limited them, at least for a time, in the way that it was hoped 'appeasement' might check Germany in Europe. The USA and the UK had asserted the validity of the Washington system in 1932, but did no more, partly because they believed China must outlast Japan. That belief remained, even as Japan pressed ahead, and continued endorsement of the Washington system became more deeply embedded in Western policy, as a means, alongside some other gestures, of encouraging China. Deals with Japan were thus ruled out. The weakness of the Western powers led them to adopt an inflexible stance, partly as a deterrent. They believed Japan would in the end have to comply.

The position in Asia differed from that in Europe. Asia was indeed a second priority for the UK, since in Europe its own security was in question, and thus it was a second priority for the USA, too. In Asia, moreover, they both believed, with undue optimism, that there was a way of handling Japan, a combination of Western disapproval with encouragement for China. With Germany there was no such option, and so appeasement was attempted. Some conceived that the Soviet Union might absorb German energies as China would absorb Japan's. But there was no confidence that the Soviet Union would be able to bring Germany to a halt, nor any identification between the Soviet Union's interests and the Versailles system to compare with those of China with the Washington system.

Yet while Britain would not and could not appease Japan, it had to take the threat of Japan into account. The burden on its naval policy was apparent. Though the Singapore graving dock was completed, the prospect of promptly despatching a fleet was diminishing, and Australia was becoming increasingly apprehensive. Denuding the Far East of naval forces was impossible, and US gestures of help insufficient.

## Germany and Japan

A change in Germany's policy in Asia directly helped Japan. Like other powers, it had been anxious not to alienate China, where it had commercial opportunities and with which it had military links. Army and business were hostile to the new Japanese venture, and the German foreign office, pointing to the non-aggression pact between China and the Soviet Union in August, argued that Japan's activities were likely to foster communism, not to inhibit it. The dilemma inherent in the Anti-Comintern Pact became apparent. Japan itself pressed for the removal of the German advisers in China and the cessation of arms supplies. In December German officials and military advisers were involved in the short-lived attempts at mediation, but they were cut off by Japan's moves early in 1938. That precipitated the solution of the German dilemma. In February Hitler told the Reichstag that he would recognise Manchukuo. He instructed Ribbentrop, now foreign minister, to have the military advisers recalled, and the arms contracts were cancelled. Chiang Kai-shek gave Falkenhausen a farewell banquet on 2 July.[82]

Italy's rapprochement with Germany also had its effect. It was a Washington signatory, but it had little China trade to sacrifice, though it had an air training mission in China from 1933.[83] In the midst of the Brussels conference it joined the Anti-Comintern Pact, leaving the League of Nations a month later. Italy recognised Manchukuo in November, fulfilling a bargain made when Japan had recognised Abyssinia in 1936.[84] The effect on China was limited; the effect on Britain, and thus on its ability to support China, considerable. Italy's sea-power in the Mediterranean made the 'main fleet to the East' policy still more problematical. Ciano had pointed out to ambassador Hotta that in an Anglo-Japanese war, Italian friendship might be valuable.[85]

The chief concern of the Japanese army, however, was with the Soviet Union, not with the maritime powers. Clashes on the frontier with Russia only increased its concern, and made the general staff urge closer relations with Germany. In July–August 1938 the Red Army gave a better account of itself at Changkufeng on the Manchukuo–Russia border than the British Foreign Office thought.[86] More pressure on Russia in the West would make it easier for the Japanese to focus on defeating the Chinese. The navy's priority was different, and it opposed a closer relationship, the price of which was a greater risk of a clash with the maritime powers.

If, however, there were limits to the co-operation of Germany and Japan, the Western powers could not co-operate with the Soviet Union. Earlier the British had hesitated to approach the Soviet Union, partly for fear that would encourage the rapprochement of Germany and Japan. They still hesitated for that reason, and for others that may be compared with those that influenced their policy in Europe. They distrusted Stalin and had a low estimate of Russia's strength. Ideology also stood in the way. The British feared that the Soviet Union's influence in China, and indeed in India and Burma, would be increased.[87]

The question the emperor had asked was a valid one. Japan could not take on both the Soviet Union and the maritime powers. It hoped, in fact, to achieve its objectives in East Asia without arousing the active antagonism of Russia and the USA. A closer relationship with Germany would help, at once weakening the UK, cautioning the USA, and giving the Soviet Union cause for concern. Germany's strategy at this juncture was not dissimilar. Subsequently, however, it was to activate the USA. With that the risk that Japan would fail became overwhelming, however effective the mobilisation of its resources to which it had committed itself. At this juncture, however, the Japanese could still hope that the major powers would continue to offer no effective opposition. Those powers contributed to that impression, partly because they were busy elsewhere, and partly because they underestimated Japan's determination.

# Chapter 7

# The War of 1939

At Munich Britain and France demonstrated the lengths they were prepared to go in order to preserve the peace. France sacrificed a major military ally and tacitly admitted that its whole post-war diplomacy and strategy of alliance with the eastern European states was in ruins. Hitler, according to Cadogan, 'had got all that he said he wanted' but he admitted that that was not to say that 'he has got all that he wants'.[1] The latter point was crucial. It was recognised that future international developments in Europe would depend largely upon the policy of Hitler's Germany. Would he abide by the commitment which he had made with Chamberlain to eschew war between their two countries and to seek to resolve any disputes by conciliation? Would Germany remain content with the gains which it had made and seek to consolidate them, or would it continue a policy of aggressive expansion?

### German policy from Munich to Prague

The Germans pursued a number of policy options in the immediate post-Munich period but peaceful consolidation was not one of them. In a secret speech to the German press in November 1938, Hitler outlined the importance of preparing the German people for war. 'It was now necessary gradually to re-educate the German people psychologically to make it clear that there are things which must be achieved by force if peaceful means fail.' Not content with imposing the harshest possible terms and humiliations upon the Czechs in the implementation of the Munich settlement, Hitler quickly made it clear to his subordinates that 'the liquidation of the remainder of the Czech state' was his ultimate goal.[2] At the same time the Germans began negotiations with Poland for further changes in eastern

Europe. They had acquiesced in Poland's demand for the cession of the disputed area of Teschen from the browbeaten Czechs. They now asked Poland to cede Danzig, allow an extraterritorial road and railway across the Corridor from Germany to East Prussia and give its adherence to the Anti-Comintern Pact. In return, Germany would guarantee Poland's western frontier and extend the 1934 German–Polish non-aggression pact. Success in the Polish negotiations would have given Germany greater freedom of action in the west and tentative plans for a war against Britain and France backed by an alliance with Italy and Japan were also under consideration.

The identification of Britain as a potential major enemy was already established. First Ribbentrop, who was embittered by his lack of success as ambassador in London, and then Hitler had come to accept that their hopes of an Anglo-German alliance were futile. Britain would not allow Germany the free hand in Europe for which it had hoped in exchange for a guarantee of the British empire. Immediately after the May 1938 crisis over Czechoslovakia, Hitler had ordered an acceleration in the German naval building programme. His plans to deal with Czechoslovakia, however, meant that the army and the airforce entered into fierce competition with the navy for the limited resources of raw materials and skilled manpower. Hitler was prepared to make few concessions over naval building. He insisted that submarine construction should continue but that priority should be given to the building of four pocket battleships and six larger battleships which were to be ready by 1944. Such a fleet could only have been designed to fight a major naval power – Britain or possibly the United States – but not in 1939. In most of his recorded musings, Hitler contended that the British were not prepared to fight, that they would be deterred by the known German military preparations and by the threat to their situation in the Far East. There would be time for Germany to make further gains and consolidate its hold on continental Europe.

The German overtures to the Poles, to the Italians and to the Japanese all failed to achieve quick results. The Poles procrastinated even when they were convinced in January 1939 that the proposals emanated from Hitler rather than Ribbentrop. They had no desire to be so closely tied to Germany. The Italians were unwilling to commit themselves before they had obtained the ratification of the Anglo-Italian agreement and before they had obtained colonial concessions from France in North Africa. The Japanese, divided amongst themselves as to their best course of action, would also make no firm commitment.

The plan to crush the Czech state was not dependent on the success of any of these negotiations. Hitler utilised the remaining ethnic grievances within the rump of Czechoslovakia to achieve his purpose. The Slovaks, who had been given much greater autonomy after Munich, were encouraged by the Germans to demand further concessions. The Czechs reacted sharply to the ensuing disturbances and declared martial law but it was not until Germany threatened to allow Hungary to occupy their country that the Slovak government declared its complete independence. Once that declaration had been made, Hitler could maintain that the state which the Western powers had guaranteed at Munich had disintegrated from within. On 15 March 1939, German troops marched unopposed into the Czech areas of Bohemia and Moravia. Threatened with the devastation of Prague by aerial bombardment and bullied to the point of physical collapse in an interview with Hitler, the Czech president, Hacha, had agreed not to order his troops to resist but to place 'the fate of his country and his people in the hands of the Führer of the German Reich'. A euphoric Hitler claimed, 'this is the greatest day of my life. I shall enter history as the greatest German of them all'.[3] Germany had eliminated any threat from the Czech army, acquired its still significant number of weapons and gained possession of the great Skoda arms factory. For the first time, however, Germany could not claim that it was redressing a grievance from Versailles nor satisfying the wishes of Germans to belong to the Reich. Hitler, even so, did not anticipate any significant reaction from Britain and France. They had taken little interest in the state which they had guaranteed and had continued to pursue conciliatory policies towards Germany.

### French and British Policy from Munich to Prague

At French instigation, a Franco-German declaration was signed in December 1938 similar to the Anglo-German declaration which had been signed at Munich. Britain ratified the Anglo-Italian agreement and, in January 1939, Chamberlain and Halifax made a pilgrimage to Rome in the hope that 'an hour or two's *tête à tête* with Musso might be extraordinarily valuable in making plans for talks with Germany'.[4] In public as in private, Chamberlain continued to express optimism about the future and to try to tempt Germany into a settlement by the promise of economic concessions. A little knowledge of the problems of the German economy was a dangerous encouragement to his optimism. Six days before the occupation of Prague, Chamberlain told the press of his high hopes for the successful outcome of a visit by a British Foreign Office minister to Berlin and for the holding of a disarmament conference before the end of the year.

Not everyone in Britain showed such optimism. Support for a policy of continuing to appease Italy and Germany was eroding. Duff Cooper, the first lord of the admiralty, had resigned from the cabinet over the Munich settlement and had joined the still small but growing number of critics of the government's foreign policy within its own party ranks. The infamous *Kristallnacht* of November 1938 aroused horror and anger. Rumours about the German oppression abounded. Although military intelligence gave little credence to predictions that Germany was about to launch a massive air strike against London or invade Holland, the War Office believed that there was an 'intense energy' about German military activities.[5] In Parliament, in some sections of the press and within the armed services there was an increasing demand that Britain should be better prepared for the eventuality of war. The chiefs of staff argued that the loss of the Low Countries would be dangerous to Britain's own security. The French pressed for an *effort du sang*, the promise of British assistance with ground forces in the event of war. The diplomats warned that if such a promise were not forthcoming French support, if Britain alone were attacked, would be in jeopardy. By March 1939 the cabinet had succumbed to the pressure and had come to accept the need to abandon its 'limited liability' policy and to make preparations for the sending of an expeditionary force to the continent.

The French had their own particular problems with the strident Italian claims for concessions about Tunis, Corsica and Nice. Bonnet and his supporters, with encouragement from the British government, were prepared to negotiate. They still clung to the hope that it would be possible to detach Mussolini from Hitler. Daladier, however, was prepared to concede nothing. He was supported by the strength of public hostility towards Italy which its demands had aroused and he was encouraged by a considerable improvement in the French economy. The 1938 devaluation of the franc, the end of the forty-hour working week and severe measures against subsequent industrial unrest had brought a new confidence in financial circles. At the British Foreign Office, Harvey recognised that there was a better spirit in France with 'less defeatism, less self-criticism, better economic outlook'.[6] Daladier also had no illusions that Italy could be appeased by small concessions. French intelligence sources warned that there was evidence of increasing collaboration between Italy and Germany and that the latter was speeding up its preparations for war. In mid-January it was reported that the German army would be ready by the beginning of March 'either for a surprise action or for another show of force'.[7]

The German occupation of Prague took place on 15 March. It was followed almost immediately by a report from the Romanian ambassador in Britain that Germany was demanding the control of his country's economy, including its considerable oil industry. The Romanian government denied that such an ultimatum had been presented but that did little to reduce the suspicion and tension. Within days Germany forced Lithuania to cede the disputed border territory of Memel and rumours were rife that it had plans for an early attack on Poland. The response of Britain and France to these developments was to issue guarantees to Poland, Greece and Romania and to make a pact with Turkey. It appeared like a revolutionary change in policy, particularly for the British who had eschewed commitments in eastern Europe since the end of the First World War. How had they come to undertake such obligations and what did they hope to achieve by them?

The guarantees were a hasty response to the new developments and gave the impression, as Cadogan himself later admitted, of 'a number of amateurs fumbling about with insoluble problems'. The government had to be seen to '*do* something now', he wrote at the time.[8] Chamberlain's initial mild reaction to the occupation of Prague brought an avalanche of criticism. Much of the press, the party whips, both sides of the Commons, the foreign secretary and his senior advisers all called for a different response. The view that one could no longer believe or hope that there was a limit to Nazi ambitions was clearly expressed by Cadogan. 'I always said that, as long as Hitler could pretend he was incorporating Germans in the Reich, we could pretend that he had a case. If he proceeded to gobble up other nationalities, that would be the time to call "Halt!" That time has come, and I must stick to my principle, because on the whole, I think it right.'[9] Pressure was also applied from outside the country, from France, the Soviet Union, smaller states of Europe and from the United States. If the British had come to believe that a 'dam' had to be constructed against German aggression, it was clear to them that they would have to take a lead in constructing it. Initially they hoped to obtain French, Soviet and Polish support for a general declaration of their intention to resist aggression.

They failed. The Poles refused to be associated with the Soviets, claiming that such an agreement would inflame Hitler. For them, as for the Romanians whom the French were most anxious to protect, the menace of a Soviet claim to disputed border territories was as great as the threat from Germany. The decision to guarantee Poland alone at the end of March was pushed by the British rather than the French and was designed to counter a 'quick putsch' by Hitler. It was a decision not without irony. The Polish part of the Versailles agreement had been most vigorously criticised by the British. They had had a jaundiced view of the authoritarian nature of the Polish regime and of that country's inclusion in the French alliance system. They had castigated the 'hyena appetite' which the Poles had displayed in the taking of Teschen.[10] While their initial intention had been to obtain Polish support for Romania, they had now given a guarantee to Poland without any reciprocal promise of support for the Balkan state. Given this background it is perhaps not surprising that some of the British press interpreted the guarantee in a limited way. In its leader on 1 April 1939, *The Times* pointed out that Britain had guaranteed the independence and not the integrity of Poland, which meant that Britain was not bound 'to defend every inch of the present frontiers of Poland' and that there was 'no blind acceptance of the status quo'. The implication that Britain would continue to negotiate with Germany over 'problems in which adjustments are still necessary' brought a fierce debate in parliament and the press. The government publicly denied that there had been any ministerial inspiration for *The Times* view and repudiated it as 'unreasonable comment' and 'unfounded gloss'. At much the same time, however, Chamberlain wrote to his sister 'stressing the important point (perceived alone by *The Times*) that what we were concerned with is not the boundaries of states but attacks upon their independence'.[11]

The guarantees to Greece and Romania were equally a hasty response to the intensification of the crisis brought about by the Italian occupation of Albania at the beginning of April. This time the pressure came from France. More convinced than the British that there was collusion between Italy and Germany, they insisted on a guarantee to Romania as well as to Greece. If Mussolini was to be deterred from further adventures in the Mediterranean, then Hitler should be deterred from striking towards the Black Sea. For the British, the guarantees were merely interim measures designed to merge into a larger security system which would include a Balkan pact and Turkish and Polish commitments to Romania. Such a system did not materialise. The Poles had not been honest about the state of their relations with Germany. Long-standing grievances and border disputes amongst the Balkan states were not easily settled. Only an Anglo-Turkish pact eventuated.

The undertaking of so many commitments was a revolution in means not ends for the British. Conciliation had failed to achieve a lasting settlement, but it was now hoped that deterrence would work. Halifax explained, 'Our policy was to resist Germany's attempts at domination . . . and the best means of stopping German aggression was almost certainly to make it clear that we should resist it by force.' At the same time he believed that they 'must try to drive into Hitler the conviction that he can satisfy every German aspiration by peaceful means'.[12] When Hitler addressed the Reichstag on 28 April and denounced the Anglo-German naval agreement and the German–Polish non-aggression pact but denied that any country was threatened by Germany, Halifax consoled himself that 'the recent alignment of the Powers had had a sobering effect'.[13] The French were more inclined to believe that Hitler had been impressed by the British introduction of conscription. A reluctant British cabinet had agreed to that move in response to mounting pressure from both France and the United States.

Other aspects of Britain's policy suggest that its main purpose was deterrence rather than serious preparation for war. Military co-operation with the guaranteed countries was minimal. Neither Poland nor Turkey could obtain the financial assistance which they sought. Military planning for a decisive blow against Italy in the Mediterranean, which had followed the occupation of Albania and the signing of the Pact of Steel between Germany and Italy on 22 May, was short-lived. The Tientsin crisis of June 1939 called into question the wisdom of a strategy which would have ensured Italian entry into a war and threatened the Mediterranean route to the east. Despite their dislike and disdain for Mussolini's 'gangster' behaviour, the British reverted to a policy of trying not to alienate Italy.

There had to be a delicate balance between what would provoke and what would deter the dictators.

### Anglo–French–Soviet negotiations

The role of the Soviet Union was seen as crucial in this balance. With significant support from his cabinet and the Foreign Office, Chamberlain opposed negotiations for a close alliance with the USSR because he feared that it would provoke Hitler and further alienate Italy and Spain. The first lord of the admiralty agreed: 'The military advantages only arise if we eventually come to war. If we assume that somehow or other we are going to avoid this I feel that more than ever the political disadvantages outweigh the possible military advantages.'[14] If the Soviets could be prevailed upon to issue a unilateral declaration of support for the victims of aggression that would be sufficient to serve as a deterrent. The Soviets refused. They wanted an alliance. Faced with increasing pressure from the Labour opposition, from a growing number of his own party, from the French, and to a certain extent from the chiefs of staff, Chamberlain agreed on 24 May to open negotiations with the Soviets for a tripartite pact. The French and the British chiefs of staff stressed the military significance of a Soviet agreement. Although they admitted that the USSR was 'militarily an uncertain quantity' and that its army was unlikely to fight beyond its own frontiers, they nevertheless believed that its supplies and support for its small neighbours would be vital in confronting Germany with serious opposition in the east. For the British military there was also the hope that the Soviets would restrain Japan in the event of a war in Europe. The crucial argument for Halifax, however, was that they could not afford a total breakdown in negotiations with the Soviets, as that would risk a Soviet–German rapprochement and totally undermine the policy of deterrence. Although the possibility of an improvement in German–Soviet relations was recognised, there was little sense of urgency or of competing for Soviet favours. Instead, there was a certain complacency that it would be 'found possible to reach a full agreement at an early date'.[15]

That agreement did not eventuate. Why it did not do so is still a matter of discussion although the deep division between Western and Soviet historians in the ideologically polarised debate of the Cold War years has been modified.[16] What remains undisputed is that deep-seated suspicion affected the perceptions and actions of both sides at every stage of the negotiations. The Soviets feared that Britain and France, despite their guarantees to Poland and Romania, would encourage Germany to turn eastwards and attack the Soviet Union. It was a point of view which was encouraged by their ambassadors in London and Paris, who chose to repeat the views of strong pro-appeasers. The British and the French remained suspicious of Soviet ideological and territorial ambitions in eastern Europe. The French, however, concerned about the implications of their renewed commitment to eastern Europe, were more willing than the British to make concessions to the Soviet point of view. The British haggled over the Soviet demand that their neighbours in eastern Europe should be guaranteed whether they wished it or not. They questioned whether indirect aggression, which was defined as a *coup d'état* or a 'reversal of policy in the interests of the aggressor' should be the trigger for a counter-attack.[17] On both issues they ultimately gave way but the Soviets believed that these hesitations showed a lack of seriousness in the negotiations and insensitivity to their fears that the Germans might attack them through their small east European neighbours. The British were not unaware of Soviet fears but they were more sympathetic to the apprehensions of the small neighbours about Soviet expansionist intentions.

When the British ambassador was taken ill, the British sent a civil servant, William Strang, to head the political negotiations. Strang, an able diplomat, was experienced in Russian and central European affairs but he was not a man of high public profile and the Russians later claimed that his selection was yet another indication that the British were lacking a seriousness of purpose. The Russian demand that military conversations should begin before a political agreement was finally settled was accepted with nervous reluctance by the British. The subsequent decision to send the British and French military delegates to Russia by a slow merchant ship has been seen as particularly symbolic of their attitude. It did reflect a lack of a sense of urgency despite the looming German–Polish crisis over Danzig. But there were also practical considerations which contributed to the decision. Was it diplomatic to cross Germany by rail or air in the circumstances? Should they risk a warship being caught in the Baltic if the German–Polish crisis deepened? The military mission finally reached Moscow on 11 August. The Russians were not impressed with the limited preparations which the British and French had made for war and particularly with their continuing defensive strategy in the west. At that point they raised what they described as the crucial issue of their right of passage across Polish and Romanian territory on the outbreak of war. While Britain and France were trying to persuade Poland and Romania to accede to this demand, an agreement between Germany and the Soviet Union was announced on 23 August.

In mid-July, Molotov, the new Russian foreign minister, had written to his ambassadors in London and Paris that it seemed that nothing would come of 'the endless negotiations' and that Britain and France would have 'no-one but themselves to blame'. The British in particular did drag their feet and in so doing fed Soviet mistrust. But in the end they conceded every point in the political negotiations. According to Geoffrey Roberts, it was only at 'the final breakdown of the military negotiations' with the Western powers that the Russians reluctantly decided to settle with Germany.[18] It is hard to believe that without an offer from Germany, the Russians would have perceived that a 'final breakdown' had been reached. Other points had taken weeks of negotiation and it was known that Poland and Romania also had to be consulted over this issue of the passage of Russian troops. Britain and France may have been remiss in not perceiving that such a Russian request was inevitable and so obtaining the agreement of the two states in advance, but it could equally be argued that Britain and France could have expected that what the Soviets described as a vital issue would have been raised at an earlier stage of the negotiations. What was surely a most important factor in the breakdown of the negotiations with Britain and France was that the Russians were presented with an attractive proposition from Germany.

Through their intelligence network, the Soviets had much more information on the plans and intentions of Britain, France and Germany than was conveyed to them through normal diplomatic channels. They knew that an agreement with the Western powers threatened them with involvement in a European war with allies who were clearly unprepared to take any offensive on Germany's western border. Their Far Eastern army was engaged in heavy fighting with the Japanese on the borders of Manchuria and Mongolia. Further war was the last thing that the Soviet government wanted. An agreement with Germany offered them the opportunity to avoid it.

### The Nazi–Soviet pact

The German path to this agreement was a tortuous one. For years the Nazis had trumpeted virulent anti-communist propaganda and Hitler had repeatedly asserted the need for *Lebensraum* for Germany at Russia's expense. Not all contacts with the Soviets, however, had been severed. Old Weimar hands who favourably remembered the pre-Nazi period of Russo-German co-operation remained in the German army and foreign office. Economic relations between the two countries had been maintained. The Germans had provided information which Stalin had used against his opponents during the purge trials. Within the Nazi leadership, Goering and Ribbentrop were both less committed to Hitler's policy of eastern expansion than the Führer himself. After the Munich settlement, these potential rivals separately worked to improve relations with the Russians, particularly with regard to trade. Hitler was only converted to this policy after the failure of the Polish negotiations and the Japanese refusal to enter a binding anti-British alliance. He determined to settle the Polish issue by force but he had no wish to face a 'simultaneous showdown with the West'.[19] An agreement with the

Soviets could be a means of achieving that objective. Britain and France could be deterred from honouring their pledges to Poland – the solution which Hitler most favoured and which he believed was most likely to happen. If he decided to attack first in the west – and in May he appeared undecided – Poland could be deterred from opening an eastern front. If deterrence failed, then a Soviet agreement would be equally valuable. The Soviets could provide much-needed food and raw materials to an already faltering German economy, which would be hard hit by a blockade.

The question of whether Germany or the USSR made the main overtures from March to late July 1939 is a matter of discussion. Stalin's speech to the 18th Party Congress in March was long thought to have been a public hint to the Germans that the Soviet Union was prepared for political negotiations. When the Nazi–Soviet Pact was signed, Molotov praised Stalin's speech for bringing about a reversal in the political relations of the two countries. Some historians are now less certain that it had been intended as a signal to Germany to begin talks. 'It was nothing of the sort' according to Douglas Watt.[20] When the speech was made it aroused relatively little diplomatic comment. The German ambassador to Russia noted that there were comparatively few denunciations of the authoritarian states but Sir William Seeds, the British ambassador, thought it contained little that 'was new or unexpected'. He warned his government, however, that the Soviet Union clearly did not 'wish to be dragged into the struggle now in progress between the Fascist states and the democracies'. He advised 'those innocents at home who believe that Soviet Russia is only awaiting an invitation to join the Western democracies' to note Stalin's 'advice to his party: "To be cautious and not allow Soviet Russia to be drawn into conflicts by warmongers who are accustomed to have others pull the chestnuts out of the fire".'[21] The message which Seeds extracted from the speech is seen as the important one by Geoffrey Roberts. It was a warning to the Western powers that Russia would not necessarily become involved in a conflict if it did not believe that its own interests were at stake.[22]

At the diplomatic level there were significant meetings between Merekalov, the Soviet ambassador to Berlin, and Weizsäcker, the German state secretary, in mid-April and between Astakhov, the Soviet chargé d'affaires, and Schnurre, the head of the economic section of the German foreign ministry, in early and mid-May. According to the German records, the initiative to expand the discussions from economic to political matters came from the Russian side, but the reports of the Soviet diplomats suggest the reverse.[23] It may well be true, as Roberts contends, that the German reports were slanted and written to persuade Ribbentrop and ultimately Hitler that a German–Soviet agreement was a possibility. Should one not also treat the Soviet reports with some caution? In the climate that had been generated by the purges in Russia, Soviet diplomats undoubtedly tried to protect their own positions. Merekalov was recalled to Moscow immediately after the meeting with Weizsäcker and never returned to his post. Soviet diplomats would need to be cautious until there were clear signs that a German agreement was a possibility and that Stalin would favour it.

The replacement of the Soviet foreign minister, Litvinov, by Molotov in May was also seen as a significant development. Litvinov was a Jew and the main architect of Russia's collective security policy, while Molotov was an intimate of Stalin and an acknowledged supporter of better relations with Germany. The German embassy in Moscow interpreted the move as a sign that the Russians would be ready for an agreement with Germany if they were approached and in Britain Harvey gloomily speculated that 'Russia will turn from the West towards isolation' and 'inevitably wobble into Germany's arms'.[24] Molotov's advent, however, did not lead to any significant change in Soviet policy. Litvinov, presumably under orders from Stalin, had been firm in his dealings with the Western powers and Molotov remained equally firm but he continued to negotiate with them.

From the end of July there was a marked change in the tempo of the German–Soviet negotiations. The pressure for a quick settlement came from the Germans. Hitler wanted the agreement before the autumn rains impeded his planned attack upon Poland. As a result of his personal request, Ribbentrop was received in Moscow on 23 August and the Nazi–Soviet non-aggression pact was signed. The Soviets had obtained their major objective. In the immediate future they would not have to fight Germany in Europe while fighting Japan in the Far East. In a secret annexe to the pact, the USSR and Germany agreed on a new partition of Poland, delimited their spheres of interest in the Baltic states and recognised Russian claims to Bessarabia. The Russians had obtained territorial concessions which Britain and France could never have made. Although they were now likely to share a border with Germany, they would also have the opportunity to construct defences outside the existing Russian borders. Stalin assured Ribbentrop that 'he gave his word of honour that the Soviet Union would not betray its partner'.[25] Could the Soviets place equal reliance upon the Nazis and be sure that they had abandoned their quest for *Lebensraum* in the east? If not, they needed a major war between Germany and the Western powers to provide them with long-term security.

### The outbreak of war

Hitler did not believe that the 'small fry' whom he had met at Munich were sufficiently prepared or determined to fight. He ordered the invasion of Poland to begin on 26 August. The news that Britain and France had ratified their agreements with Poland and that Italy was unprepared to go to war brought a temporary hesitation. Official and unofficial overtures were made to the British and French and their responses showed that they had not abandoned all hope of a settlement over Danzig. They tried to induce the Poles to negotiate and to postpone their mobilisation. Astonishingly there was a belief that Hitler was uncertain. 'Hitler is hesitant and trying all sorts of dodges', wrote Cadogan. 'Irresolution has gripped the heart of the Nazi party', advised Coulondre, the French ambassador to Berlin.[26] Bonnet, the French foreign minister, welcomed the Italian suggestion of another conference but the majority of the leadership in both countries was against any wholesale capitulation. There was no pressure on the Poles to comply with Hitler's demand that they should go immediately to Germany to negotiate. The Führer was not interested in protracted negotiations or a compromise. On 31 August, he reissued the order for the invasion of Poland. It began the next day after suitably fabricated signs of Polish aggression. Although the attack activated both the Franco-Polish alliance and the Anglo-French guarantee, Britain and France did not declare war until 3 September, and even then the French ultimatum expired six hours after the British one. Both governments wanted to make sure that war was really necessary. Hitler was given the opportunity to withdraw his troops and renew negotiations. In France, the two-day delay was used by Daladier to exert his authority over the more appeasement-minded Bonnet and by the military to complete their mobilisation. In Britain, the delay caused an uproar in the House of Commons and a near revolt against Chamberlain in the cabinet.

The governments of Britain and France had no sense of urgency, as they had no plans to give immediate military aid to the Poles. They entered the war with the sobering expectation that it would be a long, hard struggle. The prevailing opinion, however, was that there could be no question of again surrendering to German aggression. If, as his actions demonstrated, there were no recognisable limits to Hitler's ambitions then their own interests demanded that they should try to stop him before he became even more powerful.

The decisions of Britain and France may have determined the timing of the outbreak of a major European war but it was the decision of Nazi Germany which determined that there would be a war at all. By the end of 1938, Germany had regained a powerful position on continental Europe as a result of its own forceful diplomacy and the conciliatory policies of Britain and France. Only the state of the German–Polish border remained as a possible grievance from the Versailles settlement. Had Germany shown some patience and moderation, there were signs that Britain and France would have been willing to make concessions on that issue. Hitler was not prepared to be moderate. He was interested only in capitulation to his demands. He was not deterred by the increasing preparations for war that were being made by Britain and France but instead was committed to further expansion and to the achievement of it by force. The destruction of Poland was the priority in August 1939. Hitler's fear was that 'at the last moment some swine or other will yet submit to me a plan for mediation'. While he was optimistic that he would be able to isolate Poland, Hitler was prepared to risk a war against Britain and France with 'ruthless determination'.[27]

Why was Hitler prepared to take that risk? The question has produced a variety of answers. The simple answer that he had always intended to go to war is clearly insufficient. The 'structuralist' historians argue that the very nature of the regime which the Nazis had established produced pressures for a dynamic policy. The frenetic activity and high expectations which the regime generated had to find an outlet in incessant foreign adventures or pose a threat to its own internal stability. More specifically, Tim Mason has argued that it was the economic crisis that had developed in Germany which forced Hitler to risk a war. Germany's own economic policies and especially its huge investment in rearmament, combined with a worldwide recession, had brought about the crisis. Germany was faced with the possibility of inflation, shrinking export markets, difficulties in importing raw materials and a shortage of skilled labour. There was a threat of growing labour demands and social unrest, which was something Hitler always wished to avoid. In those circumstances, according to Mason, Hitler came 'to see the need for plunder through military conquest' as desirable sooner rather than later.[28] Richard Overy, however, has argued that the economic crisis prior to September 1939 was not sufficiently acute to push the German leadership into war and Mason himself has admitted that there is little evidence that Hitler's decision was a conscious response to the domestic economic situation.[29] By 1939 the sense of impending crisis in the international situation and the increasing pace of rearmament by all of the powers meant that diplomatic and strategic considerations, something in which Hitler was particularly interested, were as important as economic considerations in his decision making, if not more so. In accordance with his broad 'intentions' of the conquest of *Lebensraum* in Europe, Hitler from the beginning of his rule set the Third Reich on the road to war. The war, which he decided to take the risk of starting in 1939, was not the one which he had originally envisaged. Britain was not an ally but a foe and Russia was an associate not the object of an attack. Domestic and international developments had influenced the course which Hitler took but he made the crucial decisions and there is no evidence that he saw himself as deflected permanently from his main purpose of conquest in the east.

### The phoney war

The small amount of actual fighting between Germany and the Western powers from September 1939 to April 1940 has led to the description of that period as 'the phoney war' or the '*drôle de guerre*'. For the Poles the war was a real one. Within a week the German forces were on the outskirts of Warsaw. On 17 September Soviet forces entered the country from the east to claim their share of the spoils under the Nazi–Soviet agreement. By the beginning of October, Poland was utterly defeated and divided. France had made no attempt to distract German forces by an invasion in the west and the British had merely resorted to dropping propaganda leaflets over Germany. The main exception to this inaction was at sea. There the fighting began immediately. The Germans attacked British shipping with mines and U boats and the British had the minor triumph of sinking the German pocket battleship the *Graf Spee* in December.

The lack of other military activity was indicative of the degree of readiness for a major war on both sides. Hitler welcomed the Soviet intervention in Poland in the belief that it would ensure a short conflict. Britain and France would be willing to make a settlement with Germany on his terms. When that did not eventuate he was prepared 'to go on the offensive without delay against the West', despite the contrary advice of the German military leadership.[30] They argued that Germany was not ready to face an enemy of the calibre of the French in the immediate future and that, in particular, they needed time to replace the war *matériel* which had been depleted by the Polish campaign. The Führer was unconvinced but a lack of transport and persistent inclement weather resulted in repeated postponements until the spring of 1940. There was no lack of will and determination on the part of Hitler to 'smash the enemy until he collapses'. He wanted to 'destroy France' and 'bring England to its knees'.[31]

On the British and French side lack of previous preparations for war was also a factor in their failure to undertake major military operations. It was particularly true of the British. They had a mere 160,000 men ready to despatch to France in September 1939, which was totally insufficient to reassure the French. More men had to be trained and British industry had to be geared to war production. It was anticipated that it would be eighteen months to two years before the army which was planned on paper would be 'an Army in the flesh'.[32]

Britain and France were also constrained by the lack of a ruthless determination in the pursuit of a clear goal. They had taken a moral stand in declaring war and wanted to 'stop Hitler' but they hesitated about going on the offensive and extending the scale and scope of the fighting. They had entered the war in the belief that the war would be a long one and that their ultimate success would depend on their greater economic strength and access to resources. Germany, it was hoped, would be brought to its knees by the long-term effects of the blockade rather than by actual fighting.

In France, however, confidence in that outcome began to erode. The increasing signs of the close co-operation of Russia and Germany led to fears that the effectiveness of the blockade would be undermined. The size of the British military contribution was disappointing. Political divisions became more apparent. The French cabinet was weakened by in-fighting. Daladier was finally forced to resign in March 1940 and was replaced by Paul Reynaud, who was well known for his long-standing criticism of the former appeasement policy. Unfortunately he had no strong political following and within the cabinet his position was undermined by the constant criticism of his predecessor. Outside the cabinet, there was some ambivalence towards the war. French communists, who had been some of the most ardent anti-fascists, responded to the Nazi–Soviet pact by denouncing the French declaration of war. Their right-wing opponents questioned whether France was fighting the right enemy. In their ranks there was more enthusiasm for going to war to aid Finland when it was attacked by the Soviet Union than for launching an offensive against Germany.

In Britain dynamic political leadership was also lacking. The government was enlarged by the addition of Winston Churchill as first lord of the admiralty and by Anthony Eden as secretary of state for the dominions, a non-cabinet post. It was insufficient to generate confidence that the men who had so vigorously pursued peace would now pursue war with equal vigour and enthusiasm. Industry was slow to move into war production and there was a disappointing response from the banks to the attempt to raise a war loan.

Tension in Anglo-French relations had not evaporated with the declaration of war. The French constantly asked for the promise of more military assistance in the event of a German attack than the British were able or, in some instances, willing to give. The British for their part were unenthusiastic about French schemes to deflect the war from the borders of France, whether it was the opening of a front in the Balkans or the more controversial proposal to bomb the Russian oil refineries of Batum and Baku which were thought to be supplying Germany with oil. The possibility of bringing the Soviets fully into the war on the German side or of provoking the Italians to abandon the neutrality which they had declared at the beginning of the war was alarming to the British. While convinced that they had to prepare for a German attack against France, they could not ignore the continuing dangers to their interests elsewhere. The security of the Middle East and the freedom of passage through the Mediterranean remained major concerns. In its unprepared state and still faced with a potential major enemy in the Far East as well as with an actual enemy in Europe, Britain remained nervous that it would become committed to a war 'in the wrong direction'.[33]

### Japan and the Opening of the War in Europe

The Japanese had late in 1938 set themselves the task of creating a New Order in East Asia, 'a veritable "Pike's Peak or Bust"', as ambassador

Joseph Grew put it.[34] For that they recognised that they had to mobilise the resources at their disposal but mobilisation would not be sufficient on its own. Japan needed, particularly while that task was under way, to take advantage of the opportunities others offered. In that sense, indeed, it was continuing a traditional policy. Since the Meiji restoration, it had advanced its cause internationally, not only by building up its own strength, but by seeking the support or compliance of others. Between 1902 and 1922 it had valued the British alliance. After that it had for some time sought to avoid a total break with the Washington powers. Even after Manchuria, it tried to use the divisions among the outside powers, convinced that a closer connection with Germany would make the maritime powers more compliant and the Soviet Union less threatening, and convinced, too, that this would bring the Chinese, under the weak KMT, to heel. The policy persisted while total mobilisation got under way. Europe seemed still to offer opportunities. The pursuit of them proved frustrating. Perhaps, like its earlier policy, the policy also tended to reaffirm the Western tendency to depreciate Japan's capacity and determination.

Increasing the diplomatic pressure early in 1939 implied a closer relationship with Nazi Germany. The latter's seizure of the rest of Czechoslovakia in March and the Italian move on Albania in April weakened Britain's capacity to oppose the Japanese in Asia. In February they had occupied Hainan and in March the Spratlys. But the Japanese army was more concerned about the Soviet Union. Bringing pressure to bear on Stalin would involve intensifying the ties with Hitler, and he would demand a commitment in return. Such a commitment would be against the maritime powers, and in particular designed to deter the USA from intervening in support of Britain. That concerned the Japanese navy, as well as the foreign ministry, and the Japanese system did not readily provide for resolving priorities between army and navy. Partly as a result, the negotiations were frustrating and ultimately vain.

Early in 1939 the navy had somewhat shifted its ground. In a Japanese struggle with the Soviet Union, Britain and France might join Russia. A larger alliance would, moreover, give the navy the chance to expand its forces. It was thus agreed that, while the USA would be excluded from the application of a Germany–Japan alliance, Japan would consider giving military aid to Germany and Italy if they were involved in a war with Britain and France. The Japanese reservations over the USA were still too apparent for this to be acceptable to the Germans. The Japanese tried again. A meeting of the five ministers early in June developed a new formula: Japan might intervene if Germany and Italy were involved in a war with a power other than the Soviet Union, though the treaty should be regarded as an extension of the Anti-Comintern Pact, and it would operate only after some date to be determined by Japan. The reservations remained because of the emperor, even more because of the navy minister, Yonai Mitsumasa. The

153

army made one more effort following more fighting with the Russians, but in vain. No new pact with Germany was made. The 'lacquered half-monkeys', as Hitler called them,[35] did not join the Pact of Steel, made on 22 May by Italy and Germany.

The Führer was already changing his strategy. It was partly because he was unable to get the Japanese sufficiently to stress the anti-Western aspect of the Anti-Comintern Pact, and so face the West with a united front which would facilitate the further changes in Europe he now sought, that he determined to make a short-term deal with the Soviet Union with the same objective. If Britain's approaches to the Soviet Union prompted the Japanese to stress the anti-Russian aspect of the Anti-Comintern Pact, they prompted Hitler to pursue a revised strategy that led to the Nazi–Soviet non-aggression pact and then to war. In Tokyo the Hiranuma cabinet resigned. 'The next cabinet is beyond me,' declared Saionji, '. . . Our foreign policy is now the biggest failure since the beginning of our history.'[36]

Germany's change of strategy was indeed a shock to the Japanese, undermining the policy they had been following since 1936. The army's position in the north was already exposed by the major clashes at Nomon-han in July–August: 'thousands of dead or severely wounded Japanese soldiers lay abandoned at desolate Balshagal'.[37] Now it was further weakened – indeed Zhukov had begun a destructive counter-offensive on 20 August – and border differences were now patched up on terms advantageous to the Soviet Union. But the European war yet offered Japan some diplomatic opportunities, since Britain and France could be subjected to pressure.

Already in July Japan had been able to settle the dispute with Britain at Tientsin to its advantage. With the outbreak of war in early September, the new Abe cabinet invited the belligerent nations to withdraw their remaining troops from China, and Britain more or less did so. The USA was less compliant. During the Tientsin dispute, it had given six months' notice of its intention to terminate its commercial treaty with Japan. Now it declined to accept the request of Nomura Kichisaburo, the new foreign minister, that it recognise Japan's special position in East Asia. Ambassador Grew declared on 19 October that the American people were opposed to the effort 'to establish control, in Japan's own interest, of large areas on the continent of Asia and to impose upon those areas a system of closed economy'.[38]

During the 'phoney war', Japanese caution continued. The German invasion of Norway and Denmark in April presaged a change. The prospect of a German invasion of the Netherlands brought reports that Japan was considering 'vigorous diplomatic action' to forestall military intervention in the Indies.[39] But it wanted to avoid a take-over by the Germans as much as a take-over by their opponents. Arita Hachiro expressed Japan's concern 'over any development accompanying aggravation of war in Europe that may affect status quo in Netherlands East Indies'.[40] That was an approach that the USA, Britain and France were able to endorse.

The Japanese adhered to this policy when the Germans invaded the Netherlands and its government went into exile in London. The American acting consul-general had suggested that the Indies government would 'strive to exist...as an independent nation', even if the Netherlands were conquered by Germany, though he was not sure that the 1922 guarantee would then apply. There had also been some concern lest the Germans in the Indies might stage a coup and give the Japanese an excuse to step in.[41] In the event the governor-general declared that government authority could be maintained: 'Assistance to this end from abroad from whatever side it may be offered will be refused as being unwelcome.' The Dutch were 'clinging to the shibboleth of neutrality' in an attempt 'to maintain the status quo to please Japan', as the British consul-general put it.[42] In fact they were also having to deal with a range of economic demands that the Japanese had put in shortly after the termination of their commercial treaty with the USA of 1911 had come into effect in January 1940. Could the Dutch frame their responses so as neither to appease nor provoke the Japanese? Though they were unwilling to see the Dutch follow the former course, neither the British nor the Americans were at this time prepared to guarantee to come to their support if it was required.

### Britain and the United States in East Asia

Before the summer of 1939, the British had remained optimistic about East Asia. Japan's morale was slipping, they believed, and it was fearful of Britain and the USA. The Tientsin crisis that began in April 1939 shook that optimism. The immediate issue was the question of surrendering for trial by the Peking authorities of four alleged Chinese terrorists arrested in the British concession in Tientsin. The concession harboured Chinese guerrillas and was a base for 'terrorism' and anti-Japanese propaganda.[43] In a sense, the unequal treaties with the British were a source of practical support for China in its struggle with Japan. A surrender would afford a kind of recognition of the Japanese position. The Foreign Office in London argued against compromise. But if Japan retaliated, would the USA support the UK? And if Germany and Italy acted at the same time, could a British fleet be sent to the Far East? The answers were doubtful at best, and the British government decided to negotiate. Indeed, it agreed to a preliminary formula that substantially accepted the Japanese position: a 'Far Eastern Munich', as Clark Kerr, the ambassador in China, put it.[44] Appeasement in Asia, begun late, was quickly checked by an unexpected US reaction: it was then that the USA announced the termination of the 1911 treaty. In the subsequent Tientsin negotiations Britain took a stiffer line. It also announced a new loan to China. A Japanese reaction was expected. But the Japanese were then stunned by the conclusion of the Nazi–Soviet pact in August.

The European war that followed, however, still further underlined Britain's dependence on the USA in East Asia. The Nazi–Soviet pact and the conclusion of the frontier hostilities between Japan and the Soviet Union revived the idea of some kind of British attempt at a Far Eastern settlement. 'Russia and Japan are bound to remain enemies', R. A. Butler, the parliamentary under-secretary at the Foreign Office, declared, 'and with our position in India and the East it would pay us to make a return to the Anglo-Japanese alliance possible. It does not appear that there are the makings of a war between America and Japan; the American interests in the Far East are insufficient to justify a major war. I do not believe that it will in the end pay us to keep Japan at arm's length, and distrust everything she does, for the sake of American opinion.'[45] But the idea was dropped. Britain must continue its moral support of China and its disapproval of Japan, despite the value in an end to the Far Eastern conflict. What was at issue – as before the war, even more now – was American support, not merely in Asia but in Europe: it was not certain, but the possibility of it must not be foreclosed. 'We...constantly made it plain that we had no intention of disrupting the general principles that had governed our policy *vis-à-vis* the Chinese Government, and we certainly had no intention of getting ourselves out of step with the United States Government....'[46] 'American support in our present struggle is vital,' the foreign secretary, Lord Halifax, said, 'and it is impossible entirely to ignore the fact that what Japan is doing in East Asia is very closely akin to what Germany has done in Europe.'[47]

The war in Europe, wrote Lord Lothian, the British ambassador in Washington, meant that Britain was 'really dependent on the United States for security in the Pacific...and if we decided to come to terms with Japan at the expense of China, American opinion would certainly turn against us, and leave us to fend for ourselves'.[48] Britain had to follow a middle course: firm enough to satisfy Washington, not so rigid as to clash with the Japanese. It must court the sympathy of the USA, important in Europe as well as in Asia, but not appear to be dragging it into war. 'There is much in the American attitude which strikes us as unfair, illogical, even perverse. But the rules of American conduct of foreign affairs are fairly well known to us now, and our need for American support is such that we are bound to shape our own action according to those rules.'[49] The US reaction to the Tientsin affair encouraged the British to think that they were moving along the right lines.

The termination of the commercial treaty was not, however, followed by further action of the same kind. It was the climax in a series of moves that stiffened US policy in East Asia in late 1939 and early 1940. The United

States of America had protested against the New Order late in 1938, but its preference was still for sustaining China rather than retaliating against the Japanese. Newspaper editorials reminded the president that US trade with China was less than the cost of a week's war with Japan. In 1939 aid to China was stepped up, and some economic pressure was applied to Japan. The prevailing belief was that Japan was susceptible to economic pressure and as such would moderate its policies. Grew was doubtful: he argued that pressure would weaken moderate civilian leaders and strengthen the military. Whatever the strength of his analysis, the termination of the commercial treaty was not followed up.

Some, indeed, pressed Roosevelt for stronger action, though still, of course, in an economic field. 'War with us would ruin Japan without a shot being fired', a Chicagoan assured him. 'A successful embargo on all war materials to Japan would in six months or a year weaken Japan severely.'[50] In January 1940 Stimson, as secretary of state for war, came out in favour of an embargo on all war materials: this would entail no risk, he said, for Japan was determined to avoid war with the USA. But Roosevelt heeded Grew's view that further measures would inflame Japan, and the lapse of the treaty was not followed by new restrictions or trade discrimination against Japan. Nor, indeed, was there a further increase in direct aid to China. The prospect, however, helped to keep KMT resistance alive.

The British were somewhat apprehensive of the consequences of a stronger US policy. If, Lothian told under-secretary Welles, US action were strong enough to produce Japanese retaliation, that retaliation would not be against the USA, but 'southwards to us and the Dutch islands', and unless it were known that the USA would assist, Britain would have to yield or weaken itself in Europe and the Mediterranean.[51] The general conclusion at the Foreign Office early in 1940 was that it would nevertheless be a mistake to dissuade the USA from exerting pressure on Japan in order to frustrate the New Order.

In May it seemed possible that the Japanese government might move on the Indies, even without the provocation of an embargo. Lothian approached the president. 'He said that in view of the situation in Europe he thought it improbable that the United States would declare war on Japan over Dutch East Indies, though it would probably impose embargo.' Anglo-American staff talks he thought 'too full of political dynamite at the moment'. Yet, as Esler Dening put it at the Foreign Office, they were vital if the USA was prepared to risk an embargo: 'only the threat of force by the USA and the obvious intention to employ it would act as a deterrent in the circumstances', and if there were to be concerted action, it needed to be planned in advance.[52] No such step was yet taken.

'The American policy was to hold the threat of an embargo like a Sword of Damocles over Japan, but to avoid provoking the Japanese into action by going any further for the present,' Ashley Clarke told the French chargé in London. The latter had suggested that the USA might be encouraged to renew commercial negotiations with Japan. But the USA, Clarke added, was also against any kind of appeasement. 'While it was true that the Americans did not want a conflict in the Pacific, they were equally resolutely opposed to conciliating the Japanese, and we should probably arouse suspicion and resentment in America if we were to propose a policy of this kind.'[53] In fact Grew had been authorised to talk to Arita, though stressing 'that there can be no fundamentally friendly relations between our two countries so long as the Japanese continue to endeavour to achieve various positive national objectives by use of force'.[54]

### Japan and the crisis in Europe

By this time, indeed, the crisis in Europe was reaching its height, and the fall of France was at hand. The Japanese were to seize opportunities that opened up in mainland South-east Asia. Their actions there prompted some embargoes, but the sword of Damocles remained suspended. The Japanese, though thus cautioned, did not back down. In the rather longer term, the chances that they would do so were to be reduced by another outcome of the German victories on the continent in 1940, the American determination to build a two-ocean fleet.

Japan, it was often argued, would act in Asia only when the situation elsewhere made it possible. So far Japan's actions since the opening of the war in Europe had appeared to support that view, which was the legacy of a longer experience, and associated, too, with a tendency to depreciate Japan's determination. In 1940–1 the European situation seemed at first to offer opportunities on a new scale, and then to set new obstacles. That was because of its impact on the Americans. The Japanese were to react in an unexpected way.

While the British generally believed that Japan acted only if opportunities had been created by others, that had not enabled them to omit it from their calculations. Britain's priorities, however, lay elsewhere. The first was, of course, the security of the homeland. The security of the Middle East, and of their links with India, was put into question when Italy joined the war. That was the second priority. Not much could be promised, still less sent, to Singapore. The priorities were elsewhere, and the assessment of Japan largely supported that view. The Australians were concerned at the possible threat to their security, and indeed Britain really needed, despite its limited forces, to meet all three priorities, deploying such forces as it possessed as they were actually needed.

Lothian had pointed to the answer with characteristic perspicacity. In the USA, he had written late in 1939, army, navy, many publicists, though not yet public opinion,

> recognise clearly that the present form of American security and the Monroe Doctrine is, in the long run, just as dependent upon the British as on the American Navy. If the United States is to rely upon Great Britain to prevent totalitarian Europe from entering the Atlantic through the Straits of Gibraltar and the exits from the North Sea, the United States must themselves underwrite the security of the British Empire in the Pacific because they cannot afford the weakening of Great Britain itself which would follow the collapse of her dominions in the Pacific.[55]

Early in 1939, the British had finally moved away from seeking a settlement with Hitler towards an attempt to deter him by guaranteeing Poland, Greece and Romania. It was a vain endeavour. Indeed, it invited him to make a deal with the Soviet Union, and Japan's pressure on the Soviet Union helped him to achieve that objective. That change was a setback for the Japanese. Yet they, too, could benefit in China and Southeast Asia from the pressure that Hitler was able to exert on the maritime powers. So far the inaction of the West had encouraged them to see it as a paper tiger, and insistence on the Washington treaties was, like the new guarantees in Europe, an ineffective deterrent. By contrast, their own policies had encouraged the Western powers still to think that they would act only if others created the opportunity and, equally, would not act if that opportunity were cut off. Japan's activities had influenced the policies of Britain, as it had those of the Soviet Union. But the basic Western view had not shifted: that what was needed as far as Japan was concerned was precaution, and that a Japanese break-out was unlikely.

*Chapter 8*

# The War of 1941

In the spring of 1940, Britain and France on one side and Germany on the other began military measures which brought to an end the so-called 'phoney war'. Both sides began operations in Scandinavia. In an extension their strategy of blockade, Britain and France were anxious to deprive Germany of supplies of Swedish iron ore. They had originally contemplated sending troops across northern Norway and Sweden to help the Finns in their war against Russia and hoped, in the process, to obtain control of the export of the iron ore fields. When the Finns capitulated, the British and French adopted the alternative plan of laying mines in Norwegian territorial waters to block the ice-free route down the Norwegian coast which the Germans used. Unprepared themselves to go so far as violating Norwegian neutral territory, they anticipated that their measures could provoke a German attack upon the Scandinavian countries, to which they could respond by seizing the iron ore fields. Anglo-French disagreements delayed the operation. The mine laying began on 8 April, but the Germans had already despatched forces to occupy Denmark and Norway.

Economic and military considerations were both important in the German decision. To maintain its state of readiness for war Germany needed not merely the iron ore, but all the resources of the Scandinavian states at its disposal. On the military side, Admiral Raeder, deeply pessimistic about the outbreak of war against Britain before the navy was 'at all adequately armed for the great struggle', pressed Hitler to obtain bases on the Norwegian coast which would give them access to the Atlantic, vital in Germany's U-boat warfare.[1] The British and French were caught by surprise and their countermeasures were hampered by serious disagreements between the two allies, between the British naval and army commands and between various segments of the British cabinet. Militarily the Germans had the advantage of superior air power and of the successful decoding of much of the British naval cipher. At sea the Germans did lose many of their

160

limited number of modern destroyers but on land their success was complete. The Allies gained a foothold only at the northernmost port of Narvik and even that had to be abandoned in the face of the German attack on France in May.

### The fall of France

The long-delayed German attack began on 10 May. The Netherlands and Belgium were quickly overwhelmed and by 22 June the major part of the British forces that had been sent to France, had been evacuated from continental Europe. The French government signed an armistice with Germany in the very same railway carriage at Compiègne in which the armistice of 1918 had been signed. In little more time than it had taken to defeat the Poles, the French and British forces had been defeated by Germany. The extent and speed of the Allied collapse had been totally unexpected. How did one explain such a catastrophe? 'It was ridiculous to think that the French could be conquered by 120 tanks', Churchill had exploded at one point in the battle.[2]

In the immediate post-defeat period the idea quickly developed that such a disaster could not be explained by military factors alone. Gamelin, the French commander-in-chief, who had been replaced in the middle of the battle, understandably tried to spread the responsibility for the defeat and expounded the view that it was not a simple military matter but the result 'of all French policy domestic and foreign since 1918'.[3] The distinguished historian Marc Bloch, in his influential study *Strange Defeat*, also subjected the whole of French society to critical scrutiny and not just the military. The deep divisions in French social and political life were thought to have impeded the country's preparations for war and sapped French morale and the will to fight. More recently these views have equally been subject to critical scrutiny.[4] Military preparations had been sufficient to enable the British and French to match the Germans in numbers of men and machines on the ground, although this was not true in the air. There is no evidence that the French soldiers did not fight and fight well. It was a French rearguard action, for instance, that enabled so many men to be evacuated from Dunkirk. What is now stressed is that it was an Allied failure. The British and French military leadership failed in their planning and command compared to the Germans.

The Allied leadership anticipated that the German advance would take much the same route as the one in 1914 through Belgium and were confirmed in this expectation by the discovery of invasion plans in a shot-down German aircraft. The French had not extended the Maginot Line along the Franco-Belgian frontier but they were hampered in any joint planning by Belgium's persistence in its neutrality. They nevertheless determined that at the first sign of an attack they would advance into Belgium to meet the enemy. In itself it was a plan that had some merit. It was hoped to keep the fighting away from northern France, one of the most important industrial parts of the country. The main German advance, however, came through the Ardennes, a wooded area with narrow roads through which it had been thought that tanks would not be able to pass. That was an opinion which some of the German high command also shared, and it was only Hitler's support for the ideas of the panzer commander Guderian and General von Manstein which had led to the adoption of this radical plan of attack. When the Germans attacked along a broad front, the Allies acted according to their pre-ordained plans. The British expeditionary force and some of the most highly trained French forces moved into Belgium to meet the German advance while the Ardennes was lightly covered by largely reservist forces. The consequent German breakthrough and drive to the coast bisected the Allied armies. At that point the battle was as good as lost. Lack of imagination and flexibility in military thinking, inadequate co-ordination and co-operation between the Allies, poor communication within the French high command, antagonism between the French commander-in-chief and the French prime minister, all combined to make a successful counter-attack to the German thrust a virtual impossibility.

Inter-war developments, however, cannot be totally excluded from the explanation for the defeat. As a result of the previous appeasement policies of Britain and France, Germany had greatly increased resources at its command. Its agreement with the Soviet Union meant that it could commit the weight of its forces in the west without any fears for its eastern border. The failure of Britain and France to develop their air forces to match those of Germany proved a serious miscalculation. So did the reluctance of the French military leadership to embrace new methods of mobile warfare. One can only speculate whether earlier preparedness on the part of Britain to promise and plan for greater military participation in a European conflict would have encouraged greater confidence and flexibility in Allied military strategy as a whole.

The way in which the French coped with the defeat more clearly reflected the divisions of their society. The majority of the French cabinet chose to accept an armistice with Germany rather than attempt to rally the French empire and continue the struggle as a government in exile. Reynaud, the prime minister, resigned and was replaced by Marshal Pétain, the hero of the defence of Verdun during the First World War. In his support for the armistice, he was joined by those who feared the impact of a continuing struggle on France and also by those who saw the opportunity to rebuild French society on a different basis. Their decision was made easier by the fact that the Germans did not demand total control of the country. 'Our terms are so moderate that sheer common sense ought to make them accept', wrote Halder, chief of the German general staff.[5] Germany seized the important economic and strategic areas of northern France and the Atlantic coast but left the rest of the country as an unoccupied zone under French authority with its capital at Vichy. The Germans hoped, in the event correctly, that most of the French empire would also cease fighting and pledge its loyalty to the Vichy regime and that the French fleet would not join the Royal Navy.

## The consequences of the fall of France

The result of the battle for France, and the reaction of other powers to it, shaped the future course of the war. France would remain in humiliating subordination to Germany and would have to rely on liberation at the hands of other powers. The main question in June 1940 was whether the British government would also choose to make peace and retire from the fight. The change in the leadership of the British government, which had taken place in May 1940, was probably vital in the British decision to fight on. Chamberlain had resigned and been replaced by Winston Churchill, under whom Labour and Liberal MPs as well as Conservatives were willing to serve. While Halifax and Chamberlain, who remained in the cabinet, were prepared to support a French proposal to try to use Mussolini as an intermediary with Hitler, Churchill, after the briefest of hesitations, adopted a defiant and belligerent tone. On the eve of the French collapse he re-assured them: 'we shall listen to no peace proposals emanating from Hitler', and 'we shall never turn from the conflict until ... the wronged and enslaved states and peoples have been liberated and until civilisation is free from the nightmare of Nazism'. To his fellow prime ministers in the Dominions he pledged 'Hitler will have to break us in this island or lose the war'.[6] Rhetoric, however important it was for morale, was not enough to defeat Germany or even defend Britain. What the British could not risk was Germany's appropriation of the French fleet. Under the terms of the armistice, French warships were supposed to be disarmed but there was always the chance that they would fall intact into enemy hands. On 3 July, British warships bombarded the French fleet at Mers-el-Kebir, near Oran, sinking amongst others three major warships and killing 1250 French soldiers. The British were optimistic that they could successfully defend their island base and even indulged in some hope that a long drawn out war would weaken Germany. They knew, however, that their resources and manpower could only maintain a defensive operation at best and that to do more they needed 'the resources of America and perhaps America herself'.[7]

In the United States the Roosevelt administration reconsidered its situation in the light of the disaster in Europe. While sympathetic to the cause of Britain and France, the Americans had given only limited support even in the face of desperate appeals from the French in the last days of the fighting. With the German conquest of western Europe, there was now a more obvious potential threat to America's own position from a German-dominated continent, particularly if it could supplement its naval power. While there was still widespread opposition within the country to American participation in the war, the administration took immediate measures to increase its preparedness for such an eventuality. Appropriation bills to establish a two-ocean navy, to speed up aircraft production and to establish a sizeable army were introduced into Congress and ultimately passed. The British refusal to accept defeat and particularly their determined if ruthless action over the French fleet brought them approbation and more tangible support from the American administration. The maintenance of Britain in the war was seen as serving America's own best interests. While Britain could fight, there remained a chance that the United States would not have to do so.

The United States supplied Britain with arms, allowed it to take over French contracts to buy aircraft and provided fifty rather dated destroyers to be used as escorts for merchant ships. Ninety-nine year leases of air and naval bases in the British West Indies and Newfoundland were granted in exchange for the destroyers but all the rest was to be paid for, as loans to belligerent states were forbidden by United States law. By the end of 1940 Britain had used up its reserves and Churchill had to admit to Roosevelt, 'The moment approaches when we shall no longer be able to pay cash for shipping and other supplies'. Roosevelt had recently been re-elected president for an unprecedented third term. 'Hitler had re-elected him', it was said.[8] Faced with a threatening international scene the American people had opted for an experienced leadership but not necessarily one that would lead them into war. Roosevelt himself had no wish to do so but he responded as favourably as he could to Churchill's appeal. He used all his powers of rhetoric to persuade the Americans that their country should become 'the arsenal of democracy' and set in train the measures which led to the Lend Lease Act of March 1941. Under its terms British orders for equipment were to be paid for by the American government and then lent or leased to Britain. The United States, however, expected some return. The extent of British competition in the international market was to be limited. The British had to agree that their level of commercial exports should be the minimum that was necessary for their continuation of the war. In addition, the British were asked to abandon imperial preference and work for an open free-trade world economy at the end of the war. American support was vital to keep Britain in the war but the arrangement was not intended to be without other benefits to the United States. Britain, it was anticipated, would no longer be able to challenge the American view of how the world economy should be run. The arrangement also had less anticipated benefits.

When the United States was attacked eighteen months later, it did not have to begin from scratch to gear up its war production, and when the time came to take the offensive against Germany, Britain was an experienced, well-equipped ally which provided a secure base within striking distance of continental Europe.

The impending defeat of France in June 1940 lured Italy into the war on the German side. Mussolini had been restless for some time. He had been irritated by the Nazi–Soviet pact, jealous of the territorial gains of those two countries and had made an unsuccessful attempt to persuade Hitler to revert to an 'anti-Bolshevik banner'. 'Musso is more and more restless' and 'the position of playing a neutral part in a Europe that is fighting or getting ready to fight humiliates him', Ciano, his son-in law and foreign minister, noted in his diary.[9] He hoped for easy gains from France but Italy was so unprepared for war that it made a poor showing against the beleaguered French and later against the British in North Africa. For the British, however, the entry of Italy into the war brought additional problems. Their interests in the Middle East and their passage through the Mediterranean were more vulnerable and they had to provide and supply an army in North Africa.

The benevolent attitude of the Soviet Union towards the Germans had contributed to their victory in the west by enabling them to deploy almost their entire army in the battle. A few divisions only had been left to guard the entire eastern frontier. The speed and extent of the German victory, however, prompted Stalin to take immediate measures to consolidate the Russian position in eastern Europe. The Baltic states and the recently acquired territory from Finland were incorporated into the Russian state and Romania was pressured to cede Bessarabia and northern Bukovina. When the Germans intervened to force Romania to make further concessions – Transylvania to Hungary and the south Dobruja to Bulgaria – the Russians protested. They did not wish an extension of German influence in that area. The signature of the tripartite pact between Germany, Italy and Japan in September 1940 further alarmed the Russians, despite Ribbentrop's assurances that it was directed at the 'democratic warmongers'. For Ribbentrop this may well have been the case. He hoped to be able to convert the three-power pact into a four-power one including Russia which 'would neutralise the USA, isolate Britain and threaten her position in the Near East'.[10] When Molotov went to Berlin at the beginning of November 1940 Ribbentrop expounded on this theme, presenting schemes for the division of the world between the victorious powers largely at the expense of what he described as 'the virtually defeated' British empire. Japan could move into South-east Asia, Italy into the Mediterranean, Germany into Equatorial Africa and the Soviet Union into the area of the Persian Gulf and towards India. Molotov was unmoved by the promise of such booty. As they conversed in an underground bunker, he enjoyed the opportunity to ask, if

Britain were already defeated, whose bombs were falling on Berlin? He also brought the conversation back to the European areas of Russian concern – Turkey, the Balkan states, Poland, Sweden and Finland. The Russian conditions for joining the triple alliance were a demand that no German troops should be deployed in Finland or Bulgaria and that Russia should secure control of the Straits of the Dardanelles. Hitler would make no such commitment. Instead, on 18 December 1940, he signed a military directive for the invasion of Russia, which had the code name 'Operation Barbarossa'.

### Barbarossa

The German decision to move from co-operation with the Soviet Union to an attack upon it was one of the most momentous of the war. The reasons for the decision have been hotly debated between the intentionalist and structuralist historians. Some on the extreme are those who see it as the inevitable outcome of Hitler's ideology, of his opposition to Bolshevism and his commitment to the acquisition of *Lebensraum* in the east for Germany. 'Hitler invaded Russia for the simple but sufficient reason that he had always meant to establish the foundation of his thousand-year Reich by the annexation of the territory between the Vistula and the Urals', wrote Alan Bullock. Others believe that the decision arose out of the particular strategic and economic circumstances in which Germany found itself in 1940–1.[11] Each side can assemble evidence to support its point of view. In a much-quoted statement to Carl Burckhardt, the League of Nations Commissioner for Danzig, Hitler said in August 1939: 'Everything I undertake is directed against the Russians; if the West is too stupid and blind to grasp this, then I shall be obliged to come to an agreement with the Russians, beat the West and then after their defeat turn against the Soviet Union with all my forces.' In November 1939 he gave the same message to two hundred senior members of the armed services. 'We can oppose Russia when we are free in the West.'[12] To General von Rundstedt, at the end of the battle for France, Hitler is reported as saying that if England would 'come to a sensible peace arrangement, I shall at last have my hands free for the real major task, the conflict with Bolshevism'. At the end of the war Ribbentrop reflected that his efforts to develop a lasting Russo-German alliance 'would have succeeded in the end had there not been that resistance on ideological grounds which always made the conduct of foreign policy impossible'.[13] In the planning of the Russian campaign Hitler stressed that it was a clash of ideologies which would be reflected in the nature of the fighting. It would be very different from the war in the West. There would be no 'concept of comradeship between soldiers' but it would be a 'war of extermination', particularly of the political and intellectual leadership of the Soviet Union.[14]

Evidence in support of the importance of immediate economic and strategic pressures is also strong. Hitler himself, on more than one occasion, used the argument that the defeat of Russia would be more effective in prevailing on Britain to surrender than air and submarine warfare. His argument was that Britain was refusing to make peace because of its hope of future assistance from Russia and the United States. In particular he believed that 'Russia is the factor on which Britain is relying the most'. If Russia were smashed, Britain would have no hope of a continental ally. An added advantage, he maintained, was that Britain's hopes of support from the United States would also 'fall by the wayside' because the latter would have to concentrate on the Far East, where Japan's power would be tremendously increased by the elimination of the Soviet Union.[15]

The force of such arguments naturally increased when the German plans to invade the British Isles were postponed in the autumn of 1940 owing to the failure of the German air force to gain air supremacy over Britain and the English Channel during the Battle of Britain. While planning for a war against Russia continued, an alternative strategy for the defeat of Britain was considered. This strategy , which was urged by the naval high command, was to build up a coalition of Germany, Italy, Spain and Vichy France which would attack Britain in North Africa and the Mediterranean, capturing Gibraltar at one end and the Suez Canal at the other. Such a strategy would have been compatible with the anti-Anglo-Saxon coalition which was favoured by Ribbentrop, and Hitler did not immediately dismiss the idea. He himself went to see Franco and Pétain but neither would agree to commit their country to the Axis side without guarantees of their national interests in north Africa, which the Germans would not give. Ribbentrop's plans for an anti-Anglo-Saxon coalition foundered at the same time because of the Russian refusal to abandon its interests in eastern Europe. It was that refusal, some argue, rather than long-held ideological views, which determined Hitler's decision to commit himself to the invasion of Russia in December 1940. 'It was only as a last resort that he found himself forced in the interests of Germany and Europe, as he interpreted it, to point to the Soviets the limits of their power.'[16]

The potential extent of Soviet economic power was something of which the Germans were well aware. They twice renegotiated the German–Soviet economic agreement to obtain more supplies of raw materials, particularly oil, grain, iron and chrome, in exchange for manufactured goods including armaments. While Germany was at war the continuation of these supplies was vital. Could Russia be trusted? Twice in 1940 the Soviets held up supplies until the Germans had provided the requisite amount of manufactured goods. If Germany controlled the sources of these raw materials, its ability to face any continuation of the war against

167

Britain and possibly the United States would be assured. The *Wehrmacht* (German armed forces) was instructed that the newly won eastern territory was to be 'organised, secured and ... economically exploited' and Mussolini was told that the war in the east would secure for them 'a common food supply base in the Ukraine ... which will furnish us such additional supplies as we may need in the future'.[17]

Hitler also claimed that with the Soviet build-up of their armed forces, Germany was vulnerable to Soviet pressure and attack. If he risked deploying a major part of his forces elsewhere, there was a danger that Russia would then begin its strategy of extortion in the south and the north. If he did not 'eliminate' Russia, Germany would be paralysed and 'the whole year of 1941 will go by without any change in the general situation'.[18] The last point may well have been a crucial one. There was little evidence that the Soviets were planning an early attack upon Germany. The reports reaching the Soviet leadership in the spring of 1941 emphasised that militarily the country was unprepared for war. The state of readiness of the air force was 'unsatisfactory', the majority of troops on the western frontiers were not 'battle ready' and the rate at which 'arms and weapons and equipment' was being delivered by industry was 'totally unsatisfactory'.[19] What Hitler wished to avoid was the prolongation of a stalemate in the fighting which would give Britain's potential allies, Russia and the United States, the time to build up their resources and their readiness for war. Strategic and economic considerations coincided with Hitler's ideological convictions. 'I feel spiritually free', he told Mussolini on launching the attack.[20] The elimination of Russia would provide Germany with its *Lebensraum*, remove the plague of Jewish Bolshevism and either persuade Britain to make peace or provide Germany with the necessary resources to continue the struggle against the Anglo-Saxon powers. Hitler's ideological belief in the racial superiority of the Germans contributed to his assumption that it would be possible to crush the Soviet Union in a quick campaign and achieve the desired results before the end of 1941.

The planned attack on Russia, however, had to be delayed owing to developments in the Balkans. Mussolini, once again seeking to demonstrate his independence, launched an attack on Greece from Albania without prior consultation with his ally. It was not so much the humiliating retreat of the Italians as the opening of Greece to British troops which alarmed the Germans. The Romanian oil fields and the flank of the proposed Russian invasion force would be open to British air attack. Greece therefore had to be invaded and a pro-British coup in Yugoslavia meant that that country had to suffer the same fate. By June 1941 the Balkans were in German hands. British forces had once again been evicted from mainland Europe and even more ignominiously from the island of Crete. In North Africa too, German assistance had enabled the Italians to retain Libya and prepare to go on the offensive against the British. Hitler was not tempted to commit more troops to exploit these victories and challenge the whole British position in the Middle East. He would not be deflected further from the preparations for Barbarossa. That remained the priority and on 22 June 1941 the German invasion of Russia began.

Initially the German forces made the rapid progress which they had anticipated. In his diary entry for 3 July General Halder, the German army chief of staff, wrote: 'it is probably no overstatement to say that the Russian campaign has been won in the space of two weeks'.[21] The three-pronged German attack had advanced some 350 miles in the south, 600 miles in the centre and 500 miles in the north. Most of the Russian airforce had been destroyed on the ground. A contributory factor in the German success was that they caught the Soviets by surprise. Despite warnings from the British and from his own diplomatic, military and intelligence staffs, Stalin refused to believe that an attack was imminent. In the preceding months the Soviets had pursued a particularly conciliatory policy towards Germany. They recognised the anti-British regime in Iraq and repeatedly refused to receive the British special envoy, Sir Stafford Cripps. They sent a steady supply of raw materials into Germany. Soviet troops were ordered to ignore the increasing number of German reconnaissance flights over their territory. Soviet policy, according to the admittedly Russophile German ambassador, was 'above all directed at the avoidance of a conflict with Germany'. The desire to avoid or at least postpone such a conflict was understandable. The failure to be prepared for its advent in the face of the 'continuous and accurate intelligence of German intentions' is less easy to understand.[22]

Stalin apparently had his own interpretation of the German actions. The build-up of German forces was not the preliminary for an attack but for an ultimatum to demand further economic concessions. He convinced himself that Germany would not risk a two-front war but would pursue further operations against the British in the Middle East. As for the British warnings, they were discounted as an attempt by the British to provoke the Russo-German conflict which they desired. Such a scenario may have had a rational basis, as Geoffrey Roberts has claimed, and it was certainly fed by the deception operation launched by the Germans but Stalin's failure was to make little provision for the possibility that his interpretation was wrong. Not only were the Russian troops unprepared for the attack but they were further demoralised by the contradictory and unrealistic orders which emanated from Moscow in the early days of the fighting.

Despite the loss of thousands of miles of territory and the death or capitulation of millions of men, the Russian state did not collapse. Ill prepared for the conditions produced by the normal Russian autumn rains and the following winter weather, the German advance became bogged down before it reached its objectives of Moscow and the Caucasus. They were thwarted by the 'geographical vastness of the country',[23] by the extent of the Russian reserves of men and resources, and by the fierceness of the

169

resistance which they had helped to provoke by the brutal and ruthless nature of the fighting. The Russians had survived as a fighting force and were able to regroup and counter-attack. Well informed by their agent, Richard Sorge, in Japan, they knew that they were no longer in danger from the Japanese and so many of their battle-hardened troops from the Far East could be moved to the German front .

## The Tripartite Pact

The fall of France expanded the opportunities for Japan and, again led by Konoe, it expanded its objectives. The fall of France, however, also imposed new restraints on Japan. For Hitler's success threatened Atlantic security, and the USA decided that it had to build a two-ocean fleet if the hemisphere was to be secure. At the same time, it hoped to keep Britain's resistance alive, and offered it greater help. That gave South-east Asia, where the Japanese had found new scope, a new importance: it had indeed to be denied to the Japanese if Britain's resistance was to be sustained by access to the men and resources of Asia and Australasia. Once more Konoe's optimism was unfounded: a 'grand slam' once more failed. Indeed, it led to disaster.

The French defeat brought the future of French Indo-China into question. Geographically it was significant for the security of Thailand, Malaya and Singapore, and the Indies. It was also significant in relation to China – munitions crossed the frontier – and it was this that was the initial focus of Japanese action. In 1939 Governor-General Catroux had told the US consul-general that, while France was sympathetic to China, it could 'not afford to jeopardise Indo-China' and would therefore 'follow a policy of purely political expediency'.[24] The French had taken a keen interest in the Japanese approach to Netherlands India early in 1940. Now they were more exposed. Could they expect support from the UK or the USA? Neither was likely: the British were being pressed to close the Burma Road; the USA confined itself to words. Would the Germans support or oppose Japanese pressure? A statement Arita made on 29 June 1940 was partly designed to warn them off, but the Germans might work through the Vichy regime, which claimed allegiance over the colonial authorities.

The aim of the French was to preserve the continuity of their rule in Indo-China: once it was broken off, they believed it would be difficult, if not impossible, to re-establish. Catroux thus redoubled the policy of concession, finally agreeing to close the frontier and to accept Japanese inspection. But such a policy had risks: if it were to be sufficient to pre-empt Japanese demands, it might destroy the autonomy of Indo-China in any case. Indeed, what Catroux granted was not enough. His successor Decoux faced new

170

demands. The negotiations were moved to Tokyo. But there a new government had taken over, and its foreign minister, Matsuoka, adopted a more aggressive line than his predecessor.

The new government was headed by Konoe. He had been impatient with his predecessor, Yonai, who, he thought, had been too cautious, too anxious to await the outcome of the war in Europe, too apprehensive that an early move on South-east Asia would provoke the USA. As earlier, Konoe saw the international crisis through the lens of domestic politics: he was constructing a new political movement, with the support of Kido Koichi and leaders of the Minseito and Seiyukai, that aimed to 'strengthen the national defence state', 'renovate foreign policy', and establish a new political system.[25] The resources of South-east Asia were required. But those, Konoe argued with an insouciance unchanged by his blunder in 1937–8, could be secured without war by making a pact with the Axis. 'The Tripartite Pact was the centre of Konoe's world policy', as his adviser, Kazami Akira, put it.[26] His new government was installed on 17 July, with Tojo Hideki as war minister and Yoshida Zengo as navy minister, and its policy, hammered out at a conference in Ogikubo, was adopted by the cabinet on 26 July and the civilian–military Liaison Conference on 27 July.

The 'Outline of Fundamental National Policy' was based on strengthening ties with the Axis. That would neutralise the Soviet Union, promote the 'southern policy', and prevent the USA from entering the war in Europe or interfering in South-east Asia. Chiang Kai-shek was to be subjugated; Indo-China controlled; the Burma Road closed; the resources of Netherlands India secured, preferably by negotiation. Relations with the USA would deteriorate, but war, it was hoped, could be avoided. But if the China war were settled, military force might be used in the south, and then a clash could become unavoidable.[27] Great hopes were entertained. A panel of academics, businessmen and former government officials thought 1940 offered a chance to build the New Order, and quoted a nationalist of the Tokugawa era: 'This is a great opportunity such as comes once in a thousand years. It must not be lost.'[28] Konoe told the Privy Council: 'a humble attitude will only prompt the United States to become domineering'.[29]

For his part, despite his great victories on the continent, Hitler had become more ready to turn to Japan as a means of bringing Britain to terms. The British had not given up following the French surrender, and indeed the USA increasingly indicated confidence in their survival, notably with the 'destroyers for bases' agreement, a confidence extended by their enduring the Battle of Britain. Hitler sought to cut Britain's imperial lifelines, just as the USA sought to keep them open. The pact he saw as a warning to the USA to stand off while the status quo in Europe was again decisively altered in his favour: the USA must be 'neutralised' so that Britain would give in. At first unresponsive to the Japanese, Hitler moved towards them with the

171

announcement of the bases agreement, and Stahmer, one of Ribbentrop's entourage, was sent to Tokyo. The agreement was negotiated between 9 and 22 September 1940 and finalised on 27 September.

The earlier discussions over strengthening the Anti-Comintern Pact had been unsuccessful. The differences remained, but were partially covered over, if not resolved: Hitler still wanted a commitment against the USA, and Japan still wanted to avoid it. In the agreement, Germany, Italy and Japan undertook 'to assist one another with all political, economic and military means when one of the three Contracting Parties is attacked by a power at present not involved in the European war or in the Sino-Japanese conflict'. From this the Soviet Union was specifically excluded, so that the Japanese army's reservations were met. The USA was in mind, but the navy sought to ensure its freedom of action in an exchange of letters made at the same time as the agreement: Matsuoka endeavoured to insist that the question whether an attack had taken place must be the subject of consultation. What mattered was the public part of the pact: it was a statement that in itself was expected to affect the international situation rather than constitute a commitment to action. 'Germany and Italy intended to establish a New Order in Europe, and Japan will do likewise in Greater East Asia', Konoe declared, '. . . it is inevitable that Japan, Germany and Italy should assist one another, and the pact may acquire the force of military alliance according to the circumstances.'[30]

'The twilight of the gods of the plutocratic world order has now begun.'[31] The Japanese carried out other aspects of the Ogikubo programme: the creation of the Imperial Rule Assistance Association in October, other parties ceasing to exist; the public recognition of the puppet Wang Ching-wei regime in China; and the announcement in November that the major objective of imperial foreign policy was now the Greater East Asia Co-Prosperity Sphere. But the results of the tripartite pact were disappointing; indeed in some measure it was counter-productive. Perhaps its major achievement was to end any risk that its German ally planned to rival Japan in seeking to control colonial South-east Asia.

### South-east Asia

Success of a kind had already been secured in Indo-China before the pact was concluded, though it was true that the Germans had not at first been very helpful. On 10 August Matsuoka had demanded the right to send troops across Tonkin in pursuit of military operations against China. Baudouin, the Vichy foreign minister, believed that, in the absence of American and British support, France could not resist. By coming to terms with Japan, however, it might secure Japan's recognition of its sovereignty, and not all would be lost: 'we shall only partly lose the colony. It is true that the Japanese troops might remain in the country and annex it, but they might also respect French sovereignty, and withdraw once the fight against Chiang Kai-Shek is at an end.'[32] The agreement in principle was not implemented without a Japanese ultimatum and an attack on Langson. The process, too, prompted an American reaction, though that did not destroy the hopes Konoe had of the subsequently-announced tripartite pact.

The Burma Road had been closed by the British for three months as a result of pressure from Konoe's predecessor. It was a decision Churchill advocated, but it was controversial, and Hull 'expressed much regret and disappointment'.[33] The pact encouraged rather than discouraged the British: reopening the Road after the expiry of the three months would at once assist China and indicate a congruence with US policy when the pact seemed to be emphasising it. Indeed the pact alerted American public opinion and helped to align the USA more closely with the UK. For a time its impact was muted by the approach of the American elections. But the re-elected Roosevelt was to speak of the USA as the 'arsenal of democracy' and lend-lease was introduced.

Nor were the Japanese negotiations with the Netherlands Indies productive, despite the inability of the British to promise to come to the support of the Dutch in a conflict, given the absence of any American promise. In August the Japanese had appointed Kobayashi Ichiro as head of their economic mission, the plan, it seems, being that he would offer to guarantee the territorial integrity of the Indies in return for 'a free hand economically'.[34] The Dutch resisted the attempt to shift the discussions to the political sphere: Netherlands India did not fall within the 'living space of any Power'.[35] American action in the Indo-China episode prompted the Japanese greatly to increase their demand for oil. They secured about half of what they sought. The Dutch negotiator, H. J. van Mook, declined to discuss supplying other products until the Japanese produced an agenda. This they did, under a new head of mission, Yoshizawa Kenkichi, only in February, but the Dutch stonewalled, and in June 1941 returned a largely negative reply.

Only in regard to Thailand did the Japanese achieve some success, and only partly as a result of the tripartite pact. The Thais had been anxious about their own security, but also tempted to take advantage of the weakness of the Vichy regime in Indo-China to regain territory in Laos and Cambodia lost to France at the beginning of the century. Pibun, the prime minister, appears to have pledged himself to Japan in October, shortly after the pact was made.[36] The Japanese had recently committed themselves to upholding the integrity of Indo-China. After conferring with the army and navy, Matsuoka decided to offer mediation in the dispute, in which Japan would take Thailand's side in return for its adhesion to the New Order. Mediation was reluctantly accepted by the French in January. 'And it would appear that the Thai leaders in order to acquire their mess of pottage from the prostrate French in Indo-China have gone along and deliberately put their heads into the Japanese noose.'[37] Agreement was reached only on 11 March, and the treaty signed only on 9 May 1941. Under it much of north-western Cambodia went to Thailand. Neither France nor Thailand were to make pacts with third countries that could be considered hostile to Japan.

This was Japan's one substantial success in this phase. The diplomacy of the tripartite pact had not brought it the advantages Konoe had anticipated. Japan's approach changed. To Germany's concern there were negotiations with the USA, though the 1937 principles and the pact put major obstacles in their way. At the same time Matsuoka sought to improve relations with the Soviet Union. That could not be achieved through Berlin, as he had hoped. It was instead achieved in what Matsuoka termed 'diplomatic Blitzkrieg'[38] as a result of the worsening relations between Germany and Russia. Japan and the Soviet Union concluded a five-year neutrality pact on 13 April 1941.

Then, as in 1939, their partner confronted the Japanese with an abrupt change of policy and a challenge. Hitler's invasion of the Soviet Union offered a choice. Should Japan abandon the move south and join Germany against Russia, seizing its maritime provinces? Or should it continue its southward policy at the risk of a conflict with the USA now that the Soviet threat in the north had been eliminated? Matsuoka favoured going along with the Germans, despite the neutrality pact he had so recently signed in Moscow. 'Great men change their minds. Previously, I advocated going south, but now I favour north.'[39] In the event the decision went the other way. 'Regardless of whatever changes may occur in the world situation, Japan will adhere to the established policy of creating a Greater East Asia Co-Prosperity Sphere and thereby contribute to the establishment of world peace.' The southern area was vital. 'To attain this objective, we shall not hesitate to engage in war with Britain and the United States.'[40] Matsuoka was squeezed out of office.

Japan moved on southern Indo-China, pressing Vichy to agree to the use of air and naval bases in return for a renewed guarantee of Indo-China's integrity. Vichy agreed, holding to the earlier line of reasoning: 'the most important question for France is to remain with some authority on the spot regardless of how restricted that authority may be or how humiliating its curtailment'.[41] But the American government responded on 26 July with the freezing of Japanese assets in the USA, which was furthermore interpreted more rigidly than the president expected, and on 30 July announced that defending the Philippines was now official policy.[42] After 5 August no oil was reaching Japan from the USA or the Indies. Japan produced 400 000 kilolitres a year: its navy used that in a month. Its stock-pile of 9,400,000 kilolitres would last two years.

In early August the Japanese sought to renew the conversations with the USA that had been suspended. The USA should restore normal trade and co-operate with Japan in procuring the resources it needed, especially from the Indies. It should also help to initiate negotiations between Japan and the Chiang Kai-shek regime for 'a speedy settlement of the China Incident'. Japan would withdraw its troops from Indo-China when the Incident was settled and guarantee the neutrality of the Philippines.[43] These ideas the USA found inadequate, and while Hull modified the warning proposed by the president after he had met Churchill at Placentia Bay, he was not prepared to take up Konoe's suggestion of a meeting with Roosevelt without there being some prior understandings: the very holding of a meeting would 'cause China grave uneasiness, unless an agreement had already been reached that would protect China's sovereignty'.[44]

On 6 September the Japanese presented their policy in a somewhat different form. They would not advance beyond Indo-China without justifi-able reason, and would withdraw their forces from China when relations had been normalised. The USA was not to oppose the China settlement and was to discontinue the freezing act. Neither these ideas, nor the renewed suggestion of a high-level meeting, were accepted. Konoe's policy called for war if he could not achieve his objectives by diplomacy. He now resigned. His successor, Tojo, made a final diplomatic effort, while preparing for war against a deadline dictated by the monsoon. The negotiations did not succeed, and Japan began the war by bombing Pearl Harbor and invading Malaya early in December.

### The decision for war

In reaching their decision, the Japanese had been conscious that their pos-ition was deteriorating. At the 50th Liaison Conference, Admiral Nagano Osami, the navy chief of staff, declared that Japan was getting weaker, the enemy stronger. 'Although I am confident that at the present time we have a chance to win a war, I fear that this opportunity will disappear with the passage of time.'[45] It was not merely a question of materials. The US navy was expanding: at the end of 1941 Japan would have 70 per cent of US strength; in 1942 65 per cent; 1943 50 per cent; 1944 30 per cent. In the first stage of the war Nagano envisaged if diplomacy failed, the empire could secure a position in the south-west Pacific, by which 'we shall be able to establish the foundation for a long war by maintaining an invincible position'.[46]

Tojo reflected the same mixture of determination and desperation, of aspiration and apprehension. 'If we enter a protracted war', he told the Imperial Conference on 5 November,

> there will be difficulties.... The first stage of the war will not be difficult. We have some uneasiness about a protracted war. But how can we let the United States continue to do as she pleases, even though there is some uneasiness? Two years from now we will have no petroleum for military use. Ships will stop moving. When I think about the strengthening of American defences in the south-west Pacific, the expansion of the American fleet, the unfinished China Incident, and so on, I see no end to difficulties.... I fear that we would become a third-class nation after two or three years if we just sat tight.[47]

On 1 December, when the Imperial Conference took the final decision, Tojo declared: 'our Empire stands on the threshold of glory or oblivion'.[48]

If diplomacy failed, the Japanese had concluded, force must be attempted, though their confidence in the outcome was limited. 'The government has decided that if there is no war, the fate of the nation is sealed', Nagano had commented in September. 'Even if there is war, the country may be ruined. Nevertheless, a nation which does not fight in this plight has lost its spirit and is already a doomed country.'[49] The momentum built up in Japan played a part in this decision. The Japanese had pursued an expansive policy. Could they stop now? The world was, it seemed, being divided anew. Germany was pressing the Soviet Union, but the USA was activating its power by building a two-ocean navy. Japan must try to guarantee its future in the new world that was emerging before it was too late by securing its dominance in South-east Asia. But that the USA wished to prevent. The policies of other powers indeed played a part in Japan's decision making, now as earlier, and, as before, they tended to underestimate the determination of the Japanese. Just as they had earlier thought there was no call to do much to stop the Japanese, so now they thought they could stop them without much difficulty.

### British reaction

Though able to do little themselves, the British tended to share that view. They were, however, not without apprehensions, and, as before, tried neither to provoke Japan, nor to appease it. Without a promise of US support, the former was essential; both the former and the latter might foreclose that support. Closing the Burma Road immediately after the French surrender was done for three months, during which special attempts were to be made to bring about a just and equitable peace. Nothing came of that, and, surviving the German bombardment, and securing a demonstration of American conviction in Britain's future, the British decided to reopen the Road. They were not able to offer Thailand any guarantees, and their idea of pre-empting Japanese mediation was not supported by the USA, even though they argued that it 'would clearly not infringe United States principle that forcible annexation of territory should not be recognised'.[50] In Indo-China the British dealt with the Decoux regime, though at odds with Vichy elsewhere: indeed a De Gaulle movement was discouraged, lest it 'give the Japanese a heaven-sent opportunity for further penetration'.[51] Even after the Japanese mediation, the British preferred to keep the modus vivendi going. 'So long as we maintain some form of agreement with Admiral Decoux from which he himself derives some advantage, we shall continue to be able to exert some influence on the extent to which Indo-China comes under Japanese domination.'[52] Nor was it immediately cancelled after the Japanese move into southern Indo-China.

The British had, however, gone along with the freezing of Japanese assets following that move. Any Japanese retaliation, they realised, might fall upon them and the Dutch, rather than on the USA. They could get no guarantee of US support if it did, but determined to act even so: 'the United States Government could not be expected to give an unconditional guarantee that they would intervene with armed action; all that was possible was to explain to them that we should expect them to face any consequences which might flow from their own retaliatory measures, even if these involved an attack by Japan either on ourselves or on the Dutch'.[53] The Dutch indeed followed suit, too, and again without guarantees. The lack of any American guarantee for Netherlands India prevented the British from offering a guarantee either. The Foreign Office advocated it: Britain would have to aid the Dutch anyway, and an undertaking would facilitate advance collaborative planning. 'The reluctance ... to make a frank agreement with the Dutch seems ... like saying that when invasion comes we will defend Hampshire and of course Devonshire, but we are short of anti-tank guns and will therefore not commit ourselves to defend Dorsetshire unless we can get some backing from the president of the United States.'[54] Only on 1 December did Roosevelt indicate 'that in the case of any direct attack on ourselves or the Dutch, we should obviously all be together'.[55]

### US embargoes

The Americans had intensified their economic restrictions in July 1940, as it seemed Japan might take advantage of the European crisis. On 2 July the National Defense Act gave the president power to place certain products under an export licence system in the interests of defence. Oil and scrap iron were included, but on 1 August the restrictions were limited to aviation motor fuel and heavy iron and steel scrap. Following the moves on northern Indo-China, all grades of iron and steel scrap were included. 'Tougher measures might appear provocative', it was argued.[56] The steps taken certainly did not stop the announcement of the tripartite pact, but that did not destroy the US belief that economic measures would be effective. That view prevailed the following year when, following the move on southern Indo-China and the failure of the Japanese to accept his proposal to neutralise Indo-China, the president froze their assets. He was convinced that Japan would not fight the USA and the UK simultaneously. He was wrong. The 'firmer your attitude and ours', Churchill told him in November, 'the less chance of their taking the plunge'.[57] He was wrong, too.

Roosevelt's policies were certainly not designed to bring about war in the Pacific. Indeed he still hoped to keep the USA out of the European war as well. But two main policies he adopted helped, in the context of his and others' analysis of Japan, to bring about a war in the East that led to one in the West. One policy, less often discussed than the other, but clearly affecting the Japanese, was the building of the two-ocean fleet, a response to the crisis in Europe that threatened hemispheric defence. Japan's reaction to the other policy, better known and in some ways complementary, was affected by this. That policy was to keep available, not so much to the USA itself as to Britain, the resources of South-east Asia and Australasia, so that Britain might more effectively resist Germany in Europe, and thus again help to preserve the Atlantic security of the USA.

The policy had been defined by Grew: 'American security has admittedly depended in a measure upon the British Fleet, which in turn has been, and could only have been, supported by the British Empire...we must strive by every means to preserve the *status quo* in the Pacific at least until the war in Europe has been won or lost.'[58] Turner told Nomura in July 1941 that 'anything that affects the future security of the United Kingdom, in any part of the world, also is of interest to the United States from a defensive standpoint'. The occupation of Indo-China would threaten the British position in Singapore and the Dutch in the Indies. 'Were they to pass out of their present control, a very severe blow would be struck at the integrity of the defence of the British Isles, and the Isles might well then be overcome by the Germans.'[59] 'Any weakening of Britain, as by a Japanese attack on the Orient which interfered with the supplies she needed from the Indian Ocean and Australia area for her struggle in Europe, would be indirectly an attack on us, and could not leave us indifferent.'[60]

The USA–Japan negotiations, which had made a muddled start and had been interrupted by the move on southern Indo-China in July 1941, were subsequently renewed. Hull had insisted on a statement of fundamental principles that recalled those of 1937, themselves in some sense a restatement of earlier American views. These he reiterated in October. The following month both parties talked of a modus vivendi but he abandoned the idea. It was not that idealism got in the way of realism or that China obtruded into what was now more of a South-east Asian dispute. The practical side of idealism, never perhaps absent, had increased in importance. The Covenant and the Kellogg pact, Lytton had argued, would be weakened everywhere if breached anywhere. Laurence Salisbury had said the same of the US principles. Reiterating them would keep them alive until the world came to its senses: 'surrender or compromise of those principles in any given case would act merely as the breaking of a link in a chain which must depend for its strength as a whole upon the strength of its individual component parts'.[61] By 1941 reasserting the principles was not only a reminder of the Washington settlement: it had become even more a means of encouraging the Chinese. Their continued struggle was also part of the security system: they could not be abandoned lest they abandoned that struggle.

'[T]he same linkage that served to strengthen the American position against Japan also served to define it as peripheral: a function of America's much greater and more vital interest in the survival of the anti-fascist allies in Europe.'[62] Hull had hoped at least to win time. Winning time might be useful to the USA: it might even avoid war in the Pacific. But time could not be won in this way, and the Tojo timetable took over. 'What America wants is time to complete her preparations for a Pacific war', a Japanese editorial declared, 'America has everything to gain and nothing to lose; Japan has everything to lose and nothing to gain.... Japan has exposed herself to disdain by placing three months in the opponents' hands.'[63]

### The coming of worldwide war

Four days after the Japanese attack on Pearl Harbor Hitler, with Mussolini in tow, declared war on the United States, although Germany's formal agreements with Japan did not bind him to do so. In the preceding months Hitler had appeared to wish to avoid a conflict with the United States. He had resisted the requests of his naval commanders to pursue unrestricted submarine warfare in the Atlantic, despite his knowledge of the large amount of American aid which was reaching Britain and the increasing involvement of the American navy in escorting British as well as American merchant shipping. By December German hopes of a quick, successful campaign against Russia had failed. They were now committed to the continuation of a major war in the East. In that situation, one might have expected that Hitler would seek to avoid any further escalation of the conflict. The Japanese decision to attack the Americans, however, freed him from the fear that the USA could concentrate solely upon the European theatre of war. It would have to deflect some, if not the major part, of its resources to the Far East. If Germany declared war upon the USA, Japan would be encouraged and would not seek an early negotiated settlement with the Americans, and while the latter remained involved in the Far East they would need more time to prepare for a major participation in the European war. In the meantime he hoped that Russia would be defeated in another campaign and that Britain would be crippled by the massive success at sea which his naval commanders promised him would be the result of unrestricted submarine operations. Hitler's decision may well have been influenced by his own over-confidence and by the fact that the majority of the Nazi leadership underestimated the political will and economic and military potential of the United States. It is significant in this regard that there was no openly voiced disagreement with Hitler's decision amongst the German military and party leaders. On the other hand, however, there also appears to have been a certain element of fatalism in Hitler's action. He accepted that a conflict with the USA was inevitable and determined that he would decide the timing of it. Preparations for such a conflict had begun almost as soon as Barbarossa had been launched, with the transfer of resources from the army to air and naval programmes. War on such a scale appealed to Hitler's sense of destiny, to his sense of being involved in a life-or-death struggle for himself and for Germany. In the speech in which he declared war on the USA, he said 'I can only be grateful to Providence that it entrusted me with the leadership in this historic struggle which, for the next 500 or 1000 years, will be described as decisive, not only for the history of Germany but for the whole of Europe and indeed for the whole world. . . . A historical revision on a unique scale has been imposed on us by the Creator.'[64]

Without Hitler's declaration of war American popular resistance to participation in the European war could still have been very strong. It would have been particularly difficult for the Roosevelt administration to have carried out the pre-arranged Anglo-American strategy that the war in the Atlantic should have priority over the war in the Pacific. In an opinion poll in September 1941, nearly 80 per cent of the American population had opposed their country's involvement in the European war. The repeal of sections of the Neutrality Act which had allowed American merchant vessels to be armed and to go into the combat zone had been passed with narrow margins in both houses of Congress. Roosevelt had felt unable to go further and ask for a declaration of war on Germany and Italy. Even after Pearl Harbor he hesitated, although he denounced Germany and Italy as much as he denounced Japan in his fireside chat to the American people on 9 December, warning that 'Germany and Italy regardless of any formal declaration of war, consider themselves at war with the United States'.[65] Hitler's decision solved Roosevelt's dilemma. It also made the European and Asian wars appear as one world war, the result of which, as Hitler himself had foreseen, would be decisive for the future development of the whole world.

*Chapter 9*

# Conclusions

The nineteenth-century prophecy that Russia and the United States would be the dominant powers of the twentieth century was fulfilled at the end of the Second World War. None of the other former major powers could have any pretensions to the superpower status which it was recognised the United States and the Soviet Union occupied. Japan and Germany were defeated and the latter was about to be divided. France was recovering from the humiliation of defeat in 1940 and from the divisions caused by the Vichy regime. Britain, despite retaining the trappings of an imperial power, was financially broke. As the war had progressed its relative contribution of men and material to the fighting forces had steadily declined. Britain, Churchill ruefully acknowledged, was a 'little donkey' compared to 'the great Russian bear' and 'the great American buffalo'.[1] While the manpower and economic resources of the United States and the Soviet Union were fundamental to their leading positions, the dramatic extent of their predominance owed much to the involvement of the European powers in a second major war little more than twenty years after the end of the first.

The irony of the situation was that both Germany and Japan on one side and France and Britain on the other had pursued policies in the 1930s which were designed to prevent such a transformation in the international power balance. While Stalin was concentrating upon the consolidation of his power within the Soviet Union, and the United States was unwilling to become deeply involved in European or Asian affairs, Germany and Japan had sought to use the perceived opportunity to extend their own political and territorial power. Britain and France, on the other hand, were strongly influenced in their efforts to avoid war by the fear of its effect upon their international positions. War – and they believed if it came it would be a long one – could not fail to hasten their decline. It would be economically exhausting and the continued possession of their empires could be under threat. There was a danger that the Soviets could use the opportunity to expand territorially and ideologically. Even American assistance, which it was recognised would be vital to ensure victory in any war, would come at the price of American domination of any new peace settlement.

Britain and France were the powers who were most wedded to the preservation of the status quo at the end of the First World War. Much of the peace settlement had been constructed to protect their interests. France hoped that Germany's territorial losses and the economic constraints upon it would compensate for France's relative weakness in manpower and resources. Britain hoped that the destruction of German naval power would ensure its own safety and that of its imperial trading routes. Although the protection of their imperial possessions was a considerable drain upon their depleted resources, there was a strong assumption that the preservation of empire was a vital element in their prestige and standing as great powers. This was particularly true for the British. In 1938 General Edmund Ironside defended the British decision not to fight over Czechoslovakia on the grounds that 'it was risking the Empire and unjustifiable'.[2]

The problem for Britain and France was that the status quo which they wished to uphold was being challenged in many areas. Though it had been defeated in World War I Germany had not abandoned its ambitions to become the major power on the Continent and began agitating immediately for modifications to the treaty of Versailles. The Italians were dissatisfied with their spoils of victory. National tensions and festering resentments were ongoing threats to the settlement in eastern Europe. The Soviet Union was looking for an opportunity to revise the Polish–Russian boundary. Its support for communist parties in other countries and for the opponents of imperial rule in Asia was perceived as a threat to the internal stability of all capitalist states. Even the policy of the USA contained elements that were challenging to the French and British position – the Americans were anti-imperialist and they were trying to reorganise the world economic system in their own interest. Their reluctance to participate fully in international politics meant that they could not be relied upon but nor could they be ignored. In the Far East the instability in China was further increased by warlordism and civil war, by the KMT–CCP conflict, and by the intervention of the Japanese. The latter had not abandoned that ambition to dominate China which they had manifested in the Twenty-one Demands imposed upon the Chinese during the First World War. Within their own imperial possessions the British and French were also facing demands for change, in India and Egypt, in North Africa and Indo-China, and in their newly acquired mandate territories in the Middle East.

This is not to say that the existence of so many challenges to the system made war inevitable. By 1930 negotiated changes were taking place. Britain and, with somewhat more reluctance, France had agreed to moderate some of the terms of Versailles. Germany had become a member of the League of Nations and the Soviet Union had established normal diplomatic relations with most states. Britain was about to redefine its relationship with its Dominions in the Statute of Westminster and to make concessions to nationalist demands in India and Egypt.

The effects of the Depression, however, brought greater instability and increased the pace of change and the number of challenges to the international status quo. The governments of Japan, Italy and Germany chose to pursue their expansionist aims much more aggressively than they had done in the previous decade. The sequence of crises which their policies precipitated heightened international tension to the point where it was recognised that another war was a possibility.

The response of the other powers to the aggressor states affected not only the timing of the outbreak of that war, but also the extent of the conflict when it ultimately occurred. Britain, France, the United States and the USSR, at different times and in different degrees, made concessions to the aggressors. By 1939, as a result, Germany had succeeded in removing all its grievances from Versailles apart from the German–Polish border. It had broken up the Czech state, struck a body blow at France's alliance system, and was in the process of a steady economic penetration of eastern Europe. German and Italian assistance had assured Franco of victory in the Spanish Civil War. Germany was once more the dominant power on the continent. In the Far East Japan without impediment from the other powers had resumed major hostilities against China. The extent of the concessions which had been made meant that when first Britain and France, and then the Soviet Union and the United States, decided to resist, Germany and Japan were considerably strengthened and had much greater resources at their command. The resulting war would inevitably be a major one.

The simultaneous challenge to the status quo from all three aggressive powers had contributed to the decisions of Britain, France, the Soviet Union and the United States to make concessions and so try to avoid war. France did not want to alienate Italy in 1935 because of its greater fear of Germany. The conclusion of the Anti-Comintern Pact in 1936 was a warning that 'the most powerful disturbers of the peace in Europe and Asia had drawn together...England, France, the Soviet Union and the United States all had to remember that if they were in difficulties on one side of the globe they were threatened on the other side as well.'[3] For the British the hostility of Italy was an additional reason not to risk war. 'We are in the position of having threats at both ends of the Empire from strong military Powers, that is Germany and Japan, while in the centre we have lost our traditional security in the Mediterranean owing to the rise of an aggressive spirit in Italy', declared the Chiefs of Staff in 1937.[4] The Soviet Union was already involved in fighting with Japan when it was confronted with the possibility of war in Europe in 1939. In that difficult situation Stalin chose to make an agreement with Hitler rather than risk an additional war. In the preceding years the statesmen of Britain and France had also chosen to try to reach agreements with Italy and Germany. The domestic and international pressures to do so were strong – indeed they were so strong that they could be seen as making any other choice impossible. No leader, however, was 'the mere puppet of circumstantial constraints'.[5] Statesmen like Chamberlain and Bonnet abhorred the idea of war and such sentiments also helped to shape their choices and to deter them from courses which could have precipitated an earlier conflict.

In the spring of 1939, although there were only small changes in the underlying circumstances of the two countries, the leaders of Britain and France decided to change their policy towards Germany from one of conciliation to deterrence. The developments between Munich and the occupation of Prague in March 1939 convinced the majority of the leadership of both countries that Hitler would impose no limits upon himself and that therefore there would be no end to his demands for concessions. Such unlimited expansion would impose a direct threat to British and French vital interests – indeed to their very security. Whatever their concerns about other parts of the world, protection of the homeland had to come first. Deterrence succeeded no better than appeasement in curbing German aggression, partly because it was inadequate without a Soviet alliance. In the final analysis, however, deterrence failed to prevent war because Hitler was totally dissatisfied with the great change in the international power balance which he had already achieved. He remained unprepared to limit his enormous ambitions for territorial conquest and political control. Like other statesmen Hitler was subject to 'circumstantial constraints' – notably the pressures of an impending economic crisis and the restless dynamism of the Nazi party – but he was 'the prime mover who made the critical decisions'.[6]

In 1939 Hitler was prepared to risk embarking on a major European war and in 1941 he chose to expand the scope and alter the nature of the war by invading the Soviet Union. Hitler was not interested in a 'new European order' where Germany would have been the leading power but other states retained their independence. He wanted a new 'German order' which stretched beyond the European heartland and where all others were subordinate to the Nazi ideological vision.[7]

To achieve his goals Hitler exploited the international disarray which was caused by the expansionism of Italy and Japan. German expansionism in its turn provided opportunities for the other two aggressive powers. It created the background and the incentive for Italy and Japan to extend their own ambitions and risk becoming embroiled in a major war. Hitler's victory in the west in 1940 was a crucial point in this regard. The overseas possessions of the European colonial powers became particularly vulnerable and were a temptation to Italy and Japan. The British decision to fight on was equally crucial to the development of the war at that point. The choice of a negotiated settlement with Germany could have brought immediate safety to the United Kingdom and a reprieve for the empire, but it would also have brought humiliation and the chance that the reprieve was only temporary. Choosing to fight was equally hazardous. The British knew that alone, apart from their Dominions, they could only hope to survive until further assistance was forthcoming. The German decision to attack Russia brought some relief but what the British wanted, and what they knew they needed, to achieve victory over Germany was the full support of the United States. The Americans had been alarmed by the extent of the German successes but their total commitment to the war on the British side only came when Hitler declared war on them following the Japanese attack on Pearl Harbor.

### The role of the Japanese

In the inter-war phase the isolationism of the USA and the weakness of the Soviet Union opened the way not only to a revival of Germany's bid for world power, but to a bolder, if riskier, policy on the part of the Japanese. This book has argued that 'Asian affairs' were ever more closely 'intertwined' with European. That was true before 1939 because Japan's ambitions affected powers that had both Asian and European interests – the USA, the Soviet Union, and above all the UK, whose position had been further undermined by the First World War and the Depression. Britain could not appease Japan, lest that sacrificed China, and with it the sympathy of the USA, on which it might ultimately be necessary to draw once more if there were to be another European war. That position was easier to adopt because it was believed that Japan would not be able to sustain its expansionism, and that the USA could, if it so chose, bring it to a halt without even going to war, a belief widely shared within the USA itself.

In the meantime, however, there were no guarantees from the USA in Asia or in Europe. The British still needed to provide as best they could for the protection of their interests in the Far East. That contributed to their concern over Italy's antagonism in the Mediterranean, and to their policy of appeasing Germany. Trying to maintain the status quo as far as possible in one way in East Asia, the British tried, partly as a result, to do the same in Europe by a different method. For a time at least it was easier, as well as more necessary, to think of appeasing Germany: the Germans surely had a better case in the Rhineland, in the Sudetenland and in Austria, than the Japanese had in China. But the main reason that Britain's policies diverged is to be found in the attitudes of the USA. It was not an ally. But its alliance would be needed if the redistribution of power again took a warlike form.

The appeasement policy did not work, and reluctantly Britain and France went to war, ostensibly over Poland. The German triumph over France deeply affected the USA. It prompted the building of a two-ocean navy as a means of providing for hemispheric defence. It also prompted attempts to sustain Britain's resistance, in part by keeping open its access to the raw materials of its Asian and Australasian empire. These moves deeply affected Japan. The USA may have believed that it would bring its expansion to a halt, enabling Britain more easily to fight Germany, perhaps even avoiding the need for US intervention in that struggle. The Japanese did not, however, react as expected. Instead, while Germany and the Soviet Union engaged in an all-out struggle, they implemented hastily prepared plans to invade South-east Asia before, as they conceived, it was too late. The USA was thus committed to a Pacific war, and by that route to the European war. Only then, indeed, was there world war.

'Pearl Harbor' has been the subject of much controversy. Craigie believed that war in the Pacific could have been deferred, even avoided.[8] The decision, so far as the Western powers were concerned, was, however, an American decision, not a British. On Roosevelt's part it was not a device for getting his country into the European war; it seems clear that it was rather the result of a diplomacy designed to avoid it. The stance the Americans finally adopted was consistent with the policy they had pursued ever since the European war had ceased to be phoney. Britain had, if possible, to be kept going, and the resources of Asia and Australasia kept available to it. China had to be kept fighting, and the Japanese prevented from moving on South-east Asia.

This book has thus argued the interconnection of events in East Asia and events in Europe. To suggest that the Second World War indeed began with the 'undeclared' war of 1937 is to go further than the present authors, but they would not accept D. C. Watt's view. He suggests that the Sino-Japanese conflict represented 'a linear development from the 1890s onwards which has nothing to do with Europe. That is to say, its motivations and causes are native to the Far East. Even if Japan had not felt cribbed, confined, and threatened by the two great Anglo-Saxon naval powers . . . there would still have been a Sino-Japanese conflict and a war in the Far East which had nothing to do with that in Europe.'[9] Is that so certain? The situation in East Asia cannot be dissociated from previous European action. From the nineteenth century Japan had been seeking security over against the Western powers, who had defeated China, and against the Russians, who had founded Vladivostok after China's defeat in 1860. The absorption of Russia and the West in the First World War encouraged Japan to move ahead in China at a time of post-revolutionary chaos, while both their opposition and their example prevented a pan-Asian approach. In the 1930s the Western powers sought to sustain China in order to restrain Japan, while the Soviet Union encouraged the creation of the

Chinese Communist Party and thus gave the Japanese a new mission. Its frustration, also, of course, caused by the military success of the Soviet Union, encouraged it to look to opportunities in the south, which the involvement of the Western powers in the European war seemed to offer. Conflict in China might have been settled, but for the West and the Soviet Union, and a war in the Pacific avoided, but for the mobilisation of American power prompted by the unexpected turn taken by the war in Europe.

When it nevertheless came to war, the magnitude of the disaster for the Western powers was unexpected. The fall of France had shocked the British, as it had the Americans. The fall of Singapore on 15 February – thirty days ahead of the Japanese schedule – Churchill described as 'the worst disaster and largest capitulation in British history'.[10] Already overburdened in Europe and the Mediterranean, Britain had put little into the defence of Southeast Asia; its leaders depreciated the Japanese, and in any case Europe had priority. In the ensuing struggle Europe still had priority. The Allies would fight against Japan meanwhile, but it would be given their full attention only after the victory in Europe.

Germany and Japan only made this decision easier to take by their failure to co-operate more fully. They were allies only in words, if that, not deeds. As in the first war, so in the second, Germany chose a weak partner, while Japan had lost its one-time alliance with the major European maritime power. But they made even less of their connection than they might have done, though they acted together, yet still not simultaneously, in the month that they both went to war with the USA. For both, of course, that was fatal. They were only precipitating what they had hoped to anticipate, the succession to Britain's primacy in the world on the part of just two 'superpowers', of which the USA turned out to be the stronger.

The Japanese had not joined in the attack on the Soviet Union, but, influenced by the failure of his *Blitzkrieg* in Russia, Hitler declared war on the USA a few days after Pearl Harbor. On 11 December Germany and Japan had agreed to make no separate peace, and on 18 January they concluded a treaty of co-operation. It was, however, really a treaty for dividing the spoils, and stood in the way of co-operative action that might have succeeded, either against the Soviet Union, or against the Middle East and India. Only in January 1943 did Hitler seek Japan's entry into the Soviet war, but his ally, never keen after Nomonhan, had now suffered the naval setback at Midway, and did not respond. Nor did the Axis co-operate in the Indian Ocean. The Germans did not attack Suez early in 1942, even though the Japanese attacked Ceylon. By the time Tobruk had fallen to the Germans in June, the Japanese had been defeated at Midway. Neither could Germany and Japan agree on a declaration in favour of Indian freedom, and they failed to take advantage of the Quit India movement.

Like the First World War, however, the second developed and expanded in ways that contemporaries had generally not anticipated.

It became more fully a world war than its predecessor. The struggle was indeed on an immense scale. It suggested why leaders had attempted appeasement, and it suggested why it could be argued that appeasement had gone on too long. Could or should Germany and Japan have been stopped earlier? Those were matters of judgement. Human factors, as Hinsley says, were involved in policy-making.

### Circumstances and decisions

In an article on the causes of the two world wars, F. H. Hinsley argued for distinguishing 'more rigorously than we do between the causes of war and the given conditions in which war has broken out,... confining the causes wholly to the aims and policies of the powers', and regarding 'all other considerations as constituting only the given conditions in which the powers had to conduct themselves'. They formed 'a challenge thrown down to governments', and the failure or refusal of governments to meet the challenge brought about the wars.[11]

Governments and their leaders may, of course, take an ideological approach, allowing that to shape their policy. But even a more pragmatic or prudential statesman may absorb the intellectual atmosphere of the day – what James Joll called the 'unspoken assumptions' – and can hardly be expected entirely to rise above the current assumptions.[12] The distinction between personal factors and prevailing circumstances is nevertheless a useful one. Indeed, it seems that there is no other way of providing a satisfactory account of the causes of the world wars, if not of other historical events as well. Even if circumstances are shown to be too strong for the statesman, the question of their relationship still has to be considered.

If the system of international relations that had emerged by the late nineteenth century was to work with a minimum of violence, it was necessary for governments to define their national interests and then to pursue them in the context of an understanding of the defined interests of other states. The exchanges among them were the stuff of diplomacy, and the outcome adjustments and agreements, often represented by treaties and conventions that, unless backed by sanctions, had in themselves no binding power other than their ability to satisfy, at least for a period, the respective interests of the signatories, and form part of an otherwise anarchic system in which expectation and reputation at least provided some certainty. It was in this sense that inter-war statesmen sought 'settlements' – perhaps with too great a hope that they would last, or too little readiness to alter them – and it was their disruption by Japan and especially by Germany that undermined any sense of security.

Such a system will indeed work best when the potential for change is limited. What it will find most difficult to handle are changes of a more basic kind, in particular changes in the distribution of power among the major participants, which may, at the same time, make lesser problems more difficult to handle. It was just this that was occurring before the First World War, but particularly between the wars. The primacy of Britain that had marked the world of the nineteenth century was passing. What role would other states assume in the future? That was the core question for the diplomacy of the whole period, solved in the event by the wars that diplomacy failed to avoid.

The challenges these circumstances presented were very great, but an account of them does not of itself provide a satisfactory explanation of the war. We need also to include an account of the aims and policies governments adopted in these circumstances, and of the perceptions and judgements on which they were based.

The powers most interested in maintaining the status quo themselves had somewhat different policies. The British wanted to maintain it as far as possible, but recognised that in order to do so it was necessary to make adjustments and concessions that might win the support of some and mitigate the antagonism of others. Their worldwide interests made this both necessary and extraordinarily difficult and involved many attempts to allocate, prioritise and juggle. The Americans recognised the importance of Britain's independence to their own security, but their approach was not identical. More isolated and more powerful, the USA tended to see foreign policy more in terms of moral principle than negotiated understanding, as was evident in East Asia. Britain's global concerns also made it more difficult to sympathise and co-operate with the more Eurocentric France. Both Britain and France, apprehensive of internal crisis, were fearful of communism, and that nervousness, and Russia's suspicions of the capitalist states, inhibited the development of measures to restrain Germany. But if the interests and attitudes of these powers differed, so too did those of Germany and Japan, though neither was interested in maintaining the status quo.

Before the First World War Germany's leaders had put their wish to change its position in the world in rather confused, though apparently ambitious, forms: they wanted, it seemed, to stake a claim to the leadership of Europe, and thus to a place among the world powers of the future. Under Hitler Germany became ever more uncompromising. Claiming that conflict between individuals and states was the very essence of life, glorifying war, thriving on crises and utilising terror and propaganda to maintain its hold on power, the Nazi regime was not geared to negotiation and moderation. 'A state which dedicates itself to cherishing the best racial elements must some day be master of the world', Hitler had written in *Mein Kampf*.[13]

Japan had framed its foreign policy since the Meiji restoration in terms of a search for 'equality' with other powers. That again was an ill-defined concept. Before the First World War it was pursued in an opportunist way, taking advantage of Britain's need for an alliance and of China's post-revolution chaos. A change of method was prompted both by the Washington treaties and the successful expansion of Japan's international trade, but the Depression undermined it. In the 1930s its military leaders, and those who went along with them, interpreted the quest for equality in an increasingly expansionist way. By the time the USA decided to bring their venture into South-east Asia to a halt, the Japanese had come to see it as a matter of life and death.

Timing was important both to the German leaders and the Japanese. Before the first war, the Germans believed that the opportunity to realise their objectives was short term. The growth of Russia and the USA would foreclose the chance that the relative decline of Great Britain offered. Hitler, too, perceived short-term opportunities that, if a forceful diplomacy could not fulfil, a war could. While the USA hesitated, and with the Soviet Union still weak, he could change the status quo in Europe, perhaps even securing the compliance of the British. For the Japanese, too, timing was important, though they were even more aware than the Germans that the pace was set by others, and their deference to others indeed proved misleading.

The coupling of ambition and uncertainty was a marked feature in the policies of both Germany and Japan as they tried to establish their position in a changing world, combining with – maybe even reinforcing – the *va banque* of Hitler, the insouciance of Konoe, the fatalism of Tojo. It helps to account for their tendency to gamble on the attitudes of others and their practice of applying what force they had with the unusual degree of ruthlessness associated with *Blitzkrieg* and the rape of Nanking and Singapore. It also helps to explain the controversy over the nature of their preparations.

Were they short term or long term? The answer was, surely, both. They had to go for what they could get whenever the opportunity arose, but also to accept that the struggle might be a long-term one, and sometimes the priorities conflicted.

Germany and Japan, and the men who represented and interpreted their interests, were handled by others in different ways. That was a result not only of their own behaviour, but also of the judgements others made about them. Policies towards them were shaped by what statesmen hoped or assumed rather than what they knew: the information they were given was often fitted into a pre-existing pattern. Prolonged attempts were made to 'appease' Hitler, so prolonged in fact that 'appeasement' was later seen as a pejorative term. For Hitler, whatever was offered was but an argument for asking for more: 'settlements' with him were not made in an atmosphere of confidence, nor could they build it up. The Japanese were not 'appeased'. 'If the European Powers would apply to the Far East even a tenth of the flexibility of attitude which they display in dealing with the problems of their own continent', Konoe maintained early in 1938, 'the attainment of stability in this part of the world would be very simple indeed.'[14] It was widely believed that the Japanese would have to give up their attempt to dominate China in any case. Surely, too, they would not dare to fight both the USA and the UK. In the mistaken foreign estimate of the Japanese, which seems widespread throughout the period, there was an element of racial superiority, sustained despite all the evidence of Japanese efficiency and determination. The embargoes did not stop them, though their effects weakened Japan later in the war.

In dealing with Germany, both the Weimar and the Nazi regimes, the British had a passionate belief that there were 'moderates' to whom they could appeal. And moderates were expected to react much as the British did. They would accept limited change brought about by peaceful means. If Phipps could console himself that Hitler had disposed of 'the wild men' in 1934, his successor, Henderson, placed a good deal of faith in the moderating influence of Goering whose hunting and fishing interests seemed to give him some kinship with the English country gentleman. With his passionate hatred of war, Chamberlain found it hard to comprehend that others could desire it. In 1939 he admitted that he had not believed that any 'Government with the interests of its own people at heart would expose them . . . to the horrors of world war.'[15]

A similar difficulty hindered understanding of the Japanese. If there were extremists, there were also 'moderates'. Grew indeed endorsed a pendulum theory: 'Japanese history shows that the country has passed through periodical cycles of intense nationalism attended by anti-foreign sentiment, but these periods have always been followed by other periods of international conciliation and co-operation.'[16] But, as he found, it was easy to exaggerate the potential influence of the moderates and to minimise the extent to which they shared the views of the extremists. 'The difference between the extremists and the moderates', Sir George Sansom concluded in August 1939, 'is not one of destination, but of the road by which that destination is to be reached and the speed at which it is to be travelled.'[17]

Japan's attack on the territories of the USA and the UK was not marked by the hubris of Hitler's attack on the Soviet Union. The Japanese had little hope of long-term success. 'Inevitably, we shall lose this war', wrote Ishiwara Kanji. 'It will be a struggle in which Japan, even though it has only a thousand yen in its pocket, plans to spend ten thousand, while the United States has a hundred thousand, but only needs to spend ten thousand.'[18] The Japanese were conscious of the fragility of their position, which they had been endeavouring to strengthen by implementing the concept of the national defence state. But they were more determined than their opponents realised. Their hope, it seems, was a compromise peace. The aim, said Admiral Tomioka Sadatoshi, was a limited war: attain an overwhelming superiority in the early stages, then seek 'a favourable opportunity' for negotiations.[19] But the Japanese government had not worked out how that might be achieved, so that their attack on South-east Asia resembled in some ways their attack on China in 1937–8: a dramatic exertion of force, unaccompanied by a realistic concept of a new 'settlement' or a means of returning to the diplomatic mode that that would require.

# Epilogue

After the war world politics was dominated by the USA and the Soviet Union, a situation long foreseen. The way the war was fought, however, clearly affected the kind of relationship those superpowers had, one influenced by ideological conflict and the existence of the atomic bomb. Britain and the USA fought on three fronts: in Europe, in the Mediterranean and in East Asia and the Pacific. The Soviet Union fought on one front. It survived the German onslaught and, turning it back, was able to dominate much of eastern and parts of central Europe. Its unprecedented position, and the sense of unity the Great Patriotic War had evoked, encouraged its hopes in the post-war period and aroused the fears of others.

Britain and the USA had expressed their wartime collaboration in terms of a struggle against totalitarianism. That was designed to consolidate the American people, to inspire the mass support the war needed, and to rally the opposition to Germany in the lands it had conquered. The principles had been hammered out in the Atlantic Charter at Placentia Bay in August 1941, after the Japanese had moved on southern Indo-China but before the Pacific war had begun, and after the German attack on the Soviet Union. The alliance with the Soviet Union which that attack precipitated indeed tied the Western allies to a different kind of totalitarianism, that of the communists, who had seized power in the regime crisis precipitated by the pressures of the First World War. Though closer than the connection between Germany and Japan, it was an alliance against a common enemy, rather than one based on common principle. When a 'cold war' developed among the former allies after 1945 it again took an ideological turn. It pitted democracy against communism in Europe, the 'free world' against the communist world, and set the conflicts in the 'third world' in a framework of 'imperialism' and 'liberation'. International relations had been 'globalised', but they had also been 'ideologised'.

Amid the changes the war brought, there were continuities. It is hard to imagine a Europe, united or otherwise, in which a German state of any size did not play a leading role. The war was, however, significant in determining what kind of a German state it would be. Germany was to be divided, initially, into zones of occupation controlled by the Allied powers but later, under the pressure of the cold war, into the longer-term division between the eastern Democratic Republic and the western Federal Republic. The former was a communist state and the latter a democratic one.

The French, as in 1919, had hoped to weaken Germany by detaching part of the Rhineland but, for a second time, they were thwarted by British and American opposition. The French solution on this occasion was to seek an agreement between 'the victors and the vanquished' to 'exercise joint sovereignty over part of their joint resources'.[1] Their recent experience of war and their fear of Soviet expansion led Germany and France to agree to sacrifice something of their sovereignty for the sake of peaceful development and security. From the initial 'Schuman Plan' of 1950, which set up an international authority over the coal and steel production of France, Germany, Italy and the Benelux countries (Belgium, the Netherlands and Luxembourg), other developments towards European unity have followed. The maintenance of Franco-German co-operation has been essential. That provided, according to Alan Milward, 'the central tie in European reconstruction' which had been 'so conspicuously missing in the 1920s'.[2]

Britain was victorious in 1945, but victory had been bought at a high price, as its interwar leaders had feared that it would have to be. Its commitments at the end of the war were very great but its means of meeting them yet more inadequate than pre-war. The first priority was security in Europe. Britain sought closer ties with France and some thought that Britain could lead a 'third force' to balance the United States and the Soviet Union. By 1947, however, Britain felt the need to shed some of its commitments, and by 1949 it was focusing on a 'special relationship' with the USA. That, and its long-standing imperial and commonwealth connections, took precedence over joining the community that France and Germany were developing.

In the 'third world' the imperial relics of the primacy of the British were extensive. They sought not to abandon the relationships with its peoples, but to put them on a new basis. In South-east Asia the British sought to come to terms with nationalism in the territories the Japanese had occupied, though – and once more their policies in different parts of the world were at odds – they found that their European partners, the French and the Dutch, were less ready to do so. 'We must not appear to be ganging up with Western powers against Eastern peoples striving for independence', wrote Esler Dening at the Foreign Office in London in 1947. 'Rather our aim should be to contrive a general partnership between independent or about-to-be-independent Eastern peoples and the Western Powers who by their past experience are best able to give them help.'[3] The advance of communism and the onset of the cold war made it more necessary, the British believed, though their American allies did not always accept their analysis.

The Second World War had indeed changed the position in Asia far more dramatically than the First World War. Again it is hard in the longer term to imagine an East Asia in which, unless it fell apart, China did not resume the major role it had lost in the nineteenth century. The Washington conference of 1921–2 had envisaged a gradual change. The assessments made in the 1930s by those who believed that China would outlast the Japanese had a core of truth, though their estimate of the timing may have been too optimistic, and they neglected to distinguish between China and the regime that rules China. The Sino-Japanese and Pacific wars ensured that it would be a communist regime. The struggle with the Japanese forced Chiang Kai-shek to reduce his struggle against the communists, but the Pacific war prevented his coming to terms with the Japanese. The communists survived and were indeed able to appear as patriots in an anti-foreign struggle. Partly in order to sustain continued Chinese resistance, the Americans had identified Chiang as a major ally, one of the 'Big Four'. Their disappointment, and their sense of failure, were all the greater when the communists triumphed and set up the People's Republic in October 1949.

In South-east Asia the Japanese overthrew colonial regimes which the colonial peoples, despite their restiveness, had not succeeded in overthrowing pre-war. Yet again it might be argued that what happened was a question of timing and that the intervention of the Japanese decided rather the way in which the colonial regimes should end rather than whether they should end at all. The colonial relationship was unlikely to survive the process of modernisation, for which it was necessary to offer education and training on a considerable scale. What might have taken place was a more gradual process of decolonisation, which the British had indeed begun in Burma, and which the USA had advanced in the Philippines. The conquest precipitated the fall of the colonial regimes, the Japanese even finally disposing of the French in March 1945. Nor, as the French had realised, was it easy for a colonial power, once dislodged, to return. None of the colonial powers really succeeded in so doing. With their belief that the Europeans should come to terms with the nationalism the war had unleashed, and so provide a basis for a continued European presence in South-east Asia, the British set an example in Burma, and wanted their allies in Europe – France and the Netherlands – to follow it. Conflict, not compromise, resulted. Burma itself, becoming independent early in 1948, almost collapsed, and in Malaya the British faced the 'Emergency', ascribing it, however, to communism rather than nationalism.

The Japanese had rationalised their action as they failed to secure a settlement and defeat faced them. What they had done would have long-term significance: the Europeans would not again be able to dominate South-east Asia. The Japanese Foreign Office had argued 'that the ideo-logical foundation developed during the war of liberation in Greater East Asia by the Empire, is, regardless of the course of the war, an eventuality which even the enemy must follow and accept.'[4] It was a reasonable assessment. In the future, too, the area was to be open to investment on the part of the revived Japanese economy, so that, although the range of that economy became worldwide, some saw South-east Asia as after all forming part of a co-prosperity sphere. Certainly the Japanese benefited from the knowledge of the resources they had acquired during the occupation, and, somewhat paradoxically, from the links they established with the regional commercial networks of the Chinese. The USA sought to restore Japan's prosperity as a bulwark against communism, and, when it recovered, encouraged it to invest in South-east Asia with the same objective. The payment of relatively modest reparations paved the way.

Indeed, the Japanese role in the world at large, as in South-east Asia, became predominantly an economic one, concerned with export and invest-ment. If there were comparisons with the past, it was with the Japan of Shidehara. 'Even if China becomes a communist nation', he had said in 1927, 'foreigners could live and trade with China after a few years.'[5] But it is also true that the 'economic miracle' owed a great deal to the planning Japan developed during the war, masterminded by Kishi Nobusuke, a member of Tojo's cabinet, who became premier in 1957, and to the nature of the work-force that the war helped to create: subservient, but ready to accept innovation. Probably at MacArthur's instance,[6] an anti-war clause was included in the constitution, and Japan abandoned the concept of army and navy, committing itself only to a self-defence force. Unsurprisingly, being the only state on which atomic bombs had been dropped, it forswore nuclear weapons, and it played a limited role in international politics. The war thus affected the nature of the Japanese state and the way it exerted its power.

The dropping of the atomic bombs on Hiroshima and Nagasaki was significant in other ways. But for the war, not only would their development have been slower but their power would have been less signally demon-strated. That helped to bring the war to an unexpectedly early end. It also helped to determine the nature of the cold war that followed. It was marked by conflict, sometimes traumatic, as in Korea and Vietnam, but never by direct conflict among the major powers. Wars were fought within a fabric of understandings and a web of cautions. Korea was a major conflict, but no bomb was dropped; the UN flag was used, Chinese 'volunteers' were sent. Vietnam was again a major conflict, but only one major power directly involved itself, the USA, and it curbed the use of its power. The Second World War, it can be argued, ensured that there would be no third world war. It, not the First, was 'the war to end war'.

The League of Nations, set up in the aftermath of the First World War, had been paralysed in the 1930s. In the Second World War the Allies resolved not to abandon the attempt to create an effective international organisation, but to set up a more effective one. The United Nations yet remained supplementary to interstate diplomacy. That diplomacy itself underwent other changes, some of them already begun during the war. Conferences and congresses were not new, nor was 'summit diplomacy', but it assumed a larger role. More openness had been sought, at least since the First World War, and certainly interstate issues were now brought into the public domain in a new way, especially with the extension of television. It is doubtful, however, that this means open diplomacy. That is indeed not a credible concept. Apparent openness can conceal rather than reveal, or become part of the diplomacy itself. Widely distributed pictorial evidence of war may limit its role. It may, on the other hand, make the use of power more secretive or more convulsive.

Such forms of conflict and such diplomatic practices developed in the Cold War phase in interstate relations. A major shift followed the collapse of the Soviet Union after 1989. That shift, unlike earlier ones, was managed without major conflict. In the emerging pattern the European powers, drawing together in a union, may seek to play a larger role, and so, of course, will China. The reaction of Japan is still uncertain. A new kind of international politics is in fact being worked out. Knowledge of the past will still be helpful, but it will have to be combined with a recognition that the present is different. The lessons that history may teach are always less precise than those that have been learned. That indeed is a lesson itself. 'Munich', for example, was invoked perhaps too readily by President Truman in the Korean struggle, but also by President Johnson in Vietnam, and comparing Nasser with Hitler could only mislead Anthony Eden. Yet looking back with due caution to a world in which one power enjoyed primacy may still be worthwhile in a world in which, whatever the ambitions of others, one power again enjoys primacy.

And what should popular memory centre upon? The memorials in our villages and towns tend to remind us more of the first war than the second, and more of the soldiers than the civilians. Yet the loss of civilian life was unprecedented. Some 55 million died, perhaps more: about 39 million in the West and the Soviet Union, the rest in Asia. At least a million died in Vietnam, where there was no conflict, and between 2 and 3 million in Java, where there was virtually none. Their memorial might best be found in the contemporary concern for human rights. Though millions have died while international peace prevailed, particularly in Russia and China, '[t]he belief that it is both desirable and possible to guarantee to individuals, through international mechanisms, that certain basic entitlements will be respected, and certain forms of inhumane treatment will be proscribed, is largely a product of the Second World War'.[7]

The scale of the conflict and its atrocities led to the war crimes trials and to the punishment of 'war criminals'. 'Victor's justice' though it might be, it set a precedent of wider relevance. Historians have found it difficult to deal with the question of 'responsibility', still more with that of 'guilt', though, if personal factors are an element in causation, they cannot entirely dismiss those questions. Statesmen have found the questions difficult for other reasons. At the end of the First World War the Allies completely failed to bring the German emperor to account, while giving the impression of punishing the German people as a whole. At the end of the Second World War, as the Allies had promised in the declaration of St James in January 1942 and the Moscow Declaration of November 1943, individuals in Germany and Japan were tried for war crimes, some executed, others imprisoned. The proceedings of the Nuremberg and Tokyo tribunals can be criticised, but they advanced the idea that officials bear individual responsibility for war crimes and crimes against humanity. 'Further, by punishing named individuals for specific acts, they may have helped to reduce pressures for collective punishment, substituting a legal process for the urge for revenge.'[8]

The war had, of course, ended quite differently, with surrender not armistice, and the Allies were in a position, in both Germany and Japan, not only to punish individuals, but also to make drastic changes to their social and political systems. Both Germany and Japan made reparations. The Germans have accepted their defeat, even their responsibility, more fully than the Japanese. The Holocaust, the climax of Hitler's anti-Semitic policies, helped to bring that about. It has no Japanese equivalent. In Japan there is no clarity about responsibility for the war, nor any official interest in encouraging public debate about it. Behind this lies, perhaps, not only a deep conservatism, but a continuing sense among the Japanese of the justice of their cause, and a continued sense that they are treated differently. The post-war settlement left Japan short of the full powers of a state, in some resentful eyes a puppet, an American 'Manchukuo'. In such circumstances apology was more difficult to make, not less.

International history, the late Christopher Thorne suggested, is much more than the history of relations among states. It comprises, too, the relations among peoples, cultural as well as political. It seemed almost unavoidable, he felt, 'that international historians should pursue their enquiries into areas which are usually thought of as the domain of the sociologist or social-psychologist, say, or of the economic or intellectual historian'.[9] Yet in a history of international relations there is an advantage in making the states and their relations with each other the focus of the narrative and of the analysis, while not omitting the other issues that affect those dealings. It makes for a clarity that can too easily be lost in a different kind of international history when not in the hands of a master like Thorne.

It is also helpful in the world of states in which we live. The state has certainly not withered away, as Marx foretold. Nor has it been displaced by triumphant or triumphalist capitalism, of which he predicted the collapse. Its role in economic 'globalisation' is still at the very least a contested one. Nor is the future of the nation state clear. There are moves, for example, both towards European unity and towards the break-up of states into smaller national units. With the collapse of the Soviet Union, Francis Fukuyama wrote of the 'end' of history.[10] Other observers perceive the 'end' of the nation state. But a less dramatic view of these trends is more credible. And even if over time the contemporary system disintegrates, the nature of what replaces it will be better understood if its 'internationalism' has been better understood. The international history of the period of the two world wars, and in particular of the relationship among the states in that period, is of great intrinsic interest, and has had outcomes that have affected the world since the conclusion of the Second World War. But it also offers insights into the way the system worked, and the way men worked within the system, that have an enduring value.

# Notes

## Introduction

1  Akira Iriye, in G. Martel (ed.), *The Origins of the Second World War Reconsidered* (London: Allen and Unwin, 1986), p. 232.
2  F. II. Hinsley, *Power and the Pursuit of Peace* (Cambridge: Cambridge University Press, 1963), p. 302.

## Chapter 1: The First World War

1  Quoted in Keith Wilson in K. M. Wilson (ed.), *British Foreign Secretaries and Foreign Policy: From Crimean War to First World War* (London: Croom Helm, 1987), p. 180.
2  P. M. Kennedy, *The Rise and Fall of the Great Powers: Economic Change and Military Conflict from 1500 to 2000* (London: Fontana, 1989), p. 314.
3  Quoted in H. Rogger, *Russia in the Age of Modernisation and Revolution, 1881–1917* (London: Longman, 1983), p. 247.
4  Quoted in Z. S. Steiner, *The Foreign Office and Foreign Policy, 1898–1914* (Cambridge: Cambridge University Press, 1969), p. 115.
5  Quoted in J. M. Bourne, *Britain and the Great War, 1914–1918* (London: Edward Arnold, 1989), p. 7.
6  Quoted in A. Adamthwaite, *Grandeur and Misery: France's Bid for Power in Europe, 1914–1940* (London: Edward Arnold, 1995), pp. 37–8.
7  Ibid., p. 39.
8  Quoted in M. L. Dockrill and J. D. Goold, *Peace without Promise: Britain and the Peace Conferences, 1919–1923* (London: Batsford, 1981), p. 19.
9  Quoted in A. Sharp, *The Versailles Settlement: Peacemaking in Paris, 1919* (London: Macmillan, 1991), p. 15.
10  Quoted in Dockrill and Goold, *Peace without Promise*, p. 23.
11  E. C. J. Hahn, 'The German Foreign Ministry and the Question of War Guilt, 1918–1919', in C. Fink (ed.), *German Nationalism and the European Response, 1890–1945* (Norman: University of Oklahoma Press, 1985).

12  Akira Iriye, *Pacific Estrangement* (Cambridge, Mass.: Harvard University Press, 1972), pp. 18–19.

13  Cf. Hagihara Nobutoshi's comment in Ian Nish (ed.), *Anglo-Japanese Alienation* (Cambridge University Press, 1982), p. 100.

14  Quoted in Roger F. Hackett, *Yamagata Aritomo in the Rise of Modern Japan* (Cambridge, Mass.: Harvard University Press, 1971), p. 285.

15  Quoted in Barbara Evans Clements, *Bolshevik Feminist* (Bloomington: Indiana University Press, 1980), p. 142.

16  Quoted in Paul Dukes, *October and the World* (London: Macmillan, 1975), p. 96.

17  Quoted in N. Tarling, 'The Singapore Mutiny', *Journal of the Malaysian Branch of the Royal Asiatic Society*, LV (1982) 26.

18  Minute by Langley, n.d., FO 371/2691 (235431/31446), Public Record Office, London.

19  John Tully, *Cambodia under the Tricolour* (Clayton: Monash Asia Institute, 1996), p. 169.

## Chapter 2: The Peace Settlements

1  Quoted in A. Sharp, *The Versailles Settlement: Peacemaking in Paris, 1919* (London: Macmillan, 1991), p. 194.

2  Quoted in A. Adamthwaite, *Grandeur and Misery: France's Bid for Power in Europe, 1914–1940* (London: Edward Arnold, 1995), p. 53.

3  Quoted in Sharp, *Versailles Settlement*, p. 51; quoted in G. H. Bennett, *British Foreign Policy during the Curzon Period, 1919–24* (London: Macmillan, 1995) p. 10.

4  S. Roskill, *Hankey, Man of Secrets*, vol. II: *1919–1931* (London: Collins, 1972) p. 67.

5  *The Treaty of Versailles and After: Annotations of the Text of the Treaty* (Grosse Pointe: Michigan Scholarly Press, 1969), p. 413.

6  Quoted in Sharp, *Versailles Settlement*, p. 109.

7  Quoted in ibid., p. 123.

8  R. C. Self (ed.), *The Austen Chamberlain Diary Letters: The Correspondence of Sir Austen Chamberlain with his Sisters Hilda and Ida, 1916–1937* (Cambridge: Royal Historical Association, 1995), p. 116 (hereafter cited as Chamberlain Diary).

9  Ibid., p. 110.

10  M. Trachtenberg, 'Reparation at the Paris Peace Conference', *The Journal of Modern History*, 51, 1 (1979) 24–55; D. Stevenson, 'France at the Paris Peace Conference', in R. Boyce (ed.), *French Foreign and Defence Policy, 1918–1940* (London: Routledge, 1998).

11  *Papers Relating to the Foreign Relations of the United States: The Paris Peace Conference*, vol. 6 (Washington, 1948) p. 261.

12  Quoted in M. L. Dockrill and J. D. Goold, *Peace without Promise: Britain and the Peace Conferences, 1919–23* (London: Batsford, 1981), p. 111.

13  J. Hiden, *Germany and Europe 1919–1939*, 2nd edn (London: Longman, 1993) pp. 29, 30.

14  M. Trachtenberg, 'Versailles after Sixty Years', *Journal of Contemporary History*, 17, 3 (1982), 487–506.

15  Quoted in A. Lentin, *The Versailles Peace Settlement: Peacemaking with Germany* (London: The Historical Association, 1991), p. 27.

16  Quoted in H. W. V. Temperley (ed.), *A History of the Peace Conference of Paris*, vol. 4 (London: Frowde, 1920–4), p. 429.

17  Quoted in Roskill, *Hankey, Man of Secrets*, vol. II, p. 81.

18  Quoted in Dockrill and Goold, *Peace without Promise*, p. 195.

19  M. L. Dockrill quoting Lloyd George in B. J. C. McKercher and D. J. Moss, *Shadow and Substance in British Foreign Policy, 1895–1939: Memorial Essays Honouring C. J. Lowe* (Edmonton: University of Alberta Press, 1984), p. 206.

20  Quoted in Dockrill and Goold, *Peace without Promise*, p. 147.

21  Quoted in Adamthwaite, *Grandeur*, p. 95.

22  M. S. Anderson, *The Rise of Modern Diplomacy, 1450–1919* (London: Longman, 1994), p. 148; quoted in Sharp, *Versailles Settlement*, p. 157.

23  Quoted in Lentin, *Versailles Peace Settlement*, p.14.

24  Quoted in R. A. Stone, *The Irreconcilables: The Fight against the League of Nations* (Lexington: University Press of Kentucky, 1970), p. 88.

25  Quoted in R. E. Osgood, *Ideals and Self-Interest* (Chicago: University of Chicago Press, 1956), p. 286.

26  Quoted in Stone, *The Irreconcilables*, p. 84.

27  Quoted in Yanaga Chitoshi, *Japan since Perry* (New York: McGraw Hill, 1969), pp. 374, 375.

28  Quoted in R. Fifield, *Woodrow Wilson and the Far East* (Hamden: Archon, reprint, 1965), p. 285.

29  Naoko Shimazu, *Japan, Race and Equality* (London and New York: Routledge, 1998), pp. 49, 67, 165.

30  Akira Iriye, *Pacific Estrangement* (Cambridge, Mass.: Harvard University Press, 1972), p. 232.

31  Quoted in William Roger Louis, *British Strategy in the Far East* (Oxford: Clarendon Press, 1971), p. 64.

32  Quoted in ibid., p. 65.

33  William F. Morton, *Tanaka Giichi and Japan's China Policy* (Folkestone: Dawson, 1980), p. 46.

34  Eliot to Curzon, 17 June, quoted by R. Butler and J. P. T. Bury, *Documents on British Foreign Policy* (London: HMSO, 1966), XIV, p. 43.

35  See Saduo Oba, *The Japanese War*, trans. Anne Kareko (Sandgate: Japan Library, 1995), p.20.

36  James B. Crowley, *Japan's Quest for Autonomy* (Princeton University Press, 1966), p. 27.

37  Quoted in C. Thorne, *The Limits of Foreign Policy* (London: Hamilton, 1972), p. 51.

38  Ibid., p. 28.

39  Quoted in W. G. Beasley, *Japanese Imperialism* (Oxford: Clarendon, 1987), p. 118.

40  Quoted in Joyce C. Lebra, *Okuma Shigenobu: Statesman of Meiji Japan* (Canberra: Australian National University Press, 1973) p. 119.

41  Quoted in Peter Duus, *Party Rivalry and Political Change in Taisho Japan* (Cambridge, Mass.: Harvard University Press, 1968), pp. 63–4.

42  Gordon M. Berger, *Parties Out of Power in Japan* (Princeton University Press, 1977), p. 354.
43  Quoted in N. Tarling, 'A Vital British Interest', *Journal of Southeast Asian Studies*, 9, 2 (1978) 190.
44  Ibid., p.191.
45  Quoted in ibid., p.192.

# Chapter 3: The Implementation of the Peace Settlements

1  S. Marks, *The Illusion of Peace: International Relations in Europe, 1918–1933* (London: Macmillan, 1976); P. M. H. Bell, *The Origins of the Second World War in Europe*, 2nd edn (London: Longman, 1997). Bell's first two chapters provide a useful summary of the arguments for and against the view that the whole interwar period was part of a thirty-year war against German expansion.
2  Forty volumes of German documents on the origin of the war, *Die Grosse Politik der Europäischen Kabinette, 1871–1914*, were published between 1922 and 1927. The British began publication of their documents in 1926 and the French in 1929.
3  J. Jacobson, 'Is there a New International History of the 1920s?', *American Historical Review*, 88 (1983), 623. This article and J. Jacobson 'Strategies of French Foreign Policy after World War I', *Journal of Modern History*, 55 (1983), 78–95 provide a good introduction and commentary on much of this new material.
4  Carole Fink, 'German Revisionspolitik, 1919–1933', paper delivered at the Canadian Historical Association meeting, Winnipeg, 7 June 1986.
5  Quoted in A. Adamthwaite, *Grandeur and Misery: France's Bid for Power in Europe, 1914–1940* (London: Edward Arnold, 1995), p. 74; G. H. Bennett, *British Foreign Policy during the Curzon Period, 1919–24* (London: Macmillan, 1995), pp. 23, 27.
6  Adamthwaite, *Grandeur*, p. 75.
7  *Times*, 7 October 1922.
8  Quoted in W. N. Medlicott, *Contemporary England, 1914–1964* (London: Longman, 1967), p. 166.
9  M. Howard, *The Continental Commitment* (London: Temple Smith, 1972), p. 75.
10  R. C. Self (ed.), *The Austen Chamberlain Diary Letters: The Correspondence of Sir Austen Chamberlain with his sisters Hilda and Ida, 1916–1937* (Cambridge: Royal Historical Association, 1995), p. 122 (hereafter cited as Chamberlain Diary).
11  Many examples of this German activity are provided by F. Carsten, *Britain and the Weimar Republic* (London: Batsford, 1984), pp. 19ff, 32, 34, 49ff.
12  Quoted in S. Roskill, *Hankey, Man of Secrets*, vol. II: *1919–1931* (London: Collins, 1972), p. 181.
13  S. Schuker in G. Martel, *The Origins of the Second World War Reconsidered: The A. J. P. Taylor Debate after Twenty-five years* (London: Allen & Unwin, 1986), p. 55.
14  Quoted in B. Kent, *The Spoils of War: The Politics, Economics and Diplomacy of Reparations, 1918–1932* (Oxford: Oxford University Press, 1989), p. 137.

15  There has been a particularly vigorous debate between Sally Marks and David Felix. S. Marks, 'Reparations Reconsidered', *Central European History*, 2 (1969), 356–65; 'Reparations Reconsidered, a Rejoinder', *Central European History*, 5 (1972), 358–61; 'The Myths of Reparations', *Central European History*, 11 (1978), 231–55; D. Felix, 'Reparations Reconsidered with a Vengeance', *Central European History*, 4 (1971), 171–9.

16  J. A. S. Grenville, *The Major International Treaties, 1914–1973* (Methuen: London, 1974), pp. 139–40.

17  S. Marks, '1918 and After: The Post-War Era', in G. Martel (ed.), *The Origins of the Second World War Reconsidered* (London: Allen & Unwin, 1986), p. 35; A. Orde, 'Britain and European Reconstruction after the Great War', in P. Catterall and C. J. Morris (eds), *Britain and the Threat to Stability in Europe, 1918–1945* (London: St Martin's Press, 1993), p. 11.

18  P. Guinn, 'Poincaré, the Entente and the Ruhr Occupation', *European History Quarterly*, 18 (1988), 427–39, and J. F. V. Keiger, 'Raymond Poincaré and the Ruhr Crisis', in R. Boyce (ed.), *French Foreign and Defence Policy, 1918–1940* (London: Routledge & Kegan Paul, 1998), pp. 49–70.

19  Quoted in S. A. Schuker, *The End of French Predominance in Europe* (Chapel Hill: University of North Carolina Press, 1976), pp. 127, 218.

20  Quoted in Chamberlain Diary, p. 265.

21  Chamberlain Diary, p. 266.

22  J. Barnes and D. Nicholson, *The Leo Amery Diaries*, vol.1: *1896–1929* (London: Hutchinson, 1980), p. 399.

23  Grenville, *Major International Treaties*, pp. 101–8.

24  Chamberlain Diary, pp. 282–3.

25  Ibid., p. 283.

26  Surveys of literature on Stresemann can be found in H. W. Gatzke, 'Gustav Stresemann: A Bibliographical Article', *Journal of Modern History*, 36 (1964), 1–13; R. Grathwol, 'Gustav Stresemann: Reflections on his Foreign Policy', *Journal of Modern History*, 45 (1973), 52–70.

27  K. Hildebrand, *The Foreign Policy of the Third Reich* (London: Batsford, 1973), pp. 9 ff; J. Hiden, *Germany and Europe, 1919–1939*, 2nd edn (Harlow: Longman, 1993), p. 79.

28  Quoted in J. M. Hughes, *To the Maginot Line: The Politics of French Military Preparation in the 1920s* (Cambridge, Mass.: Harvard University Press, 1971), pp. 141, 142.

29  Adamthwaite, *Grandeur*, p. 125.

30  Quoted in Adamthwaite, *Grandeur*, p. 134.

31  C. J. Bartlett, *British Foreign Policy in the Twentieth Century* (London: Macmillan, 1989), p. 37.

32  Chamberlain Diary, p. 314.

33  J. Jacobsen, *American Historical Review*, 88 (1983), 644.

34  See N. Clifford, *Retreat from China* (London: Longman, 1967), p. 6; also William Roger Louis, *British Strategy in the Far East* (Oxford: Clarendon Press, 1971), pp. 153–4.

35  C. Thorne, *The Limits of Foreign Policy* (London: Hamilton, 1972), p. 32.

36  Quoted in ibid., p. 35.

37  George A. Lensen, *Japanese Recognition of the USSR* (Tokyo: Sophia University Press, 1970), p. 163 ff.

38  Ibid., pp. 350–1.

39  Nobuya Bamba, *Japanese Diplomacy in a Dilemma* (Vancouver: University of British Columbia Press, 1972), pp. 163–4.

40  Quoted in Yanaga Chitoshi, *Europe since Perry* (New York: McGraw-Hill, 1969), p. 448.

41  Quoted in James B. Crowley, *Japan's Quest for Autonomy* (Princeton University Press, 1966), pp. 31–2.

42  William F. Morton, *Tanaka Giichi and Japan's China Policy* (Folkestone: Dawson, 1980), p. 130.

43  Quoted in ibid., p. 131.

44  Quoted in ibid., p. 132.

45  Quoted in Crowley, *Japan's Quest*, p. 32.

46  Quoted in Peter Duus, *Party Rivalry and Political Change in Taisho Japan* (Cambridge, Mass: Harvard University Press, 1968), p. 146.

47  Morton, *Tanaka Giichi*, pp. 65–6.

48  Quoted in Duus, *Party Rivalry*, p. 24.

49  Bamba, *Japanese Diplomacy*, p. 61.

50  G. M. Wilson, *Radical Nationalist in Japan* (Cambridge, Mass.: Harvard University Press, 1969), p. 87.

51  Quoted in Richard Storry, *The Double Patriots* (London: Chatto, 1957), p. 38.

52  Quoted in Wilson, *Radical Nationalist*, pp. 82, 86.

53  Duus, *Party Rivalry*, p. 244.

54  Ibid., p. 244.

55  Quoted in Tetsuo Najita, *Hara Kei in the Politics of Compromise* (Cambridge, Mass.: Harvard University Press, 1967), pp. 18–19.

56  Quoted in Sadako Ogata, *Defiance in Manchuria* (Berkeley and Los Angeles: University of California Press, 1964), p. 152.

57  Quoted in Richard D. Burns and E. M. Bennett (eds), *Diplomats in Crisis* (Santa Barbara: ABC-Clio, 1974), p. 276.

58  Quoted in Akira Iriye, *After Imperialism* (Cambridge, Mass.: Harvard University Press, 1965), pp. 300–1.

## Chapter 4: The Depression

1  R. Boyce, 'World Depression, World War: Some Economic Origins of the Second World War', in R. Boyce and E. M. Robertson (eds), *Paths to War: New Essays on the Origins of the Second World War* (Basingstoke: Macmillan, 1989) p. 55.

2  Some of the main sources are: J. Noakes, *The Nazi Party in Lower Saxony, 1921–1933* (Oxford University Press, 1971); G. Pridham, *Hitler's Rise to Power: The Nazi Movement in Bavaria, 1923–1933* (London: Hart-Davis MacGibbon, 1973); R. F. Hamilton, *Who Voted for Hitler?* (Princeton: Princeton University Press, 1982); M. H. Kater, *The Nazi*

*Party: A Social Profile of Members and Leaders, 1919–1945* (Oxford: Blackwell, 1983); T. Childers, *The Nazi Voter: The Social Foundation of Fascism in Germany, 1919–1933* (Chapel Hill: University of North Carolina Press, 1983).

3 Quoted in B. Kent, *The Spoils of War: The Politics, Economics and Diplomacy of Reparations, 1918–1932* (Oxford: Oxford University Press, 1989), p. 329.

4 A. Hitler, *Mein Kampf*, trans. R. Mannheim (London: Hutchinson, 1969), pp. 596–9.

5 Quoted in M. Gilbert, *Winston S. Churchill*, vol. V: *1922–1939* (London: Heinemann, 1976), p. 455.

6 Quoted in K. Feiling, *The Life of Neville Chamberlain* (London: Macmillan, 1976), p. 199.

7 Quoted in A. Adamthwaite, *Grandeur and Misery: France's Bid for Power in Europe, 1914–1940* (London: Edward Arnold, 1995), p. 135.

8 F. G. Stambrook, 'The German–Austrian Customs Union Project of 1931: A Study of German Methods and Motives', *Journal of Central European Affairs*, 21 (1961), 15–44, and A. Orde, 'The Origin of the German–Austrian Customs Union Affair of 1931', *Central European History*, 13 (1980), 34–59.

9 Quoted in N. Waites in N. Waites (ed.), *Troubled Neighbours: Franco-British Relations in the Twentieth Century* (London: Weidenfeld and Nicolson, 1971), p. 134.

10 A good introduction to the economic aspects of international relations in the early 1930s can be found in the essay by Boyce in Boyce and Robertson (eds), *Paths to War*, pp. 55–95. A more detailed discussion of French economic policy is in R. Boyce, 'Business as Usual: The Limits of French Economic Diplomacy', in R. Boyce (ed.), *French Foreign and Defence Policy, 1918–1940* (London: Routledge & Kegan Paul, 1998), pp. 107–31. On Britain, there is R. Boyce, 'Was there a "British" Alternative to the Briand Plan?' in P. Catterall and C. J. Morris (eds), *Britain and the Threat to Security in Europe, 1918–1945* (London: St Martin's Press, 1993), pp. 17–34.

11 Quoted in R. Boyce and E. R. Robertson (eds), *Paths to War*, p. 85.

12 Quoted in S. Roskill, *Hankey, Men of Secrets*, vol. II: *1919–1931* (London: Collins, 1972), p. 517.

13 Quoted in A. P. Adamthwaite, *The Making of the Second World War* (London: Allen & Unwin, 1977), p. 123; M. Gilbert, *Sir Horace Rumbold: Portrait of a Diplomat, 1869–1941* (London: Heinemann, 1973), p. 381.

14 Quoted in Adamthwaite, *Grandeur*, p. 188.

15 A. Adamthwaite, *France and the Coming of the Second World War* (London: Frank Cass, 1977), p. xiii.

16 Quoted in Feiling, *Life of Neville Chamberlain*, p. 226.

17 Quoted in James B. Crowley, *Japan's Quest for Autonomy* (Princeton University Press, 1966), p. 102.

18 James C. Thomson et al., *Sentimental Imperialists: The American Experience in East Asia* (New York: Harper, 1981). p. 154.

19 Crowley, *Japan's Quest*, p. 112.

20 Bernd Martin, *Japan and Germany in the Modern World* (Oxford: Berghahn, 1995), p. 212.

21  Sadako Ogata, *Defiance in Manchuria* (Berkeley and Los Angeles: University of California Press, 1964), pp. 58–9. Crowley, *Japan's Quest*, p.120.

22  Quoted in Ogata, p. 81.

23  Quoted in Crowley, *Japan's Quest*, p. 126.

24  Quoted in ibid., p. 150.

25  Quoted in ibid., p. 158.

26  Quoted in ibid., pp. 182–3.

27  Quoted in Richard Storry, *The Double Patriots* (London: Chatto, 1957), p. 85.

28  Quoted in Crowley, *Japan's Quest*, p. 185.

29  Quoted in William Roger Louis, *British Strategy in the Far East* (Oxford: Clarendon Press, 1971), p. 219.

30  Memo, February 1931 (*lapsus calami* for 1932), quoted in Louis, *British Strategy*, p. 187.

31  Quoted in C. Thorne, *The Limits of Foreign Policy* (London: Hamilton, 1992), p. 143.

32  Quoted in Thomson, *Sentimental Imperialists*, p. 179.

33  Quoted in Thorne, *Limits*, p. 162.

34  Quoted in Louis, *British Strategy*, p. 196.

35  Thorne, *Limits*, p. 272.

36  Quoted in ibid., p. 281.

37  Quoted in I. Nish, *Japan's Struggle with Internationalism* (London: Routledge & Kegan Paul, 1993), p. 171.

38  Quoted in Louis, *British Strategy*, p. 206.

39  Nish, *Struggle*, p. 179.

40  Quoted in ibid., p.189.

41  Thorne, *Limits*, p. 360.

42  Sir John Pratt, quoted in Crowley, *Japan's Quest*, p. 156.

43  Quoted by N. Graebner, in D. Borg and S. Okamoto (eds), *Pearl Harbor as History* (Cambridge, Mass.: Harvard University Press, 1964), p. 32.

44  Quoted in Thorne, *Limits*, p. 344.

45  Ogata, *Defiance*, p. 178.

46  Quoted in Reginald Bassett, *Democracy and Foreign Policy* (London: Longman, 1952), p. 5.

47  Quoted in Thorne, *Limits*, p. 8.

48  Quoted in ibid., p. 284.

49  J. W. Dower, *Empire and Aftermath: Yoshida Shigeru and the Japanese Experience* (Cambridge, Mass.: Harvard University Press, 1979), p. 97.

## Chapter 5: The End of Collective Security

1  Quoted in D. Mack Smith, *Mussolini* (London: Weidenfeld and Nicolson, 1981), p. 199.

2  Quoted in G. Scott, *The Rise and Fall of the League of Nations* (London: Hutchinson, 1973), p. 288.

3  Quoted in A Adamthwaite, *The Making of the Second World War* (London: Allen & Unwin, 1977), p. 139. For further discussion of British policy see H. H. Hall III, 'The Foreign Policy Making Process in Britain, 1934–35, and the Origins of the Anglo-German Naval Agreement', *The Historical Journal*, **19** (1976), 477–99.

4  Quoted in A. Adamthwaite, *The Lost Peace: International Relations in Europe, 1918–1939* (London: Edward Arnold, 1980), p. 165.

5  This argument has been put forward very strongly by R. Lamb, *Mussolini and the British* (London: John Murray, 1997), pp. 118–20.

6  Quoted in Nicole Jordan, 'The Cut Price War on the Peripheries: The French General Staff, the Rhineland and Czechoslovakia', in R. Boyce and E. M. Robertson (eds), *Paths to War: New Essays on the Origins of the Second World War* (Basingstoke: Macmillan, 1989), p. 139.

7  The importance of public opinion and the extent to which it was orchestrated by the League of Nations Union is discussed by D. Waley, *British Public Opinion and the Abyssinian War, 1935–6* (London: Temple Smith, 1975).

8  Quoted in Steven Morewood, 'The Chiefs of Staff, the Men on the Spot and the Italo-Abyssinian Emergency, 1935–36', in D. Richardson and G. Stone (eds), *Decisions and Diplomacy: Essays in Twentieth-Century International History* (London: Routledge & Kegan Paul, 1995), p. 102.

9  *The Times*, 23 December 1935.

10  A. Eden, *The Eden Memoirs: Facing the Dictators* (London: Cassell, 1962), p. 326.

11  B. Bond (ed.), *Chief of Staff: The Diaries of Lieutenant-General Sir Henry Pownall*, vol. 1: *1933–1940* (London: Leo Cooper, 1972), p. 104 (hereafter cited as Pownall Diaries).

12  Memo by Eden on 'The German Danger', 17 January 1936, Documents on British Foreign Policy (DBFP) (London: HMSO, 1946), second series, vol. xv, no. 460.

13  N. Nicolson (ed.), *Diaries and Letters, 1930–1939* (London: Collins, 1966), p. 250 (hereafter cited as Nicolson Diaries).

14  S. Azzi, 'The Historiography of Fascist Foreign Policy', *Historical Journal*, **36** (1993), 187–203.

15  Quoted in J. T. Emmerson, *The Rhineland Crisis, 7 March 1936* (London: Temple Smith, 1977), p. 237.

16  P. M. H. Bell, *The Origins of the Second World War in Europe* (Harlow: Longman 1986), p. 208; J. Harvey (ed.), *The Diplomatic Diaries of Oliver Harvey, 1937–1940* (London: Collins, 1970) [hereafter *Harvey Diary*], p. 28.

17  W. S. Churchill, *The Gathering Storm* (London: Cassell, 1948), pp. 150–70.

18  S. Schuker, 'France and the Remilitarization of the Rhineland 1936', *French Historical Studies*, **14** (1986), 299–338, defends the decision of the French government and argues that the opportunity to 'stop' Hitler had already been lost owing to the weakening of France's economic, military and diplomatic position.

19  M. Gilbert, *Churchill, 1922–39* (London: Heinemann, 1976), vol. 5, pp. 774, 775.

20  Pownall Diaries, pp. 106, 108.

21  Quoted in Nicolson Diaries, p. 258.

22  Quoted in James B. Crowley, *Japan's Quest for Autonomy* (Princeton University Press, 1966), p. 195.

*Notes*

23  James W. Morley, *The China Quagmire* (New York: Columbia University Press, 1983), pp. 79–80.
24  Quoted in Crowley, *Japan's Quest*, p. 199.
25  Ibid., p. 219.
26  Stephen E. Pelz, *Race to Pearl Harbor* (Cambridge, Mass.: Harvard University Press, 1974), p. 172.
27  Quoted in Crowley, *Japan's Quest*, pp. 295–6.
28  Ibid., p. 300.
29  F. W. Ikle, *German–Japanese Relations 1936–40* (New York: Bookman, 1956), p. 38.
30  Quoted in William Roger Louis, *British Strategy in the Far East* (Oxford: Clarendon Press, 1971), p. 241.
31  R. C. J. Butow, *Tojo and the Coming of the War* (Stanford University Press, 1961), p. 67.
32  Pelz, *Pearl Harbor*, p. 167.
33  Crowley, *Japan's Quest*, pp. 245–6.
34  See Andrew Gordon, *Labor and Imperial Dermocracy in Pre-War Japan* (Berkeley: University of California Press, 1991), p. 283 ff.
35  Quoted in C. Thorne, *The Limits of Foreign Policy* (London: Hamilton, 1972), p. 71.
36  Ann Trotter, *Britain and East Asia, 1933–1937* (Cambridge University Press, 1975), p. 193.
37  Sir John Pratt, quoted in ibid., p. 38.
38  Quoted in Pelz, *Pearl Harbor*, p. 107.
39  N. Graebner in D. Borg and S. Okamoto (eds), *Pearl Harbor as History* (Cambridge, Mass.: Harvard University Press, 1964), p. 35.
40  Quoted in Graebner, in ibid., p. 36.
41  Quoted in E. L. Presseisen, *Germany and Japan: A Study in Totalitarian Diplomacy* (The Hague: Nijhoff, 1958), p. 32.
42  Quoted in Thorne, *Limits*, p. 357.
43  Presseisen, *Germany and Japan*, p. 74.
44  Carl Boyd, *The Extraordinary Envoy: General Hiroshi Oshima and Diplomacy in the Third Reich* (Washington: University of Washington Press, 1980), p. 41.
45  Ibid., p. 44.
46  Presseisen, *Germany and Japan*, p. 107.

## Chapter 6: Appeasement

1  Examples of early post-war writing are L. B. Namier, *Europe in Decay: A Study in Disintegration* (London: Macmillan, 1949); W. J. Hofer, *War Premeditated* (London: Thames and Hudson, 1955).
2  Some idea of the nature of that debate can be gathered from E. M. Robertson (ed.), *The Origins of the Second World War* (London: Macmillan, 1971), pp. 83–224.
3  I. Kershaw, *The Nazi Dictatorship: Problems and Perspectives of Interpretation* (London: Edward Arnold, 1989), p. 120. Good introductions to the debate between 'intentionalist'

and 'structuralist' historians can be found in Kershaw, *The Nazi Dictatorship*, pp. 107–30, and in J. Hiden and J. Farquaharson, *Explaining Hitler's Germany: Historians and the Third Reich* (London: Batsford, 1989), pp. 110–29.

4 Quoted in G. L. Weinberg, *The Foreign Policy of Hitler's Germany: Diplomatic Revolution in Europe, 1933–36* (London and Chicago: University of Chicago Press, 1970), p. 355.

5 A. S. Milward, *The German Economy at War* (London: Athlone Press, 1965); B. A. Carroll, *Design for Total War: Arms and Economics in the Third Reich* (The Hague: Mouton, 1968).

6 R. J. Overy, *War and Economy in the Third Reich* (Oxford: Clarendon Press, 1994). This work contains the major articles in which Overy has argued his case.

7 Quoted in Glyn Stone, 'The European Great Powers and the Spanish Civil War, 1936–1939', in R. Boyce and E. M. Robertson (eds), *Paths to War: New Essays on the Origins of the Second World War* (Basingstoke: Macmillan, 1989), p. 201.

8 Quoted in Hiden, *Germany and Europe, 1919–1939*, 2nd edn (Harlow: Longman, 1993), p. 185.

9 Quoted in Enrique Moradiellos in P. Catterall and C. J. Morris (eds), *Britain and the Threat to Security in Europe, 1918–1945* (London: St Martin's Press, 1993) p. 97. The essay by Glyn Stone in Boyce and Robertson provides a good introduction to the whole question of foreign intervention in the Spanish civil war. D. Little, 'Red Scare 1936: Anti-Bolshevism and the Origins of British Non-Intervention in the Spanish Civil War', *Journal of Contemporary History*, 23 (1988), 292–311, argues that fear of communism rather than strategic considerations was the determining factor in Britain's policy towards Spain.

10 Quoted in D. Dilks (ed.), *The Diaries of Sir Alexander Cadogan, 1938–1945* (London: Cassell, 1971), p. 30 (hereafter cited as Cadogan Diaries).

11 Quoted in D. Dutton, *Anthony Eden: A Life and Reputation* (London: Edward Arnold, 1997), p. 108.

12 Quoted in S. Roskill, *Hankey, Man of Secrets*, vol. III: *1931–1963* (London: Collins, 1974), p. 304; quoted in G. L. Weinberg, *The Foreign Policy of Hitler's Germany: Starting World War II, 1937–1939* (Chicago and London: University of Chicago Press, 1980), p. 135.

13 Quoted in Sidney Aster in R. Boyce and E. M. Robertson (eds), *Paths to War*, p. 244.

14 Quoted in J. T. Emmerson, *The Rhineland Crisis, 7 March 1936* (London: Temple Smith, 1977), p. 244.

15 Quoted in Weinberg, *Starting World War II*, p. 296

16 Halifax to Henderson, 11 March 1938, DBFP 3rd series, vol. 1, no. 44.

17 Cadogan Diaries, p. 55; A. Adamthwaite, *France and the Coming of the Second World War* (London: Frank Cass, 1977) p. 75.

18 Quoted in K. Feiling, *The Life of Neville Chamberlain* (London: Macmillan, 1976), p. 342.

19 Quoted in Weinberg, *Starting World War II*, p. 339.

20 Halifax to Henderson, 21 May 1938, DBFP 3rd series, vol. 1, no. 250.

21 Quoted in J. Noakes and G. Pridham (eds), *Nazism, 1919–1945: A History in Documents and Eyewitness Accounts*, vol. 2 (New York: Schocken Books, 1988), p. 712.

# Notes

22  Quoted in B. Bond (ed.), *Chief of Staff: The Diaries of Lieutenant-General Sir Henry Pownall*, vol. I: *1933–1940* (London: Leo Cooper, 1972), p. 143 (hereafter cited as Pownall Diaries).

23  J. W. Wheeler-Bennett, *Munich: Prologue to Tragedy* (London: Macmillan, 1948), pp. 33–4.

24  J.-B. Duroselle, *La Decadence, 1932–39* (Paris: Impr. Nationale, 1979); M. Baumont, *Origins of the Second World War*, trans. Simone De Couvreur Ferguson (New Haven, Conn.: Yale University Press, 1978).

25  Anthony Adamthwaite in W. J. Mommsen and L. Kettenacker (eds), *The Fascist Challenge and the Policy of Appeasement* (London: Allen and Unwin, 1983), pp. 246–56; R. J. Young in G. Martel, *The Origins of the Second World War Reconsidered: The A. J. P. Taylor Debate after Twenty-five Years* (London: Allen & Unwin, 1986), pp. 97–118. Both authors stress the 'independence' of French policy makers, but while Adamthwaite is critical of the indecisive nature of their choices, Young is more sympathetic to their uncertainty.

26  R Girault, 'The Impact of the Economic Situation on the Foreign Policy of France, 1936–9', in Mommsen and Kettenacker (eds), *Fascist Challenge*, pp. 209–23.

27  Quoted in A. Adamthwaite, *Grandeur and Misery: France's Bid for Power in Europe, 1914–1940* (London: Edward Arnold, 1995), p. 208.

28  Quoted in W. D. Irvine, *French Conservatism in Crisis* (Baton Rouge: Louisiana State University Press, 1979), p. 176.

29  Y. Lacaze, 'France and the Munich Crisis', in R. Boyce (ed.), *French Foreign and Defence Policy, 1918–1940* (London: Routledge & Kegan Paul, 1998), p. 228.

30  Quoted in J. E. Dreifort, *Yvon Delbos at the Quai D'Orsay* (Lawrence: University Press of Kansas, 1973), p. 181.

31  Quoted in Lacaze in Boyce (ed.), *French Foreign and Defence Policy*, p. 225; quoted in Adamthwaite in Mommsen and Kettenacker (eds), *Fascist Challenge*, p. 247.

32  Lacaze in Boyce, *French Foreign and Defence Policy*, p. 229.

33  Quoted in Adamthwaite in Mommsen and Kettanacker, (eds), *Fascist Challenge*, pp. 250, 249.

34  G. Jukes, 'The Red Army and the Munich Crisis', *Journal of Contemporary History*, 26 (1991), 195–214; J. Haslam, *The Soviet Union and the Struggle for Collective Security in Europe, 1933–1939* (London: Macmillan, 1984); G. Roberts, *The Soviet Union and the Origins of the Second World War* (Basingstoke: Macmillan, 1995).

35  Young in Martel, *Origins*, p. 105.

36  Quoted in A. Eden, *The Eden Memoirs: Facing the Dictators* (London: Cassell, 1962), p. 478.

37  J. K. Ferris, ' "The Greatest Power on Earth": Great Britain in the 1920s' and B. J. C. McKercher, ' "Our Most Dangerous Enemy": Great Britain Pre-eminent in the 1930s', *The International History Review*, 13 (1991), 726–50, 751–83.

38  Quoted in Cadogan Diaries, p. 30.

39  Quoted in Michael Howard in D. Dilks, *Retreat from Power: Studies in British Foreign Policy in the Twentieth Century*, vol. I: *1906–1939* (London: Macmillan,1981), p. 114.

40  W. K. Wark, *The Ultimate Enemy: British Intelligence and Nazi Germany, 1933–1939* (Oxford: Oxford University Press, 1986), pp. 232, 231.

41 Quoted in Michael Howard in Dilks, *Retreat*, p. 114.

42 Quoted in Hans-Jürgen Schröder in Mommsen and Kettenacker (eds), *Fascist Challenge*, p. 395.

43 J. Harvey (ed.), *The Diplomatic Diaries of Oliver Harvey, 1937–1940* (London: Collins, 1970), pp. 69–70 (hereafter cited as Harvey Diaries).

44 Harvey Diaries, p. 69.

45 Quoted in I. Colvin, *The Chamberlain Cabinet* (London: Gollancz, 1971), p. 68; B. R. Farnham, *Roosevelt and the Munich Crisis* (Princeton: Princeton University Press, 1997), p. 49.

46 Quoted in A. Adamthwaite, *The Making of the Second World War* (London: Allen & Unwin, 1977) p. 183.

47 P. Kennedy, 'The Tradition of Appeasement in British Foreign Policy, 1865–1939', *British Journal of International Studies*, 2 (1976), 195.

48 Quoted in W. N. Medlicott in Dilks, *Retreat*, p. 83.

49 Pownall Diaries, p. 162; L. W. Fuscher, *Neville Chamberlain and Appeasement* (New York: Norton, 1982), p. 33.

50 Quoted in Lord Birkenhead, *The Life of Lord Halifax* (London: Hamish Hamilton, 1965), p. 425.

51 Cadogan Diaries, p. 63.

52 R. Cockett, *Twilight of Truth: Appeasement and the Manipulation of the Press* (New York: St Martin's Press, 1989).

53 Lord Ismay, *Memoirs* (London: Heinemann, 1960), p. 92; quoted in B. Bond, *British Military Policy between Two World Wars* (Oxford: Clarendon Press, 1980), p. 281.

54 S. Aster, ' "Guilty Men": The Case of Neville Chamberlain', in Boyce and Robertson (eds) *Paths to War*, pp. 233–68; R. A. C. Parker, *Chamberlain and Appeasement: Britain and the Coming of the Second World War* (London: Macmillan, 1988).

55 Quoted in Adamthwaite, *France and the Coming*, p. 329.

56 Quoted in James B. Crowley, *Japan's Quest for Autonomy* (Princeton University Press, 1966), p. 339.

57 Ibid., p. 350.

58 Quoted in ibid., p. 375.

59 N. Clifford, *Retreat from China* (London: Longman, 1967), p. 91.

60 Quoted in Crowley, *Japan's Quest*, p. 378.

61 Quoted in Crowley in J. W. Morley (ed.), *Japan's Foreign Policy, 1868–1941* (New York: Columbia University Press, 1974), p. 78.

62 Quoted in G. M. Berger, *Parties Out of Power in Japan* (Princeton University Press, 1977), p. 145.

63 Michael A. Barnhart, *Japan Prepares for Total War* (Ithaca: Cornell University Press, 1987), p. 105.

64 Gordon Berger, *Parties out of Power in Japan* (Princeton University Press, 1977), pp. 138–9.

65 Quoted in A. Best, *Britain, Japan and Pearl Harbor* (London: Routledge & Kegan Paul 1995), p. 43.

66 Quoted in William Louis, *British Strategy in the Far East* (Oxford: Clarendon Press, 1971), p. 241.

67 Quoted in Best, *Britain, Japan*, p. 43.

68 Louis, *British Strategy*, pp. 241–2.

69 Bradford A. Lee, *Britain and the Sino-Japanese War, 1937–9* (Stanford University Press, 1973), pp. 124–5.

70 Quoted in Louis, *British Strategy*, p. 249.

71 Lee, *Sino-Japanese War*, p. 111.

72 Cadogan, 23 December 1938, quoted in P. Lowe, *Great Britain and the Origins of the Pacific War* (Oxford: Clarendon Press, 1977), p. 53.

73 Cadogan, in Lee, *Sino-Japanese War*, p. 145.

74 Press release, 16 July 1937, *Foreign Relations of the United States, Japan*, 1 (Washington: Government Printing Office, 1943), p. 326.

75 N. Graebner, in D. Borg and S. Okamoto (eds), *Pearl Harbor as History* (Cambridge, Mass.: Harward University Press, 1964), p. 36.

76 Ibid., p. 37.

77 Quoted in Farnham, *Roosevelt and the Munich Crisis*, p. 65.

78 Quoted in Clifford, *Retreat*, p. 33.

79 Graebner, in Borg and Okamoto (eds), *Pearl Harbor as History*, p. 39.

80 Quoted in M. Murfett, *Foolproof Relations: The Search for Anglo-American Naval Cooperation during the Chamberlain Years* (Singapore University Press, 1984), p. 81.

81 David Reynolds, *The Creation of the Anglo-American Alliance, 1937–41* (London: Europa, 1981), p. 61.

82 John P. Fox, *Germany and the Far Eastern Crisis* (Oxford: Clarendon Press, 1982), p. 330.

83 E. L. Presseisen, *Germany and Japan: A Study in Totalitarian Diplomacy* (The Hague: Nijhoff, 1958), p. 164.

84 Ibid., p. 184.

85 Ibid., p. 172.

86 Alvin Coox, *Nomonhan* (Stanford University Press, 1985), vol. 1, pp. 131ff.

87 Lee, *Sino-Japanese War*, pp. 138–9.

## Chapter 7: The War of 1939

1 D. Dilks (ed.), *The Diaries of Sir Alexander Cadogan, 1938–1945* (London: Cassell, 1971), p. 120 (hereafter cited as Cadogan Diaries).

2 Quoted in Noakes and G. Pridham (eds), *Nazism, 1919–1945: A History in Documents and Eyewitness Accounts*, vol. 2 (New York: Schocken Books, 1988), pp. 721–2, 724.

3 Quoted in ibid., p. 728; quoted in D. C. Watt, *How War Came* (New York: Pantheon Books, 1989), p. 154.

4 Quoted in Watt, *How War Came*, p. 86.

5 Quoted in W. K. Wark, *The Ultimate Enemy: British Inteligence and Nazi Germany, 1933–1939* (Oxford: Oxford University Press, 1986), p. 114.

6   J. Harvey (ed.), *The Diplomatic Diaries of Oliver Harvey, 1937–1940* (London: Collins, 1970), p. 250 (hereafter cited as Harvey Diaries).

7   P. Jackson, 'Intelligence and the End of Appeasement', in R. Boyce (ed.), *French Foreign and Defence Policy* (London: Routledge & Kegan Paul, 1998), p. 241.

8   Cadogan Diaries, p. 161.

9   Ibid., p. 161.

10   W. S. Churchill, *The Second World War*, vol. I (London: Cassell, 1948), p. 271.

11   Quoted in A. J. Foster, 'An Unequivocal Guarantee? Fleet Street and the British Guarantee to Poland, 31 March 1939', *Journal of Contemporary History*, 26 (1991), 35, 41, 43.

12   Quoted in S. Aster, *1939: The Making of the Second World War* (London: History Book Club, 1973), pp. 104, 220.

13   Quoted in C. A. MacDonald, 'Britain, France and the April Crisis of 1939', *European Studies Review*, 2 (1972), 169.

14   Quoted in James Herndon in W. J. Mommsen and H. Kettenacker (eds), *The Fascist Challenge and the Policy of Appeasement* (London: Allen & Unwin, 1983), p. 310.

15   Quoted in R. Manne, 'The British Decision for Alliance with Russia, May 1939', *Journal of Contemporary History*, 9 (1974), 4, 26.

16   Many Soviet historians began to express views that were very critical of Stalinist foreign policy, while some Western historians became more sympathetic. See the discussion in Further Reading. G. Roberts, 'The Alliance that Failed: Moscow and the Triple Alliance Negotiations 1939', *European History Quarterly*, 26 (1996), 383–414 is sympathetic to the Soviet position but gives some balanced criticism of the two sides.

17   Quoted in Watt, *How War Came*, p. 377.

18   Quoted in G. Roberts, *The Soviet Union and the Origins of the Second World War* (Basingstoke: Macmillan, 1995), pp. 82, 86.

19   Quoted in Noakes and Pridham (eds), *Nazism*, p. 737.

20   Watt, *How War Came*, p. 111.

21   Seeds to Halifax, 20 March 1939, DBFP, third series, vol. 4, no. 452.

22   Roberts, *Soviet Union*, p. 68.

23   D. C. Watt, 'The Initiation of Negotiations Leading to the Nazi–Soviet Pact: An Historical Problem', in C. Abramsky and P. J. Williams (eds), *Essays in Honour of E. H. Carr* (London: Macmillan, 1974); G. Roberts, 'Infamous Encounter? The Merekalov–Weizsäcker Meeting of 17 April 1939', *Historical Journal*, 35 (1992), 921–6.

24   Harvey Diaries, p. 287.

25   Quoted in Watt, *How War Came*, p. 461.

26   Cadogan Diaries, p. 206; A. Adamthwaite, *Grandeur and Misery: France's Bid for Power in Europe, 1914–1940* (London: Edward Arnold, 1995), p. 222.

27   Quoted in Noakes and Pridham (eds), *Nazism*, p. 742.

28   T. W. Mason, *Social Policy in the Third Reich: The Working Class and the 'National Community'* (Oxford: Berg, 1993), p. 297.

29   A debate between Overy and Mason: 'Germany, "Domestic Crisis" and War in 1939', *Past and Present*, 116 (1987), 138–68 and 122 (1989), 205–21.

30   Quoted in Noakes and Pridham (eds), *Nazism*, p. 762.

31 Quoted in C. Burdick and H. A. Jacobsen, *The Halder War Diary, 1939–1942* (Novato: Presidio, 1988), p. 66.

32 B. Bond (ed.), *Chief of Staff: The Diaries of Lieutenant-General Sir Henry Pownall*, vol. I: *1933–1940* (London: Leo Cooper, 1972), p. 200 (hereafter cited as Pownall Diaries).

33 Quoted in B. Millman, *The Ill-Made Alliance: Anglo-Turkish Relations, 1934–1940* (Montreal and Kingston: McGill-Queens University Press, 1998), p. 280.

34 Quoted in K. Friedrich, 'In Search of a Far Eastern Policy: Joseph Grew, Stanley Hornbeck, and American–Japanese Relations, 1937–1941', PhD thesis, Washington State University, 1974, p. 104.

35 F. W. Ikle, *German–Japanese Relations, 1936–40* (New York: Bookman, 1956), p. 133.

36 Quoted in R. Storry, *The Double Patriots* (London: Chatto, 1957), p. 256.

37 A. Coox, *Nomonhan* (Stanford University Press, 1985), p. 841.

38 Quoted in David J. Lu, *From the Marco Polo Bridge to Pearl Harbor* (Washington: Public Affairs Press, 1961), p. 65.

39 Quoted in N. Tarling, *Britain, Southeast Asia and the Onset of the Pacific War* (Cambridge University Press, 1996), p. 83.

40 Quoted in ibid., p. 83.

41 Dickover to Secretary of State, 16 April 1940, FRUS 1940 (Washington, 1955), IV, pp. 8–9.

42 Quoted in Tarling, *Onset of the Pacific War*, pp. 88–9.

43 William Louis, *British Strategy in the Far East* (Oxford: Clarendon Press, 1971), p. 262.

44 Ibid., p. 266.

45 Quoted in P. Lowe, 'Great Britain and the Coming of the Pacific War, 1939–41', *Transactions of the Royal Historical Society*, 5th Series, **24** (1974), 44.

46 FO/Lothian, 27 November 1939, quoted in Sato Kyozo, *Japan and Britain at the Crossroads, 1939–1941* (Tokyo: Senshu University Press, Tokyo, 1986), p. 38.

47 Quoted in Lowe, *TRHS*, p. 45.

48 Quoted in Bradford A. Lee, *Britain and the Sino-Japanese War, 1937–9* (Stanford University Press, 1973), p. 204.

49 Ashley Clarke, 11 August 1939, quoted in ibid., p. 208.

50 Quoted in N. Graebner, in D. Borg and S. Okamoto (eds), *Pearl Harbor as History* (Cambridge, Mass.: Harvard University Press, 1964), p. 42.

51 Quoted in Tarling, *Onset of the Pacific War* p. 81.

52 Quoted in ibid., pp. 92, 93.

53 Quoted in ibid., pp. 93–4.

54 Hull to Grew, 4 June 1940. FRUS, IV, p. 346.

55 WP (G) (39) 92,15 November 1939, CAB 67/2, Public Record Office, London.

## Chapter 8: The War of 1941

1 Quoted in J. Noakes and G. Pridham (eds), *Nazism, 1919–1945: A History in Documents and Eyewitness Accounts*, vol. 2 (New York: Schocken Books, 1988), p. 767.

2 Quoted in D. Dilks (ed.) *The Diaries of Sir Alexander Cadogan, 1938–1945* (London: Cassell, 1971), p. 284 (hereafter cited on Cadogan Diaries).

3 Quoted in R. J. Young, *In Command of France: French Foreign Policy and Military Planning, 1933–1940* (Cambridge, Mass.: Harvard University Press, 1978), p. 252.

4 Quoted in J. Blatt (ed.), *The French Defeat of 1940: Reassessments* (Oxford: Berghahn Books, 1998); P. Jackson, 'Recent Journeys along the Road Back to France 1940', *Historical Journal*, 39 (1996), 497–510.

5 Quoted in Burdick and Jacobsen (eds), *Halder War Diary*, p. 213.

6 Quoted in Cadogan Diaries, pp. 298, 303.

7 Quoted in J. Harvey (ed.), *The Diplomatic Diaries of Oliver Harvey, 1937–1940* (London: Collins, 1970), p. 365.

8 Quoted in R. A. C. Parker, *Struggle for Survival: A History of the Second World War* (Oxford: Oxford University Press, 1989), p. 58; quoted in M. R. Zahniser, 'Rethinking the Significance of Disaster: The United States and the Fall of France in 1940', *The International History Review*, 14 (1992), 274.

9 H. Gibson (ed.), *The Ciano Diaries, 1939–1943* (New York: Heinemann, 1947), pp. 174, 178.

10 Quoted in Geoffrey Waddington in D. Dilks and J. Erickson (eds), *Barbarossa: The Axis and the Allies* (Edinburgh: Edinburgh University Press, 1994), p. 20.

11 Quoted in A. Bullock, *Hitler: A Study in Tyranny* (Harmondsworth: Pelican Books, 1962), p. 651; H. W. Koch, 'Hitler's Programme and the Genesis of Operation "Barbarossa"' in H. W. Koch (ed.), *Aspects of the Third Reich* (London: Macmillan, 1985), pp. 285–324 argues for the importance of the immediate circumstances.

12 Quoted in Noakes and Pridham, *Nazism*, pp. 739, 763.

13 Quoted in Waddington in Dilks and Erickson, *Barbarossa*, p. 26.

14 Quoted in Halder Diary, p. 346.

15 Quoted in Noakes and Pridham, *Nazism*, p. 790.

16 Quoted in Koch, *Aspects*, p. 320.

17 Quoted in Noakes and Pridham, *Nazism*, pp. 814, 816–17.

18 Quoted in ibid., p. 816.

19 Quoted in Dmitri Volkogonov in Dilks and Erickson, *Barbarossa*, p. 80.

20 Quoted in Noakes and Pridham, *Nazism*, p. 817.

21 Halder Diary, p. 446.

22 Quoted in G. Roberts, *The Soviet Union and the Origins of the Second World War* (Basingstoke: Macmillan, 1995), p. 136.

23 Halder Diary, p. 563.

24 Reed to Secretary of State, 3 October 1939, FRUS 1939, III (Washington, 1955), pp. 273–4.

25 Quoted in J. C. Crowley in J. W. Morley (ed.), *Japan's Foreign Policy, 1868–1941* (New York: Columbia University Press, 1974), p. 82.

26 Quoted in ibid., p. 83.

27 Quoted in ibid., p. 87.

28 Quoted in ibid., p. 88.

29 Quoted in ibid., p. 88.

30  Quoted in Ikeda Kiyoshi in T. G. Fraser and Peter Lowe (eds), *Conflict and Amity in East Asia* (Basingstoke: Macmillan, 1992), p. 42.

31  *Völkische Beobachter*, 28 September 1940.

32  P. Baudouin, *The Private Diaries* (London: Eyre and Spottiswoode, 1948), p. 203.

33  Memorandum, 12 July 1940, FRUS IV, pp. 46–7.

34  Quoted in N. Tarling, *Britain, Southeast Asia and the Onset of the Pacific War* (Cambridge: Cambridge University Press, 1996), p. 147.

35  Quoted in ibid., p. 215.

36  Judith A. Stowe, *Siam becomes Thailand* (London: Hurst, 1991), p. 152.

37  Grant to Hull, 27 January 1941, FRUS 1941, v (Washington, 1956), p. 44.

38  Quoted in Sato, *Japan and Britain at the Crossroads*, p. 107.

39  Quoted in ibid., p. 117.

40  Quoted in Crowley in Morley (ed.) *Japan's Foreign Policy*, p. 94.

41  Leahy to Hull, 22 July 1941, FRUS v, pp. 221–2.

42  David Reynolds, *The Creation of the Anglo-American Alliance, 1937–41* (London: Europa, 1981), p. 235.

43  Proposal, 6 August, FRUS Japan II, pp. 549–50.

44  Quoted in Jonathan Marshall, *To Have and Have Not* (Berkeley and Los Angeles: University of California Press, 1995), p. 141.

45  Quoted in Ike Nobutaka (ed.), *Japan's Decision for War* (Stanford University Press, 1967), p. 131.

46  Quoted in Crowley in Morley, *Japan's Foreign Policy*, p. 97.

47  Quoted in Ike, *Japan's Decision*, p. 238.

48  Quoted in ibid., p. 283.

49  Quoted in Crowley in Morley, *Japan's Foreign Policy*, p. 98.

50  Quoted in Tarling, *Onset of the Pacific War*, p. 258.

51  Quoted in ibid., p 241.

52  Quoted in ibid., p. 250.

53  FE (41) 27th meeting, 24 July, CAB 96/2.

54  Ashley Clarke, quoted in Tarling, *Onset of the Pacific War*, p. 309.

55  Quoted in Tarling, *Onset of the Pacific War*, p. 311.

56  Reynolds, *Onset of the Creation*, p. 140.

57  Quoted in Deborah N. Miner, 'United States Policy toward Japan 1941', PhD thesis, Columbia University, 1976, p. 344.

58  Grew to Hull, 12 September 1940, FRUS IV, p. 602.

59  Quoted in Miner, 'United States Policy', p. 243.

60  Cordell Hull, *Memoirs* (London: Hodder and Stoughton, 1948), II, p. 1059.

61  Quoted in Jonathan G. Utley, 'The Department of State and the Far East, 1937–41: A Study of the Ideas behind its Diplomacy', PhD thesis, University of Illinois, 1970, p. 165.

62  Thomson et al., *Sentimental Imperialists*, p. 193.

63  Quoted in Delmer M. Brown, *Nationalism in Japan* (New York: Russell, 1955), p. 228.

64  Quoted in A. Bullock, *Hitler and Stalin: Parallel Lives* (New York: Knopf, 1992), p. 766.

65 Quoted in S. I. Rosenman (ed.), *Public Papers and Addresses of Franklin D. Roosevelt*, vol. 10 (New York: Harper and Brothers, 1950), pp. 514–30; J. D. Doenecke, 'Historiography: US Policy and the European War, 1939–1941', *Diplomatic History*, **19** (1995), 669–98.

## Chapter 9: Conclusions

1  D. Dilks (ed.), *The Diaries of Sir Alaxander Cadogan, 1938–1945* (London: Cassell, 1971), p. 382.

2  Quoted in R. Ovendale, *Appeasement and the English-Speaking World* (Cardiff: University of Wales Press, 1975), p. 7.

3  G. L. Weinberg, *The Foreign Policy of Hitler's Germany: Diplomatic Revolution in Europe, 1933–36* (London and Chicago: University of Chicago Press, 1970), vol. 1, p. 347.

4  Quoted in W. D. McIntyre, *The Rise and Fall of the Singapore Naval Base* (London: Macmillan, 1979), p. 129.

5  R. A. C. Parker, *Chamberlain and Appeasement: Britain and the Coming of the Second World War* (London: Macmillan, 1988), p. 364. Parker made the comment specifically about Chamberlain.

6  David Kaiser, 'Hitler and the Coming of War', in G. Martel (ed.), *Modern Germany Reconsidered, 1870–1945* (London: Routledge, 1992), p. 193.

7  M. Mazower, *Dark Continent: Europe's Twentieth Century* (London: Allen Lane, 1998), p. 150.

8  N. Tarling, *Britain, South-East Asia and the Onset of the Pacific War* (Cambridge: Cambridge University Press, 1996), p. 296.

9  Foreword to S. Dockrill (ed.), *From Pearl Harbor to Hiroshima* (Basingstoke: Macmillan, 1994), p. xii.

10  W. S. Churchill, *The Second World War*, vol. iv (London: Cassell, 1948), p. 81.

11  F. H. Hinsley, 'The Causes of War', *New Zealand Journal of History*, 1:1 (April 1967) 3.

12  James Joll, *The Unspoken Assumptions* (London: Weidenfeld, 1968).

13  A. Hitler, *Mein Kampf*, trans. R. Mannheim (London: Hutchinson, 1969), p. 68.

14  Quoted in Bradford A. Lee, *Britain and the Sino-Japanese War, 1937–9* (Stanford University Press, 1973), p. 205.

15  Quoted in Larry W. Fuchser, *Neville Chamberlain and Appeasement*, p. 176.

16  Quoted in J. W. Dower, *Empire and Aftermath: Yoshida Shigeru and the Japanese Experience* (Cambridge, Mass.: Harrard University Press, 1979), p. 109.

17  Quoted in Ian Nish, *Japanese Foreign Policy: Kasumigaseki to Miyakezaka* (London: Routledge, 1977), p. 260.

18  Quoted in Mark R. Peattie, *Ishiwara Kanji and Japan's Confrontation with the West* (Princeton University Press, 1975), p. 340.

19  Quoted in Ikeda Kiyoshi in I. Nish, *Anglo-Japanese Alienation, 1919–1952* (Cambridge: Cambridge University Press, 1982), p. 144.

*Notes*

## Epilogue

1  Quoted in D. W. Ellwood, *Rebuilding Europe: Western Europe, America and Postwar Reconstruction* (London: Longman, 1992), p. 169.

2  A. S. Milward, *The Reconstruction of Western Europe, 1945–51* (Berkeley and Los Angeles: University of California Press, 1984), p. 418.

3  Quoted in N. Tarling, *Britain, Southeast Asia, and the Onset of the Cold War* (Cambridge University Press, 1998), p. 189.

4  Quoted in H. Benda et al., *Japanese Military Administration in Indonesia* (New Haven, Conn.: Yale University Press, 1965), p. 242.

5  Quoted in Sharon H. Nolte, *Liberalism in Modern Japan* (Berkeley and Los Angeles: University of California Press, 1987), p. 165.

6  Richard B. Finn, *Winners in Peace: MacArthur, Yoshida, and Postwar Japan* (Berkeley and Los Angeles: University of California Press, 1992), p. 103.

7  A. W. B. Simpson in *TLS*, 27 August 1999.

8  Adam Roberts in *TLS*, 28 January 2000.

9  C. Thorne, *The Issues of War* (London: Hamilton, 1985), p. xi.

10  F. Fukuyama, *The End of History and the Last Man* (New York: Free Press, 1992).

# Suggestions for Further Reading

The following bibliographical notes, which do not include all the works cited in the chapter notes, are designed to enable readers to follow up problems raised in the text, or to explore issues closely related to them.

## The origins of the Second World War

Most of the books on this subject focus on the origins of the war of 1939. P. M. H. Bell, *The Origins of the Second World War*, 2nd edn (London: Longman, 1997) is a masterly survey. A. Adamthwaite, *The Making of the Second World War* (London: Allen and Unwin, 1977) provides an interesting collection of documents and a good introductory essay. A. J. P. Taylor, *The Origins of the Second World War* (London: Hamish Hamilton, 1961; revised, with 'Second Thoughts', London: Harmondsworth, 1964) is dated and controversial but still stimulating and provides the background for a lot of the work which followed.

Some books cover developments in Asia more fully, though generally in a less integrated way than is attempted in the present book. R. Overy and A. Wheatcroft, *The Road to War* (London: Macmillan, 1989) is a good introduction, while A. J. Crozier, *The Causes of the Second World War* (Oxford: Blackwell, 1997) provides an impressively detailed coverage and an interesting discussion of the European historiography.

There are some good collections of essays, e.g. G. Martel (ed.), *The Origins of the Second World War Reconsidered: The A. J. P. Taylor Debate after Twenty-five Years* (London: Allen and Unwin, 1986), which includes an incisive essay by Akira Iriye, 'The Asian Factor'; R. Boyce and E. M. Robertson (eds), *Paths to War: New Essays on the Origins of the Second World War* (London: Macmillan, 1989); P. Finney (ed.), *The Origins of the Second World War* (London: Arnold, 1997), a useful collection of mainly edited extracts from previously published works, containing a challenging essay by Michael A. Barnhart, 'The Origins of the Second World War in Asia and the Pacific: Synthesis Impossible?', as well as a paper by Hosoya Chihiro.

Amongst the works that focus on the origins of the war of 1941 are William Carr, *Poland to Pearl Harbor: The Making of the Second World War* (London: Arnold, 1985) and Akira Iriye, *The Origins of the Second World War in Asia and the Pacific* (London and New York: Longman, 1987).

*Suggestions for Further Reading*

An interesting comparative approach to two of the main protagonists is offered by Bernd Martin, *Japan and Germany in the Modern World* (Oxford: Berghahn, 1995).

## The foreign policy of the European powers

### Britain

C. J. Bartlett, *British Foreign Policy in the Twentieth Century* (London: Macmillan, 1977) provides a brief introduction; J. W. Young, *Britain and the World in the Twentieth Century* (London: Arnold, 1997) particularly addresses the question of British decline. M. Howard, *The Continental Commitment* (London: Temple Smith, 1972) provides a short, stimulating discussion of the problems of British over-commitment. P. Catterall and C. J. Morris (eds), *Britain and the Threat to Security in Europe, 1918–45* (London: St Martin's Press, 1993) covers an interesting range of topics.

### France

Two interestingly different interpretations are provided by A. Adamthwaite, *Grandeur and Misery: France's Bid for Power in Europe, 1914–1940* (London: Arnold, 1995) and R. J. Young, *France and the Origins of the Second World War* (London: Macmillan, 1996). R. Boyce (ed.), *French Foreign and Defence Policy, 1918–1940* (London: Routledge & Kegan Paul, 1998) is an excellent collection of essays.

### Germany

K. Hildebrand, *German Foreign Policy from Bismarck to Adenauer: The Limits of Statecraft* (London: Unwin Hyman, 1989) provides a good broad coverage, while J. Hiden, *Germany and Europe, 1919–1939*, 2nd edn (London: Longman, 1993) compares the Weimar and Nazi periods.

### Italy

C. J. Lowe and F. Marzari, *Italian Foreign Policy, 1870–1940* (London: Routledge & Kegan Paul, 1975).

### Soviet Union

A. B. Ulam, *Expansion and Co-existence: The History of Soviet Policy, 1917–67* (London: Secker & Warburg, 1968) reflects the views of the Cold War period in which it was written; G. Gorodetsky (ed.), *Soviet Foreign Policy 1917–1991* (London: Frank Cass, 1994) contains essays from Russian and Western scholars.

### United States

The literature on American foreign policy is immense. A look at some of the debated issues is provided by G. Martel (ed.), *American Foreign Relations Reconsidered, 1890–1993* (London: Routledge & Kegan Paul, 1995).

## Japan's position in the world and the making of its foreign policy

Understanding the Meiji Restoration of 1868 is essential to understanding modern Japan. That is widely accepted. There is much less agreement on how it should be understood. At the time it seemed to some observers to be a rapid transformation: a 'political and social revolution...as sudden and complete as a theatrical transformation scene', as Sir Alexander Wedderburn put it in 1878 [see Yokoyama Toshio, *Japan in the Victorian Mind* (London: Macmillan, 1986), pp. 109–10]. It was also recognised that such a change could not have taken place unless Japan were 'ripe for revolution'. That approach has been attractive to recent scholars, who have drawn attention to the diversity and innovation barely concealed and in some ways encouraged by the Tokugawa regime. Increasingly it seems that it is necessary to study that period also in order to understand modern Japan. By contrast, indeed, Meiji Japan was highly regulated and centralised. Some have seen the Restoration as a 'revolution betrayed'. They have studied the opposition to the regime, both at the elite and the popular level. See, for example, William W. Kelly, *Defence and Defiance in Nineteenth-Century Japan* (Princeton University Press, 1985), and the contribution by H. D. Harootunian in Najita Tetsuo and J. V. Koschmann (eds), *Conflict in Modern Japanese History* (Princeton University Press, 1982). For others again Meiji seems to be a model. At the beginning of the twentieth century, other Asian leaders saw it as an example: an Asian country could modernise itself and the West could be challenged. Was there 'some kind of abacus', the hero in Pramoedhya's novel asks, to 'use to calculate how many dozens of years it will take the Javanese to reach the same level as the Japanese?' [*This Earth of Mankind*, trans. Max Lane (Melbourne: Penguin, 1982/1991), p. 315]. After the Second World War it seemed a model for 'development' in newly independent countries. The Meiji Restoration emerged from a crisis in foreign relations as well as a domestic crisis. The Japanese were determined to avoid falling under a colonial power, though they perhaps came nearer to it than is generally assumed. They were determined to undo the unequal treaties and to act like a Western power. Some, like Fukusawa Yukichi, saw that as 'leaving Asia'. The 'pan-Asian' expansion of the interwar period was thus seen as 'returning to Asia'.

Volume 5 of *The Cambridge History of Japan* (1989), edited by Marius B. Jansen, covers the nineteenth century; volume 6 (1988), edited by Peter Duus, covers the twentieth.

Three other authoritative works are Michael A. Barnhart, *Japan and the World Since 1868* (London: Arnold, 1995); W. G. Beasley, *Japanese Imperialism* (Oxford: Clarendon Press, 1987); and Ian Nish, *Japanese Foreign Policy, 1869–1941: Kasumigaseki to Miyakezaka* (London: Routledge & Kegan Paul, 1977).

Those adopting a more biographical approach could use Lesley Connors, *The Emperor's Adviser: Saionji Kinmochi and Pre-war Japanese Politics* (London: Croom Helm, 1987); J. W. Dower, *Empire and Aftermath: Yoshida Shigeru and the Japanese Experience, 1878–1954* (Cambridge, Mass.: Harvard University Press, 1979); and Mark R. Peattie, *Ishiwara Kanji and Japan's Confrontation with the West* (Princeton University Press, 1975).

## The peace settlement

G. Schulz, *Revolutions and Peace Treaties, 1917–20* (Eng. trans. London: Methuen, 1972) remains a useful general survey. A. Sharp, *The Versailles Settlement: Peacemaking in Paris in 1919* (London: Macmillan, 1991) provides a good introduction to much modern scholarship and despite its title covers the whole of the settlement. M. L. Dockrill and J. D. Goold, *Peace without Promise: Britain and the Peace Conferences, 1919–1923* (London: Batsford, 1981) is a useful guide to British policy in all parts of the settlement. A good brief introduction to the

Versailles settlement is provided by A. Lentin, *The Versailles Peace Settlement: Peacemaking with Germany* (London: Historical Association, 1991).

Early work on the peace settlement like R. S. Baker, *Woodrow Wilson and World Settlement*, 3 vols (New York: Doubleday, Page, 1923) helped to establish the view that Wilson favoured a peace of reconciliation, that Lloyd George was inconsistent but tended to favour moderation, and that the French were committed to a vindictive punitive policy. A revisionist view, more sympathetic to the French and more critical of Britain and the USA, and which placed more weight on economic and domestic political considerations, became established by such works as R. E. Bunsalmeyer, *The Cost of the War of 1914–1919: British Economic War Aims and the Origins of Reparation* (Hamden, Conn.: Archon Books, 1975), A. Lentin, *Lloyd George, Woodrow Wilson and the Guilt of Germany: An Essay in the Pre-History of Appeasement* (Leicester: Leicester University Press, 1984) republished in 1985 under the title *Guilt at Versailles: Lloyd George and the Pre-History of Appeasement*. See also D. Stevenson, *French War Aims against Germany, 1914–1919* (Oxford: Oxford University Press, 1982), K. Schwabe, *Woodrow Wilson, Revolutionary Germany and Peacemaking*, trans. R. and R. Kimber (Chapel Hill: University of North Carolina Press, 1985), and M. Trachtenberg, *Reparation in World Politics: France and European Economic Diplomacy, 1916–1923* (New York: Columbia University Press, 1980). W. A. McDougall, *France's Rhineland Diplomacy, 1914–1924: The Last Bid for a Balance of Power in Europe* (Princeton, N.J.: Princeton University Press, 1978) covers much more than Rhineland policy.

## The working-out of the peace settlement

S. Marks, *The Illusion of Peace: International Relations in Europe, 1918–1933* (London: Macmillan, 1976) provides a good introduction and, although published before most of the 'revisionist' monographs, is sympathetic towards the French and critical of Britain and Germany. She strongly criticised the view that Germany had been unable to pay reparations, which had been argued by D. Felix, *Rathenau and the Weimar Republic* (Baltimore, Md: Johns Hopkins University Press, 1971).

The complicated political and economic issues involved in the whole question of reparations is discussed by B. Kent, *The Spoils of War: The Politics, Economics and Diplomacy of Reparations, 1918–32* (Oxford: Oxford University Press, 1989). The importance of financial considerations in French foreign policy is explained by S. A. Schuker, *The End of French Predominance in Europe: The Financial Crisis of 1924 and the Adoption of the Dawes Plan* (Chapel Hill: University of North Carolina Press, 1976). A sympathetic examination of Britain's attempts to deal with the related problems of inter-Allied war debts, British debts to the United States and reparations can be found in A. Orde, *British Policy and European Reconstruction after the First World War* (Cambridge: Cambridge University Press, 1990).

E. Kolb, *The Weimar Republic*, trans. P. S. Falla (London: Unwin Hyman, 1988) provides an excellent account of the domestic context for German foreign policy. M. M. Lee and W. Michalka, *German Foreign Policy, 1917–1933: Continuity or Break?* (Leamington Spa: Berg, 1987) discuss the main issues of the continuity debate. An in-depth consideration of Stresemann is provided by R. P. Grathwol, *Stresemann and the DNVP: Reconciliation or Revenge in German Foreign Policy, 1924–1928* (Lawrence: The Regents Press of Kansas, 1980). The major book on the whole Locarno period remains J. Jacobson, *Locarno Diplomacy: Germany and the West, 1925–1929* (Princeton: Princeton University Press, 1972).

## Japan's foreign policy and the Manchuria crisis

Works dealing with Japan's foreign policy after the First World War, in particular in respect of China, include Nobuya Bamba, *Japanese Diplomacy in a Dilemma: New Light on Japan's China Policy, 1924–1929* (Vancouver: University of British Columbia Press, 1972); Akira Iriye, *After Imperialism: The Search for a New Order in the Far East, 1921–1931* (Cambridge, Mass.: Harvard University Press, 1965); and William F. Morton, *Tanaka Giichi and Japan's China Policy* (Folkestone: Dawson, 1980).

The conditions under which foreign policy was made can be further explored in Peter Duus, *Party Rivalry and Political Change in Taisho Japan* (Cambridge, Mass.: Harvard University Press, 1968); G. M. Wilson, *Radical Nationalist in Japan: Kita Ikki, 1883–1937* (Cambridge, Mass.: Harvard University Press, 1969); and Gordon M. Berger, *Parties out of Power in Japan* (Princeton University Press, 1977).

The main issues in Japan's policy these books will help you to consider are both domestic and foreign. What was the relationship of Shidehara's policy with the emergence of the so-called Taisho democracy? Why and how did Japan turn away from the 'China friendship' approach?

The considerable literature on the Manchuria crisis and the creation of Manchukuo includes Sadako Ogata, *Defiance in Manchuria* (Berkeley and Los Angeles: University of California Press, 1964); C. Thorne, *The Limits of Foreign Policy: The West, the League and the Far Eastern Crisis of 1931–1933* (London: Hamilton, 1972); and Ian Nish, *Japan's Struggle with Internationalism: Japan, China and the League of Nations, 1931–1933* (London and New York: Routledge, Kegan Paul, 1993).

*Japan Erupts: The London Naval Conference and the Manchurian Incident. 1928–1932* (New York: Columbia University Press, 1984) is one of an invaluable series of books edited by James W. Morley. They comprise articles by Japanese scholars using both Japanese and non-Japanese sources, originally written for an eight-volume study, 'The Road to the Pacific War', published by the Japan Association of International Relations.

The foreign context for the Manchuria crisis is well covered in the books listed. The central controversy among the Western powers was over the Stimson doctrine of non-recognition. It had a lasting effect on Anglo-American relations, since it seemed that the UK had failed to support a US initiative that might have restrained Japan. In retrospect it is clear that such an interpretation has little validity, if any. None of the powers was prepared to intervene to stop Japan. Manchuria looked different in hindsight.

From another perspective Manchuria marked a radical shift in Japanese policy. The radicals spoke of a 'return to Asia'. Somewhat paradoxically, that was coupled with the concept of a 'bloc economy' which was borrowed from wartime Germany, and with stage-managed development on the Soviet model. The ideas behind the Manchukuo adventure are explored in Louise Young, *Japan's Total Empire: Manchuria and the Culture of Wartime Imperialism* (Berkeley and Los Angeles: University of California Press, 1998). Other practices developed there, such as mass mobilisation, were later applied in the homeland itself and in the south-east Asian conquests.

Historians have recognised the importance in inter-war Japan of semi-governmental and political associations, especially among the military. Recent trends in historiography have reflected contemporary concern with rhetoric and its significance. Earlier works include Richard Storry, *The Double Patriots* (London: Chatto, 1957), G. M. Wilson, *Radical Nationalist in Japan: Kita Ikki, 1883–1937* (Harvard University Press, 1969), and, on the 1936 mutiny, Ben-Ami Shillony, *Revolt in Japan* (Princeton University Press, 1973). More recent studies include, besides Louise Young's book, Ken'ichi Goto', *'Returning to Asia': Japan–Indonesia Relations, 1930s–1942* (Tokyo: Ryukei Shyosha, 1997). On the importance of the backing the army received in rural Japan, see Richard J. Smethurst, *A Social Basis for Prewar Japanese Militarism* (Berkeley and Los Angeles: University of California Press, 1974).

## Europe in the 1930s

W. J. Mommsen and L. Kettenacker, *The Fascist Challenge and the Policy of Appeasement* (London: Allen and Unwin, 1983) is an excellent collection of essays on mainly European topics but there is also some consideration of British policy in Asia.

### Britain

A wholehearted defence of Chamberlain's policy is in J. Charmley, *Chamberlain and the Lost Peace* (Basingstoke: Macmillan, 1989). R. A. C. Parker, *Chamberlain and Appeasement: British Policy and the Coming of the Second World War* (London: Macmillan, 1988) provides a detailed, sustained, critical assessment of Chamberlain's policy. A useful shorter discussion is in F. McDonough, *Neville Chamberlain, Appeasement and the British Road to War* (Manchester: Manchester University Press, 1998). D. Dutton, *Anthony Eden, a Life and Reputation* (London: Edward Arnold, 1997) discusses Eden's policy in the context of the debate about British decline and appeasement. Particular aspects of British policy are covered by W. Wark, *The Ultimate Enemy: British Intelligence and Nazi Germany, 1933–1939* (Oxford: Oxford University Press, 1986); B. Bond, *British Military Policy Between the Two World Wars* (Oxford: Clarendon Press, 1980); G. C. Peden, *British Rearmament and the Treasury, 1932–39* (Edinburgh: Scottish Academic Press, 1979); R. Ovendale, *'Appeasement' and the English-Speaking World: Britain, the United States, the Dominions and the Policy of Appeasement, 1937–1939* (Cardiff: University of Wales Press, 1975).

### France

J. Jackson, *The Politics of the Depression in France, 1936–1936* (Cambridge: Cambridge University Press, 1985) and J. Jackson, *The Popular Front in France* (Cambridge: Cambridge University Press, 1988) provide a good introduction to the domestic context of foreign policy making. A. Adamthwaite, *France and the Coming of the Second World War* (London: Frank Cass, 1977) questions the judgement of French leadership, and N. Jordan, *The Popular Front and Central Europe: Dilemmas of French Impotence, 1918–1940* (Cambridge: Cambridge University Press, 1983) particularly questions military policy. R. J. Young, *In Command of France: French Foreign Policy and Military Planning, 1933–1940* (Cambridge, Mass.: Harvard University Press 1978) and M. Alexander, *The Republic in Danger: General Maurice Gamelin and the Politics of French Defence, 1935–1940* (Cambridge: Cambridge University Press 1993) are more sympathetic to the French.

### Germany

W. Carr, *Arms, Autarky and Aggression: A Study in German Foreign Policy, 1933–39* (London: Edward Arnold, 1972) still provides a good introduction. Examples of the intentionalist point of view can be found in K. Hildebrand, *The Foreign Policy of the Third Reich*, trans. A. F. Fothergill (London: Batsford, 1973); E. Jäckel, *Hitler's World View* (Cambridge, Mass.: Harvard University Press, 1981); G. L. Weinberg, *The Foreign Policy of Hitler's Germany*, 2 vols (Chicago: University of Chicago Press, 1970, 1980). Examples of the structuralist point of view can be found in R. Smelser, *The Sudeten Problem, 1933–38: Volkstumpolitik and the Formulation of Nazi Foreign Policy* (Middletown, Conn.: Wesleyan University Press, 1975); T. Childers and J. Caplan (eds), *Re-evaluating the Third Reich* (New York: Holmes and Meier, 1993); H. W. Koch (ed.), *Aspects of the Third Reich* (London: Macmillan, 1985); J. Caplan (ed.), *Fascism and the Working Class: Essays by Tim Mason* (Cambridge: Cambridge University Press, 1995). Some of Overy's arguments about the German economy can be found in R. Overy, *War and Economy in the Third Reich* (Oxford: Clarendon Press, 1994) and R. Overy, *Goering: The 'Iron Man'* (London: Routledge & Kegan Paul, 1984). I. Kershaw, *The Nazi Dictatorship* (London: Edward Arnold, 1989) and J. Hiden and J. Farquharson, *Explaining Hitler's Germany*, 2nd edn (London: Batsford, 1989) provide good discussions of Nazi foreign and economic policy.

## Italy

M. Knox, *Mussolini Unleashed, 1939–41* (Cambridge: Cambridge University Press, 1982) is the main exponent of the view that Mussolini's aggressive expansionist ideology inevitably led to his joining Nazi Germany. The view that Italy pursued the role of a 'decisive weight' in Europe has been argued by the Italian historian De Felice and appears in a modified form in H. J. Burgwyn, *Italian Foreign Policy in the Inter-war Period, 1918–1940* (Westport, Conn.: Praeger, 1997). D. Mack Smith, *Mussolini* (London: Weidenfeld and Nicolson, 1981) is very critical of the Duce. E. M. Robertson, *Mussolini as Empire Builder: Europe and Africa, 1932–1936* (London: Macmillan, 1977) provides a detailed examination of the Abyssinian adventure.

## Soviet Union

J. Haslam, *The Soviet Union and the Struggle for Collective Security in Europe, 1933–1939* (London: Macmillan, 1984) and G. Roberts, *The Soviet Union and the Origins of the Second World War: Russo-German Relations and the Road to War, 1933–1941* (London: Macmillan, 1995) argue that the Soviets were sincere in their pursuit of collective security while R. C. Tucker, *Stalin in Power: The Revolution from Above, 1928–1941* (New York: Norton, 1990) and J. Hochman, *The Soviet Union and the Failure of Collective Security* (Ithaca: Cornell University Press, 1984) argue that Stalin's consistent aim was an agreement with Hitler. A very similar view has been iterated by A. M. Nekrich, *Pariahs, Partners, Predators: German–Soviet Relations, 1922–1941* (New York: Columbia University Press, 1997).

## United States

A. A. Offner, *American Appeasement, United States Foreign Policy and Germany, 1933–1938* (New York: Norton, 1976) argued that the United States followed its own independent policy of appeasement. C. A. MacDonald, *The United States, Britain, and Appeasement, 1936–39* (London: Macmillan, 1981) takes the view that the Americans began a gradual shift towards deterrent diplomacy from 1937. D. Reynolds, *The Creation of the Anglo-American Alliance, 1937–41: A Study in Competitive Co-operation* (London: Europa, 1981) examines the difficulties in Anglo-American relations which prevented their working together before the pressures of war made co-operation desirable for both sides.

For a study of individual crises see J. T. Emmerson, *The Rhineland Crisis: 7 March 1936* (London: Temple Smith, 1977); P. Preston (ed.), *Revolution and War in Spain, 1931–39* (London: Methuen, 1984); M. Alpert, *A New International History of the Spanish Civil War* (Basingstoke: Macmillan, 1994); M. Latynski (ed.), *Reappraising the Munich Pact: Continental Perspectives* (Washington, DC: Woodrow Wilson Centre Press; Baltimore: Johns Hopkins University Press, 1992).

## Japan's foreign policy in the 1930s

The major problem for historians in this phase is to determine the origins of the undeclared war. Seeing Japan's policy in 1937–8 as a simple continuation of its policy in 1931–2 is inadequate. The present authors argue that Konoe had a major role. Army leaders, determined on 'total mobilisation', wished to avoid an incident in the meantime. But Konoe rallied support for total mobilisation by turning the clash with China into a Great Patriotic Endeavour. This approach draws on David J. Lu, *From the Marco Polo Bridge to Pearl Harbor* (Washington: Public Affairs Press, 1961) and Michael A. Barnhart, *Japan Prepares for Total War* (Cornell University Press, 1987).

The essential work is James B. Crowley, *Japan's Quest for Autonomy: National Security and Foreign Policy 1930–1938* (Princeton University Press, 1966). He follows it up in an essay in James W. Morley (ed.), *Japan's Foreign Policy, 1868–1941* (New York: Columbia University Press, 1974). The volumes in Morley's series for this period include *The Chinese Quagmire: Japan's Expansion on the Asian Continent, 1933–41* (New York: Columbia University Press, 1983) and *Deterrent Diplomacy: Japan, Germany and the U. S. S. R., 1935–1940* (New York: Columbia University Press, 1976).

There are several studies of the policies of the Western powers and their relations with Japan. On the British side, see, for example, William Roger Louis, *British Strategy in the Far East, 1919–1939* (Oxford: Clarendon Press, 1971); Ann Trotter, *Britain and East Asia 1933–1937* (Cambridge University Press, 1975): Bradford A. Lee, *Britain and the Sino-Japanese War, 1937–9* (Stanford University Press, 1973); and Ian Nish (ed.), *Anglo-Japanese Alienation, 1919–1952* (Cambridge University Press, 1982).

On the US side, see Dorothy Borg, *The United States and the Far Eastern Crisis of 1933–1938* (Cambridge, Mass.: Harvard University Press, 1964). Also worthwhile are Stephen E. Pelz, *Race to Pearl Harbor: The Failure of the Second Naval Conference and the Onset of World War II* (Cambridge, Mass.: Harvard University Press, 1974), and a collection on USA–Japan relations, 1931–41, edited by D. Borg and S. Okamoto, *Pearl Harbor as History* (New York: Columbia University Press, 1973), which includes Norman Graebner's important study on Roosevelt and the Japanese.

Germany–Japan relations are discussed in Ernst L. Presseisen, *Germany and Japan: A Study in Totalitarian Diplomacy, 1933–41* (The Hague: Nijhoff, 1958); F. W. Ikle, *German–Japanese Relations, 1936–40* (New York: Bookman, 1956); and J. M. Meskill, *Hitler and Japan: The Hollow Alliance* (New York: Atherton, 1966).

The violence of the Japanese army after the fall of Nanking in December 1937 is described in the *Cambridge History of Japan* as 'a rampage of killing, looting, and raping' (p. 320). Official texts in Japan have not fully acknowledged it, but a graphic account is found in Honda Katsuchi, *The Nanking Massacre: A Japanese Journalist Confronts Japan's National Shame*, ed. F. Gibney, trans. K. Sandness (Armonk: Sharpe, 1999). See also Iris Chang, *The Rape of Nanking* (Harmondsworth: Penguin, 1998).

## The outbreak of the European War

W. Murray, *The Change in the European Balance of Power, 1938–1939* (Princeton: Princeton University Press, 1984) is very critical of British and French decisions on strategic grounds. D. C. Watt, *How War Came: The Immediate Origins of the Second World War* (London: Heinemann, 1989) provides a gripping and authoritative account. On the Allied defeat in June 1940 see M. Bloch, *Strange Defeat*, trans. Gerard Hopkins (London: Oxford University Press,

1949); J. Blatt (ed.), *The French Defeat of 1940: Reassessments* (Oxford: Berghahn Books, 1998); E. M. Gates, *End of the Affair: The Collapse of the Anglo-French Alliance, 1939–40* (Berkeley, Cal.: University of California Press, 1981). The latter presents a favourable view of French policy.

Issues of German policy and strategy are discussed in M. van Creveld, *Hitler's Strategy, 1940–41: The Balkan Clue* (London: Cambridge University Press, 1973). R. Cecil, *Hitler's Decision to Invade Russia, 1941* (London: Davis-Poynter, 1975) discusses the mixture of ideological, racial, political and economic motives which influenced Hitler's decision. J. Erickson and D. Dilks (eds), *Barbarossa: The Axis and the Allies* (Edinburgh: Edinburgh University Press, 1994) has a good collection of essays on the diplomatic, intelligence and social aspects of the operation. Particularly illuminating is Geoffrey Waddington's analysis of Ribbentrop's global strategy which, differing from that of Hitler, was shattered by the decision to invade Russia. W. Heinrichs, *Threshold of War: Franklin D. Roosevelt and American Entry into World War II* (New York: Oxford University Press, 1988) explains the importance of Europe as well as the Far East in determining Roosevelt's policy.

## The outbreak of the Pacific war

On Japan's policy, see, for example, the books by Lu and Barnhart; R. C. J. Butow's classic work, *Tojo and the Coming of the War* (Princeton University Press, 1961); Nobutaka Ike (ed.), *Japan's Decision for War* (Stanford University Press, 1967), including minutes of the liaison and imperial conferences: and two volumes in the series edited by James W. Morley, *The Fateful Choice* (Columbia University Press, 1980) and *The Final Confrontation* (Columbia University Press, 1994).

The literature on Pearl Harbor is naturally very substantial and very controversial. Admiral Robert A. Theobald argued in *The Final Secret of Pearl Harbor* (Old Greenwich: Devin-Adair, 1954) that Roosevelt kept a weak fleet in Pearl Harbor and withheld information derived from MAGIC and other sources, in order to further 'an invitation to a surprise attack' (p. 4). James Rusbridger and Eric Nave argued, in *Betrayal at Pearl Harbor* (New York: Simon and Schuster, 1992), that Churchill lured Roosevelt into the Second World War, again by withholding information, in this case that provided by the breaking of the code JN 25.

The conspiracy theorists have not, however, found general support. The point made by Roberta Wohlstetter in *Pearl Harbor Warning and Decision* (Stanford University Press, 1962) is readily recognised by historians: the problem of hindsight. What later seems obvious because we know what happened is not so obvious at the time. That was perhaps particularly true of the information available to decision-makers in 1941. It was copious. The problem was to interpret it. It is an issue that interested Wohlstetter because of the possibility of a 'surprise attack' in the Cold War. In our 'information age', selection and interpretation remain crucial. Do we find only what we seek? Do we recognise the unexpected?

In any case Churchill's information was, it seems, passed on, as G. A. H. Gordon suggests in Robert W. Love (ed.), *Pearl Harbor Revisited* (Basingstoke: Macmillan, 1995). Stephen Ambrose finds the conspiracy charges against Roosevelt 'ridiculous', and the logic of the charges against Churchill escapes him (ibid., p. 94). Jon Bridgman's account of 6 December 1941 leans towards the views of the 'court historians', but his hour-by-hour examination of Roosevelt's day finds a certain 'murkiness'. Does that suggest a deeper truth that a common-sense approach misses? 'Or does it only reveal the commonplace – that if any highly contentious historical event is examined in great enough detail, it is likely to dissolve into a muddle?' (ibid., p. 144).

The surprise attack was seen as relieving Roosevelt of a difficulty: he did not have to carry Congress and people in a declaration of war. In fact, of course, it did not get him into the European war. It was Hitler who achieved that. Roosevelt's policy, says Ambrose, was to avoid war in the Pacific. The view has widespread acceptance. But if it was not a conspiracy, US policy was based on a misconception. It misinterpreted the Japanese by emphasising their previous caution and compliance and depreciating their determination or desperation. See also Jonathan G. Utley, *Going to War with Japan, 1937–1941* (Knoxville: University of Tennessee Press, 1985); and, though the argument is not in the end convincing, Jonathan Marshall, *To Have and Have Not: Southeast Asian Raw Materials and the Origins of the Pacific War* (Berkeley: University of California Press, 1995).

The British role in these years was relatively minor, but it, too, has been much studied. See, for example, A. Best, *Britain, Japan, and Pearl Harbor: Avoiding War in East Asia, 1936–41* (London and New York: Routledge & Kegan Paul, 1995); Peter Lowe, *Great Britain and the Origins of the Pacific War* (Oxford: Clarendon Press, 1977); Sato Kyozo, *Japan and Britain at the Crossroads, 1939–1941* (Tokyo: Senshu University Press, 1986); and N. Tarling, *Britain, Southeast Asia and the Onset of the Pacific War* (Cambridge University Press, 1996).

## The Second World War and after

The literature – narrative, analytic and reflective – is vast.

A short general account is provided by R. A. C. Parker, *Struggle for Survival: The History of the Second World War* (Oxford: Oxford University Press, 1989). A much longer coverage, particularly of political and military matters is in G. L. Weinberg, *A World at Arms: A Global History of World War II* (Cambridge: Cambridge University Press, 1994); see also I. C. B. Dear (ed.), *The Oxford Companion to World War II* (Oxford and New York: Oxford University Press, 1995). On the war in the Pacific do not miss John W. Dower, *War without Mercy: Race and Power in the Pacific War* (New York: Pantheon, 1986); or S. Dockrill (ed.), *From Pearl Harbor to Hiroshima* (Basingstoke: Macmillan, 1994).

Three issues may attract particular attention. One is the role of Emperor Hirohito. He was not tried as a war criminal, partly because he was seen as necessary to the surrender of Japan and its forces, and then to its post-war rehabilitation. If, however, he was able to call upon his people to surrender, why did he not oppose the opening of the war?

In his book *Japan's Imperial Conspiracy* (New York: Morrow, 1971), David Bergamini saw his role as that of a conspirator. An immediate response was offered by Charles D. Sheldon, who had supervised the translation of Kido's diary in 1946–7. The Emperor was bypassed or faced with *faits accomplis*: he was 'absolutely consistent in using his personal influence to induce caution and to moderate, and even to obstruct, the accumulating, snowballing impetus towards war' ('Japanese Aggression and the Emperor, 1931–1941, from Contemporary Diaries', *Modern Asian Studies*, 10, 1 (1976), pp. 1–40). Following the publication of the Emperor's 1946 monologues in 1990, the Bergamini view now has little support, if any. Critics, Japanese and non-Japanese, speak rather of his inaction. He 'lacked the will' to exert political control, writes Daikichi Irokura, *The Age of Hirohito*, trans. Mikiso Hane and John K. Urda (New York: Free Press, 1995), p. 85.

Stephen Large takes a middle ground in his 'Emperor Hirohito and Early Showa Japan', *Monumenta Nipponica*, 46, 3 (Autumn 1991), pp. 349–68, reprinted in the collection of articles Large has edited, *Showa Japan: Political, Economic and Social History, 1926–1989* (London and New York: Routledge & Kegan Paul, 1998), i, pp. 239–58; and his book *Emperor Hirohito and Showa Japan: A Political Biography* (London and New York: Routledge & Kegan Paul, 1992). He draws attention to ambiguities in the Meiji constitution, under which the emperor was both an absolute and a constitutional monarch. That tended to mean that, so far as Japanese in general were concerned, he was absolute: but that within the ruling elite he was constrained by civilian and military leaders. Large argues that he was limited not only by his wish to behave like a constitutional monarch, and by the retention of outdated court rules, but also by his own indecisive personality.

Hirohito's own argument was that to intervene in 1941 would have been a 'despotic' act. It would have aroused public opinion and a coup might have followed. In 1945 the circumstances were different. In any case in 1941 it was surely too late to intervene. If there was a time to intervene, it was early in 1938, when Konoe bypassed the opposition of the vice-chief of army staff, General Tada, to the escalation of the Sino-Japanese war. The Emperor's pre-war role is, as Large says, better understood in an institutional context. He was the 'supreme ratifier', his task 'to keep the consensus-making process honest', as David Anson Titus has written [*Palace and Politics in Prewar Japan* (Columbia University Press, 1974), pp. 11, 263]. That consensus-making was, in Titus' phrase, 'privatised': the differences among Japan's decision makers were not resolved in public process. It was not a democratic state, nor was it a fascist one.

A second controversial issue is the decision to drop the atomic bombs. It has been argued both that it shortened the war and that it was unnecessary. In his *Atomic Diplomacy* (London: Secker and Warburg, 1966; revised 1985), Gar Alperovitz focused on its diplomatic influence. An article by J. Samuel Walker revived his interest in the topic and a second book focuses more on the decision itself, *The Decision to Use the Atomic Bomb and the Architecture of an American Myth* (New York: Knopf, 1995). Walker later published *Prompt and Utter Destruction: Truman and the Use of Atomic Bombs against Japan* (Chapel Hill and London: University of North Carolina Press, 1997). He also provides a bibliographical survey in Michael J. Hogan (ed.), *Hiroshima in History and Memory* (Cambridge University Press, 1996).

A third issue is the acceptance of guilt on the part of the Japanese. Read George Hicks, *Japan's War Memories: Amnesia or Concealment?* (Aldershot: Ashgate, 1997). On reparations, see Lawrence Olson, *Japan in Postwar Asia* (London: Pall Mall, 1970) and Chaivat Khamchoo and E. Bruce Reynolds (eds), *Thai-Japanese Relations in Historical Perspective* (Bangkok: Innomedia, 1988).

On the conclusion of the war and the post-war phase see John W. Wheeler-Bennett and Anthony Nicolls, *The Semblance of Peace* (London: Macmillan, 1972); Richard B. Finn, *Winners in Peace: MacArthur, Yoshida and Postwar Japan* (Berkeley: University of California Press, 1992); and N. Tarling, *Britain, Southeast Asia and the Onset of the Cold War* (Cambridge University Press, 1998).

# Index

Abe Noboyuki, 154
Abyssinia, 91, 94–9, 101, 117, 136
Albania, 143, 153, 168
Alsace-Lorraine, 7, 9, 23, 25
Amery, Leo, 23, 55
Amo Eiji, 103, 108
Anglo-Japanese Alliance (1902), 1,
   13–14, 16, 18, 37–9, 156
Anschluss, *see under* Austria *and* Germany
Anti-Comintern Pact (1936), 105, 110, 130,
   136, 153–4, 172, 184
appeasement, xi, 111–12, 117, 121, 126–9,
   135–6, 140, 155, 158, 186–7, 189,
   191
   *see also* Great Britain *and* France
Arabs, 8, 32–3
Araki Sadao, 69, 83, 86, 106
Arita Hachuro, 110, 154, 158, 170
Astakhov, Georgei, 147
Ashton-Gwatkin, F., 42
Asia Development Board, 131
atomic bomb, 197, 231
Australia, 16, 36, 129, 133, 136, 158, 170
Austria, 21, 30, 57, 71, 74–5, 93, 122, 127
   customs union with Germany, 77–8
   Anschluss, 118–19
Austria-Hungary, 4, 6, 7, 21, 29

Baker, Newton D., 90
Baldwin, Stanley, 48
Balfour, Arthur J., 23, 30
Balkans, 4, 31, 152, 166, 168
Barthou, Louis, 93–4
Baudouin, Paul, 172
Belgium, 5, 7–9, 23, 37, 51, 54, 101, 161–2
Bladeslee, G., 89
Bloch, Ivan, 13
Blomberg, Werner von, 114

Bonnet, Georges, 123, 141, 149, 185
Borneo, 15, 18, 104
Borodin, 64
Boxer rebellion, 13
Briand, Aristide, 56–8, 60
Brüning, Heinrich, 73–4
Brussels Conference (1938), 135–6
Bulgaria, 5–6, 21, 29–31, 75, 165–6
Burckhardt, Carl, 166
Burma, 15, 137, 196
Burma Road, 133, 170–1, 173, 176–7
Butler, R. A., 156

Cadogan, Alexander, 128, 138, 142, 149
Cambodia, 14, 173–4
Canada, 37, 124
Canton, 134
Castle, William J., 70
Catroux, G., 17
Cecil, Lord Robert, 33
Chamberlain, Austen, 49, 55–6, 61, 63
Chamberlain, Neville, 76, 78, 81, 121, 124,
   126, 138, 143–4, 163, 185, 192
   and appeasement, 128–9
   and Czechoslovakia, 120, 142
   and Germany, 117–18, 140
   and Italy, 117
   and Japan, 107–9, 133–4
Chang Hsueh-liang, 64–5, 105
Chang Tso-lin, 64–5, 68, 81, 83
Changkufeng, 136
Cherry Society, 82, 86
Chiang Kai-shek, 16, 63, 65, 104–5, 107,
   130–4, 136, 171, 175, 196
China, 1–2, 8, 10–14, 16–17, 36, 41, 81, 103,
   108–10, 125, 155, 175, 179, 183, 196
   and Washington agreements, 40, 62–4, 69,
   70

and Manchuria, 84, 87–9
and undeclared war, 129–35
*see also* Chiang Kai-shek *and* Kuomintang
'China Friendship' policy, 64, 66, 70
*see also* Shidehara Kijuro
Chinese Communist Party (CCP), 62–4, 109
Chinese Eastern Railway (CER), 64
Churchill, Winston S., 31, 102, 129, 152,
    161, 163–4, 173, 175, 178, 182, 188
Ciano, Galeazzo, 110, 165
Clarke, Ashley, 157, 158
Clemenceau, Georges, 7, 9, 21–3, 27, 32
co-existence and co-prosperity, 41, 103
    *see also* Greater East Asia Co-Prosperity
        Sphere
Comintern, 41, 52, 56, 62, 105
Communism, communists, 16–17, 19, 40–1,
    62, 75, 87, 107, 116, 136, 194, 196–7
    in France, 77, 122, 152
    in Germany, 52, 54, 56, 73
    *see also* Russia *and* Chinese Communist
        Party
'Control Faction', 106, 131
Cooper, Alfred Duff, 120, 140
Craigie, R., 133–4, 187
Cripps, Stafford, 169
Crowe, Eyre, 3, 5
Crowley, James B., 83, 104, 130
Curzon, Lord, 48
Czechoslavakia, 29, 31, 50–1, 56, 75, 94, 99,
    119–23, 128, 139, 140, 153, 183–4

Daladier, Edouard, 123, 141, 149, 152
Dan Takuma, 82, 86
Danzig, 23, 25–6, 139, 145, 149
Decoux, Jean, 170, 177
Delbos, Yvon, 123
Dening, Esler, 157, 195
disarmament, 77, 79–80, 92
Dutch, *see* Netherlands India
Duus, Peter, 69

Eden, Anthony, 97–9, 101, 117, 124, 126,
    133, 135, 152
Eliot, C., 38
embargo, 'freeze', 157, 174–5, 177–8, 192
Ethiopia, *see* Abyssinia

Falkenhausen, Alexander von, 136
Finland, 152, 160, 165–6
Fisher, Warren, 108
Foch, Marshal Ferdinand, 22, 60

Fourteen Points, 7, 9, 17, 25, 28, 35
France, xi, 1, 4, 13, 56–7, 72, 78, 80, 113,
    139, 141, 143–4, 147, 165, 167,
    182–4
    and Abyssinia, 95–6, 98
    and Anschluss, 119
    and Czechoslovakia, 120, 122–3
    and East European alliances, 50, 58, 94,
        96, 120, 184
    and First World War, 5–7, 9
    and Indochina, 129, 170, 172
    and peace settlements, 24–5, 28, 31–2, 34,
        45–8
    and Rhineland, 99–100
    and Spain, 115–16
    and war, 148–9, 151–2, 160–2
    and war debts and reparations, 26–7, 48,
        51, 53, 77–8
    armed forces in, 96, 120–3
    economic situation in, 48, 54, 59, 76, 81,
        121–2
    relations with Germany, 58, 60, 140
    relations with Great Britain, 47–8, 94, 116,
        124, 142
    relations with Italy, 79, 93–6, 116,
        141
    relations with Poland, 25, 50, 149
    relations with Russia, 94, 145
Franco, General Francisco, 115–16, 167
Franz Ferdinand, Archduke of Austria, 4
Fritsch, Werner von, 114
Fukuyama, F., 200
Fundamental Principles of National Policy
    (1936), 104, 132

Gamelin, General Maurice, 96
Genoa Conference (1922), 53
genro (elder statesmen), 41, 69
Germany, x, xi, 1, 3, 4, 14–15, 17, 57, 60, 67,
    69, 77–8, 101, 124, 141, 165, 182–4,
    186, 190–2
    and Anschluss, 118–19
    and Czechoslovakia, 119–20, 138–40
    and First World War, 7–9
    and Four Year Plans, 113–14
    and peace settlements, 21, 23–9, 34–5, 46,
        72
    and reparations, 24, 26–7, 51–2, 72, 74
    and Spanish Civil War, 115
    and war, 151, 160–2, 167, 169
    armed forces in, 80, 93, 95, 113, 116, 139,
        141

# Index

Germany (*cont.*)
  economic situation in, 26, 28, 52, 59, 71,
    74, 147, 150, 167
  relations with China, 16–17, 136
  relations with France, 45, 51, 56, 60, 80,
    140, 157
  relations with Great Britain, 94, 118
  relations with Italy, 116
  relations with Japan, 12–13, 83, 105,
    109–11, 137, 153–4
  relations with Poland, 25, 28, 93, 138–9
  relations with Russia, 52–3, 56, 59, 64,
    145–8, 156, 166, 174, 184
  relations with USA, 179–80
  *see also* Hitler
Goebbels, Josef, 127
Goering, Hermann, 113, 118, 146, 192
Gondo Seikyo, 86
Great Britain, x, xi, 1–2, 111, 113, 139, 147,
    165, 182–6, 190, 192
  and Abyssinia, 96–8
  and Anschluss, 119
  and Czechoslovakia, 120, 123
  and First World War, 5–7, 9, 72, 80
  and guarantees to east European states,
    141–3
  and India, 10–11, 15–17, 19
  and League of Nations, 22–3, 93, 97–8
  and Manchuria, 87–8, 90–1
  and peace settlements, 24–5, 32–4, 37–8,
    46–7
  and Spain, 115–16
  and war, 148–9, 151–2, 160–3
  and war debts and reparations, 27, 49, 51,
    53, 77–9
  armed forces, 97, 125, 128, 141, 143
  economic situation in, 49, 55, 71, 76, 81, 125
  relations with France, 47–8, 55, 80, 100,
    116, 126
  relations with Germany, 94, 100
  relations with Italy, 102, 116–17, 143
  relations with Poland, 26, 141–2, 149
  relations with Russia, 127, 144–5
  relations with USA, 79, 126, 156–8
Greater East Asia Co-Prosperity Sphere, 172,
    174, 197
Greece, 30, 32, 141, 143, 168
Grew, Joseph C., 153–4, 157–8, 178, 192
Grey, Edward, 1
Guderian, Heinz, 162

Hainan, 153

Halder, Franz, 163, 169
Halifax, Lord, 119–20, 128, 140, 143–4,
    156, 163
Hamaguchi Yukō, 81–2
Hankey, Maurice, 23, 48, 50, 116–17
Hayashi Senjuro, 132
Harvey, Oliver, 126, 141, 148
Hay notes, 14, 37, 39–40; *see also* 'Open
    Door'
Henderson, Nevile, 117, 192
Henlein, Konrad, 119
Herriot, Edouard, 54–5, 60, 78
Hindenburg, Paul von, 74
Hinsley, F. H., xi, 189
Hiranuma Kiichiro, 154
Hirohito (Showa Emperor), 68, 84, 131, 151,
    153, 230–1
Hitler, Adolf, 74, 80, 91, 95, 100, 120, 127,
    140–1, 143–4, 146, 185, 192
  and Barbarossa, 166–9
  and declaration of war on USA, 179–81
  and foreign policy, 93, 99, 101, 113, 115,
    118–19, 154
  and Japan, 110, 136, 171–2
  and *Mein Kampf*, 75, 112
  and preparations for war, 112, 114, 138–9,
    180
  and war, 148–151
Hoare, Samuel, 97–8
Hong Kong, 37
Honjo Shigeru, 83
Hoover, Herbert, 77–8, 88, 108
Hossbach, Friedrich, 114
Hotta Masaaki, 136
Hughes, Charles E., 40
Hughes, William, 36
Hull, Cordell, 103, 109, 134, 173, 175,
    178–9
Hungary, 29–31, 140, 165

Imperial Rule Assistance Association, 172
India, 1, 10–11, 15–16, 19, 48, 81, 127, 137,
    183, 188
Indo-China, 14, 170–4, 177–8, 196
industrialisation, x, 10, 12
Ingersoll, Royal E., 135
Inoue Junnosuke, 84
Inukai Ki, 84–5, 106
Iriye Akira, xi
Ironside, Edmund, 183
Ishiwara Kanji, 192
Islam, 15

Ismay, Hastings, 128
Italy, xi, 76, 92–3, 102, 111, 124, 139, 141,
    143, 148–9, 154, 167, 180, 183–5
    and Abyssinia, 91, 95, 98, 117
    and East Asia, 110, 136, 172
    and First World War, 8
    and peace settlements, 29–31, 35
    and Spanish Civil War, 115
    and war, 165, 168
    relations with France, 61, 79, 93
    *see also* Mussolini

Japan, x, xi, 1, 6, 10–12, 18, 22, 35, 42, 71,
    81, 95, 97, 102–7, 124–5, 127, 175–6,
    182–6
    and First World War, 8, 16–17, 20
    and Germany, 139, 153–5, 165, 171–2, 188
    and Manchuria, 72, 81–91
    and Russia, 144, 148
    and Sino-Japanese War, 117, 129–137
    and South East Asia, 42, 172–4, 197
    and USA, 157–9, 177–80
    and Washington agreements, 37–41, 43
Jebb, Gladwyn, 118
Jews, 8, 33
Joll, James, 189

Kanto earthquake (1923), 67
Kato Komei, 41–2, 64–7, 81
Kato Tomasaburo, 38
Kazami Akira, 171
Kellogg–Briand Pact (1928), 58, 88–9, 179
Kenseikai, 66
Kerr, A. Clark, 155
Keynes, John Maynard, 45, 49–51, 77
Kirin, 83
Kishi Nobusuke, 197
Kita Ikki, 67–9, 86
Kobayashi Ichiro, 173
kodo (imperial way), 69, 106, 131
kokutai (national polity), 66
Kollontay, Alexandra, 16
Komoto Daisaku, 65
Konoe Fumimaro, 130–4, 170–2, 174–5,
    191–2
Korea, 12, 14, 197
Kuomintang (KMT), 62–5, 81, 87, 89,
    103–4, 107, 109, 153, 157
Kwantung army, 65, 68, 83, 86, 104

Langson, 173
Lansing–Ishii agreement (1917), 17

Laval, Pierre, 93–6, 98
Law, Andrew Bonar, 48–9
League of Nations, 27–8, 32, 34–5, 47–8,
    56, 59, 78, 92–3, 100, 135, 179, 184,
    198
    and Abyssinia, 95–6
    and draft treaty of mutual assistance, 55
    and Geneva Protocol, 55
    and Japan, 35, 84–5, 90–1, 109
    formation of, 10, 22–3
Lindley, Francis, 84, 87, 89
Lindsay, R., 88
Lithuania, 141
Litvinov, Maxim, 148
Lloyd George, David, 7, 21, 24, 26–8, 32,
    48
London naval conferences, 79, 82, 92, 103
Lothian, Lord, 156–7, 159
Loucheur, Louis, 51
Lytton, Lord, 85, 87, 89–91, 179

MacDonald, James Ramsay, 55, 61, 79
Maginot line, 58, 60, 101–2, 122, 161
Makino Shinken, 36
Malaya, 15, 170, 175, 196
Manchuria, Manchukuo, 12–14, 16, 63–5,
    68, 81–92, 95, 103–7, 127, 130–2, 136,
    199
Mander, Geoffrey, 90
Manstein, Erich von, 62
Marco Polo bridge incident (1937), 130–2,
    134
Matsuoka Yosuke, 70, 109, 171–4
May 4th Movement, 41, 62
Mediterranean, 32, 79, 97–8, 100, 102, 111,
    115–17, 124, 129–30, 143, 152, 165,
    167, 184
Meighen, Arthur, 37
Meiji restoration, 11–12, 69, 106, 153, 191
Merekalov, Alexei, 147
Middle East, 1–2, 31–4, 152, 165, 169
Midway, 188
Milner, Lord, 23
Milward, Alan, 195
Minseito, 81, 84, 106, 131, 171
Mitsubishi, 83, 86
Mitsui, 67, 82, 86
Molotov, Vyacheslav M., 145, 147–8, 165
Mongolia, 64–5, 83, 104, 130
Montagu declaration (1917), 16, 19
Mook, H. J. van, 173
Mukden, 83, 86

Munich meeting, agreement (1938), 120,
    123–4, 129, 134, 138–40, 148, 155, 185,
    198
Mussolini, Benito, 61, 91–2, 100, 113, 121,
    140–1, 143, 165, 168, 179
  and Abyssinia, 93–6, 98
  and Spain, 115
mutiny (Tokyo, 1936), 105, 131

Nagano Osami, 175–6
Nagata Tetsuzan, 83, 105
Nanking, 130, 133, 135, 191
National Mobilisation Bill (1938), 132
National Principle School, 86, 106
nationalism, xi, 4, 10, 26, 30–1, 61, 82, 93,
    195–6
naval building, 18, 37–8, 82, 94, 103, 108,
    125, 139, 158, 170
Nazis, 46, 60, 72, 80, 93, 99, 119, 121, 146,
    150
  rise to power in Germany, 60, 62, 72–5
Netherlands India, 14, 17–18, 42–3, 104,
    155, 157, 170, 173, 177–8
Neurath, Constantin von, 114
New Zealand, 32, 129
Nicolson, Harold, 100
Nish, Ian, 90
Nissan, 132
Nomonhan, 154, 188
Nomura Kichisaburo, 154, 178
'Non-recognition', 17, 88, 90, 103, 109
Northern March, 62–4

Ogata Sadako, 90
Ogikubo, 171–2
oil, 18, 39, 66, 104, 107, 173–5
Okada Keisuke, 105
Okuma Shigenobu, 16, 41
'Open Door', 2, 14, 16–17, 37, 39, 62, 64,
    88, 103; *see also* Hay notes
Orlando, Vittorio, 22, 30
Ottawa agreements (1932), 72, 79, 87
Ottoman Empire, *see* Turkey

*Panay*, USS, 135
Pan-Asianism, 12, 16–17, 85, 87
Pearl Harbor, 39, 175, 186
Pescadores, 12
Pétain, Marshal Philippe, 162, 167
Philippines, 2, 14–15, 37, 39, 175, 196
Phipps, Eric, 101, 127, 192
Pibun Songkram, 173

Piggott, F. S. L., 38
Placentia Bay, 175, 194
Poincaré, Raymond, 54
Poland, 7–9, 31, 50–1, 56, 139, 141–2,
    144–51, 159
  and peace settlements, 24–6, 30, 46
Pownall, Henry, 100, 102, 128
Pratt, John, 87, 133

'racial equality', 35–6
Raeder, Erich, 160
Rathenau, Walter, 51–2
Reed–Matsudaira compromise, 82
reparations, 7–8, 24, 26–7, 30, 51–2
  and Dawes Plan, 54
  and Hoover moratorium, 74
  and Young Plan, 59–60
Reynaud, Paul, 152, 162
Rhineland, 7, 24–5, 27, 29, 33, 54, 56–9
  remilitarisation of, 99–102
Ribbentrop, Joachim von, 114, 136, 139,
    146–8, 165–7, 172
right of supreme command, 11, 69, 82
Romania, 4–5, 8, 29–31, 141–6, 165, 168
Roosevelt, Franklin Delano, 79, 109, 126,
    134–5, 157, 164, 173, 175, 177–8,
    180–1, 187
Ruhr, 54, 58, 78, 99, 101
Rumbold, Horace, 80
Rundstedt, Gerd von, 166
Russia, x, 1–3, 13, 16, 29, 32, 35, 41–2, 56,
    61, 76, 99, 115, 123, 127, 135, 152–3,
    174, 182–4, 186
  and East Asia, 12, 36, 40, 62, 64, 83, 87–8,
    103, 105, 109, 131, 136, 154
  and war, 169
  Bolsheviks in, 25, 47, 59
  relations with France, 93–4, 116, 144–6
  relations with Germany, 52–3, 59, 94, 127,
    146–7, 151, 165, 167–9
  relations with Great Britain, 116, 127, 142,
    144–6
  relations with Japan, 127
  relations with Poland, 50, 52, 151
Russo-Japanese War (1904–5), 2–3, 13–14

Saar, 7, 23–5, 58
Saionji Kinmochi, 66, 70, 84–6, 105–6, 131
Saito Makoto, 85, 103, 105
Salisbury, Laurence, 179
Sansom, G., 87, 192
Schacht, Hjalmar, 113

Schnurre, Karl, 147
Schuman Plan, 195
Schuschnigg, Kurt von, 118–19
Seeds, William, 147
Seeley, Sir J., 10
Seiyukai, 66, 82, 84–5, 171
Shanghai incidents (1932, 1937), 85, 88, 130, 133
Shantung, 16, 36, 40, 65
Shidehara Kijuro, 64–7, 70, 81–4, 87, 197
Showa restoration, 68, 106; *see also* Hirohito
Siam (Thailand), 14, 15, 18, 36, 170, 173–4, 177
Siberia, 17, 40–1, 64, 68, 109
Sikhs, 15, 17
Silesia, 24–6
Simon, John, 90, 108
Singapore, 15, 17, 39, 107, 135–6, 170, 178, 188, 191
Sino-Japanese wars,
  (1894–5), 11–12
  'undeclared war' (1937), 130–5, 187
Smuts, Jan, 16
South Africa, 124, 127
South Manchurian Railway (SMR), 64
Sorge, Richard, 170
Soviet Union, *see* Russia
Spain, 75, 114–15, 118, 125, 144, 167
Spratly Islands, 153
Stahmer, Heinrich, 172
Stalin, Joseph, 61, 72, 137, 146–8, 169, 182, 184
Stimson, Henry L., 88, 108, 157
Strang, William, 145
Stresa meeting (1935), 93–5
Stresemann, Gustav, 54–7, 59–60, 73
Sun Yat-sen, 62

Tada Shun, 132
Taiwan, 12, 14
Tanaka Giichi, 65–6, 81
tariff autonomy, 63, 81
Tatekawa Yoshitsugu, 83
Teschen, 51, 139, 142
Thorne, C., 40, 88, 199
Tientsin crisis, 143, 154–6
*Times, The*, 98, 142–3
Tojo Hideki, 171, 175–6, 179, 191, 197
Tokugawa, 11, 171
Tomioka Sadatoshi, 192
Treaties,
  Berlin (1926), 59

Brest-Litovsk (1918), 5, 29, 53
Franco-Belgian (1920), 50
Franco-Czech (1924), 50, 120, 122
Franco-Polish (1921), 50
Lausanne (1923), 21, 31–2
Locarno (1925), 56–8, 93
Neuilly (1919), 21
Portsmouth (1905), 13–14, 67
Rapallo (1922), 53
Sèvres (1920), 21, 31
Shimonoseki (1895), 12
St Germain (1919), 21, 29, 78
Trianon (1920), 21, 29
Versailles (1919), 21, 23–9, 34, 36–7, 40–1, 43, 45, 53, 62, 70, 72, 91, 94, 127, 135, 140, 149, 183
Tripartite Pact, 165, 171–3, 178
Triple Intervention (1895), 12–13, 16, 89
Tsinan, 65
Tuan Chi-jui, 62
Turkey, 2–6, 8, 15, 19, 21, 31–2, 143, 166
Turner, Richmond K., 178
Twenty-one Demands (1915), 16–17, 40–1
Tyrol, South, 30, 93

Uchida Shinya, 85
Ugaki Issei, 69, 82
Ugaki Kazushige, 134
USA, x, xi, 1–2, 8, 12, 14, 33, 46–7, 59, 71, 79, 80, 99, 126, 142, 159, 165, 168, 182–4, 186, 194
  and China, 103, 108, 134–5
  and First World War, 5–6, 8–9
  and Great Britain, 142, 164
  and isolationism, 126
  and Japan, 11, 17, 82, 154–7, 174–5, 177–9
  and League of Nations, 22–3
  and Lend Lease, 164, 173
  and navy, 82, 158, 170, 178
  and New Deal, 81
  and non-recognition, 88, 90–1, 109
  and the war in Europe, 163–4, 180
  and war debts and reparations, 26, 53, 77–9
Vansittart, Sir Robert, 78, 97
Vietnam, 12, 14, 197; *see also* Indo-China

Wakatsuki Reijiro, 65, 83–4
Wang, C. T., 134
Wang Ching-Wei, 131, 172

# Index

Washington conferences, agreements, 'system', 36–43, 62, 69–70, 79, 81–2, 84–8, 91–2, 107–8, 131, 135, 153, 159, 179, 196

Watt, D. C., 187

Weizsäcker, Ernst von, 147

Welles, Sumner, 90–1, 157

Wellesley, V., 90

Wilson, Woodrow, 8–10, 21–6, 30, 32, 34–6, 39, 43, 87

Wirth, Josef, 52

Yamagata Aritomo, 17, 41, 66–7, 69, 103

Yonai Mitsumasa, 153, 171

Yoshida Shigeru, 91, 108, 133

Yoshida Zengo, 171

Yoshizawa Kenkichi, 173

Yuan Shih-kai, 16

Yugoslavia, 29–31, 75, 92, 168

zaibatsu, 67–8, 82, 132

Zhukov, 154

Zimmern, A., 19